Ralph Russell (1918–2008) has been widely recognized as the greatest western scholar of Urdu. Khushwant Singh described him as 'the most revered name of interpreters of Ghalib's life and works'. He headed the Urdu department at the School of Oriental and African Studies, University of London for thirty years, and was a popular visiting scholar in India and Pakistan. His unusual skill as a translator and his insightful writing have opened up an appreciation of Urdu literature to a wide range of readers. His books include *The Pursuit of Urdu Literature: A Select History* (1992), *How Not to Write the History of Urdu Literature: and Other Essays on Urdu and Islam* (1999) and *The Oxford India Ghalib: Life, Letters and Ghazals* (2003) among others.

Marion Molteno is a prize-winning novelist. She is the literary executor for Ralph Russell. She has edited several of his books, including his autobiography and his introduction to Ghalib's ghazals, *The Famous Ghalib: The Sound of My Moving Pen* (2015). Her latest novel, *Uncertain Light* (2015) has been published by Speaking Tiger.

Praise for *Hidden in the Lute: An Anthology of Two Centuries of Urdu Literature*

The most comprehensive anthology of its kind in English. It will certainly be of great help to non-Urdu readers, in India and elsewhere, who desire a preliminary yet clearly focused understanding of Urdu literature and the values, the milieu, and the ethos that inform it.

—Mohammed Asaduddin
Indian Review of Books

No one in the West today speaks with such authority about Urdu or is better able to communicate its pleasures to those who do not read the language.

—Francis Robinson
Times Literary Supplement

With Russell's almost unparalleled skill as a translator from Urdu, this eclectic, wide-ranging anthology succeeds not only in casting light on Russell's own tastes, but also in supplying some core texts for new enthusiasts of the language's heritage, and for students of history.

—Aamer Hussain
Times Higher Education Supplement

An exceptional introduction to Urdu literature organized by styles and with many very appropriate explanations of the Indo-Pakistani culture, biography and times of the authors and their relevance. Written in a pleasant, but not simplistic style, it is highly recommended for those who like me want to learn more about this literary work.

—Renata
Reader's review on *Goodreads.com*

A
Thousand
Yearnings

A Book of Urdu Poetry and Prose

Translated and introduced by
Ralph Russell

Edited and with a foreword by Marion Molteno

SPEAKING
TIGER

SPEAKING TIGER PUBLISHING PVT. LTD
4381/4 Ansari Road, Daryaganj,
New Delhi–110002, India

Published in the UK as *Hidden in the Lute: An Anthology of
Two Centuries of Urdu Literature* by Carcanet Press 1995
This revised edition first published in the Indian subcontinent as
A Thousand Yearnings: A Book of Urdu Poetry and Prose by Speaking Tiger 2017

ISBN: 978-93-86702-16-6
eISBN: 978-93-86702-15-9

10 9 8 7 6 5 4 3 2 1

For sale in South Asia only

Typeset in Bembo Std by Jojy Philip
Printed at Sanat Printers, Kundli

My love, I cannot tell the tale of all the things I want from
   you.
A hundred longings fill my soul, a thousand yearnings
   throng my heart.

   kya kahiye rakhein hain hum tujhse, yaar khvaahish
   yak jaan, sad tamanna—yak dil hazaar khvaahish
                                        —*Mir*

Contents

Ralph Russell & Urdu literature:
Foreword by Marion Molteno   xi

Introduction   xvii

SHORT STORIES AND SKETCHES   1

    Prem Chand: *A Wife's Complaint*   7

    Ismat Chughtai: *Tiny's Granny*   20

    Rashid Jahan: *Behind the Veil*   33

    Krishan Chander: *Kalu Bhangi*   47

    Saadat Hasan Manto: *The Black Shalwar*   63

    Shaukat Thanavi: *Love and Prudence*   77

    Ismat Chughtai: *Hellbound*   81

POPULAR LITERATURE   93

    Outwitting the Powerful   99

    Akbar and Birbal   104

    Mullah Dopiaza   109

    Shaikh Chilli   112

    Tales of Famous Men   115

    The Creation of Adam and the Loss of Paradise   118

Sikandar, Khizar and the Water of Life 126

Khwaja Hasan Nizami: *Guests are Pests* 130

LOVE POETRY:
THE GHAZALS OF MIR AND GHALIB 139

Hasrat Mohani and Momin: *Lovers' Meetings* 146

Mir: *The Ideal Ghazal Lover* 151

Ghalib's More Nuanced View of Love 164

Mystic Love 168

The Challenge to Orthodoxy 172

The Humanist Values of the Ghazal 182

God and Humankind 186

The Poet in Society 191

Ghalib's Personal Philosophy 202

Images and Allusions 211

Eleven Ghazals of Ghalib 216

A Living Tradition 227

THE LIVES OF POETS 231

Muhammad Husain Azad: *Nasikh:*
The Portrait of a Poet 236

Abdul Halim Sharar: *The King and the Singer* 242

Farhatullah Beg: *A Memorable Delhi Mushaira* 244

Altaf Husain Hali: *A Memoir of Ghalib* 252

Ghalib: *Letters* 260

THE 'NEW LIGHT':
RESPONDING TO SOCIAL CHANGE   279

    Sayyid Ahmad Khan and the Aligarh Movement   285

    Akbar Ilahabadi: *Satire in a Changing Society*   309

THE NOVEL   319

    Rusva: *Umrao Jan Ada*   325

EDITOR'S NOTES   375

    Urdu Pronunciation   377

    Further Reading   379

Ralph Russell and Urdu Literature

Foreword by Marion Molteno

The book you are about to read is the work of an Englishman who became an eminent scholar and translator of Urdu. He felt that his close engagement with Urdu speakers and their literature had immeasurably enriched his life. So he directed his considerable intellect and energy to sharing what he had learnt by teaching and translating Urdu literature to make it accessible to people who didn't know the language.

Ralph Russell was born in 1918, at the end of the First World War, and died at the age of 90 in 2008, when the world had changed almost unrecognizably from the one he had grown up in. Throughout his long life he was continually reading, thinking, writing, making new friends and cherishing old ones, always keen to understand how others saw the world. He was an easy communicator: warm, relaxed, open to people of all kinds. Until a month before his death he was still teaching, advising others, and writing further chapters of his autobiography.

His first encounter with Urdu was—to say the least—unusual. During the Second World War, as a young man of 22 just out of university, he was conscripted and sent to serve on an attachment to the Indian Army. He had been a communist since the age of sixteen and was a passionate believer in the cause of Indian independence. Urdu was the army's language of communication, and from his first days in India he applied himself to learning it as well as possible, so that he could get to know the people among whom he would be living. His unit was sent to Assam to supervise the building of a road to the Burma border, and in this remote area, cut off from civilian life, he spent the war years in the company of the hundred Indian sepoys in his unit. Most were from South India but they all used Urdu to communicate. The British officers around him knew little Urdu, relying on their Indian subordinates to interpret. Ralph picked up the language fairly quickly, and freely talked with the men about things which the authorities would have regarded as highly subversive. He taught himself to read, practising on leaflets from the Communist Party of India and translations of the works of Lenin.

This experience changed the direction of his life. When the war was over he was sent back to the UK, but looked for a way to maintain his connection with India. He got a scholarship to study Urdu at the School of Oriental and African Studies (SOAS) in London, with the possibility—if he did well enough—of becoming a lecturer. He describes the shock of discovering how difficult he found Urdu literature in his autobiography. It involved a huge leap in vocabulary from the kind of conversational Urdu he had acquired. Its literary forms were strange to him, particularly the poetry. Later he wrote about his personal journey in getting past this strangeness, in an article called *The Pursuit of the Urdu Ghazal*. Eventually he came to not only appreciate the ghazal, but felt a close identification with it.

Even before studying Urdu he was well read in other languages. He had studied classical Latin and Greek, and read French, Russian and several other European literatures in translation. But Urdu was not just another language, it had grown out of a culture very different from his own. Some of that culture was familiar to him from his years in India, but the literature he encountered at university took him to another level. He learnt to see from the point of view of people who had been formed by a different society, in different times. It became his pleasure to constantly extend his understanding—to learn from Urdu speakers how they understood a particular verse of poetry or a piece of prose. Then he would translate and interpret it, hoping to share with others what he had learnt.

This engagement was not just intellectual. During his thirty years as head of Urdu studies in SOAS, he spent one in every seven years in India and Pakistan, where he lived with Urdu-speaking friends and personally came to know many of the great Urdu writers of the time. He stayed in the homes of Krishan Chander, Faiz Ahmed Faiz, and knew many others prominent in the Progressive Writers' Association. He regularly spent time with staff of Aligarh Muslim University and Jamia Millia Islamia, and lectured in Delhi University. Back in the UK, he dressed for comfort in his own home in kurta and paijama, and enjoyed Indian food more than any other. He was an atheist all his life (as were many of his friends among the Urdu writers), yet he developed a respectful understanding of how his Muslim friends viewed things. He had South Asian standards of hospitality, and adapted it to his own personal lack of concern for status. When people came to stay over he insisted—even in his eighties—on them having the only bed in his small flat while he slept on rolled-out bedding on the floor. He believed deeply in the equal value of all people, and the literature that he most easily identified with shared these beliefs. Unlike many academics, he prioritized teaching, and gave immense care to producing language teaching materials that helped his students become fluent. His enthusiasm inspired his students, many of whom remained lifelong friends and went on to assist him in teaching Urdu to English speaking adults in multi-ethnic communities in the UK.

His training in other languages undoubtedly contributed to his skill as a translator, though ultimately the feel for words is something that cannot be learnt. Working alongside him for twenty-six years I was often struck by the fact that where I might remember the substance of a conversation, he would remember the actual words used. He had an instinctive feel for the rhythm of both prose and poetry. He also had an enormous store of songs learnt from childhood on, and would often spontaneously start singing something someone had just said, because the speech rhythm reminded him of a tune he knew. The translation part of his brain seemed to work effortlessly, and was something akin to the skill of interpreters in international conferences. When asked to translate prose of a not particularly literary kind—a straight narrative, or a letter—he could record a natural English translation onto cassette, without reading it through first, or pausing to think. Afterwards he would play it back and check, but he seldom needed to change anything. Literary prose was a different matter and poetry even more so. He took great care to be sure he had understood and captured the nuances; and with poetry, that he could render the poet's complex thought in natural English, within the framework of poetic metre.

Such breadth of understanding has informed his selection of this introductory taste of Urdu literature.

~

I had a small part in the origins of this book. I met Ralph in 1982, shortly after he had retired from SOAS. I was getting to know Urdu speakers through my work organizing English classes, and I asked if he would teach me Urdu. All I aimed for was to be able to have simple conversations—I had no thought that I would ever learn to read the Urdu script or explore its literature. But in our lessons Ralph would often quote a couplet of poetry, or refer to something an Urdu writer had said. I was intrigued, and asked if he could suggest something for me to read. He laughed and said, 'Well, you could read my books.' I had no idea that he had written any. He gave me two books that he and Khurshidul Islam had produced on classical poets. I loved them, and wanted more. Did he have anything I could read about the other writers he referred to? Premchand? Ismat Chugtai? Hali? Each time he would go to his filing cabinet and pull out an old copy of an article or a translation, written decades earlier and published in some obscure journal. There seemed to be something in that treasure trove on every

writer I asked about, and each opened a new door. I knew there
would be lots of other people who would find them as interesting
as I did, but would never have my luck in finding them. 'You should
get them published as a book,' I said. And that's how it started.

We planned and edited together, discussing how to arrange the
pieces to make a coherent whole. I was the test reader, suggesting
changes or additions to make the historical context intelligible
to readers who knew nothing about the society reflected in the
literature. As a result Ralph generously dedicated the first edition
of this book to me, describing me as 'the ideal audience'. All he
meant was that I was the kind of person he had in mind when
translating Urdu literature—someone who would be interested to
read it, but who could do so only through translations.

In the end two publishers were interested in taking on the
project, and because of their differing interests, it became two
books. Ralph regarded them as companion volumes. *The Pursuit
of Urdu Literature: A Select History*, was published in 1993. The first
edition of this book followed in 1995.

Before Ralph's death he asked me to be his Literary Executor,
and it is my privilege to be responsible for keeping his work in
print. We had worked so closely together that he was happy for
me to make any decisions needed in editing them. The minor
changes I have made in order, layout or text, are intended only
to make clearer what Ralph has presented. I am delighted to
have been able to include transcriptions of the Urdu originals of
ghazal verses—something Ralph had always wanted to do, but the
original publishers had not been able to accommodate. For those
new to Urdu, I have added a note on pronunciation using this
transcription, and for those who would like to read more, there is
an appendix on Ralph's other writings on Urdu literature.

The original title of this book was *Hidden in the Lute: An
Anthology of Two Centuries of Urdu Literature*. The phrase 'hidden
in the lute' comes from a translation of a couplet by Ghalib, and
Ralph's *Introduction* explains what the phrase suggested. By the
second edition, the publisher had dropped the phrase and called

the book simply *An Anthology of Urdu Literature*. That does not seem an adequate title for such a personal selection, so for this new edition we have chosen a phrase from another ghazal couplet, this time by Mir:

> *My love, I cannot tell the tale of all the things I want from you.*
> *A hundred longings fill my soul, a thousand yearnings throng my*
> *heart.*

The second line is an example of the intensity of expression for which Urdu poetry is widely known. It is a vehicle for the expression of universal emotions: desire, hopes, dreams, and tragedies. Through the breadth of Ralph's own appreciation of this literature, and his extraordinarily sensitive translations, we are offered an insight into the thoughts and concerns of people across two centuries for whom Urdu was the natural medium. The result is often entertaining, sometimes moving, and always enlightening.

Marion Molteno

Introduction

This book presents a selection of Urdu literature for anyone who cannot read Urdu but is interested to find out what it has to offer.

Apart from people who count English as their mother tongue, there are many to whom this description applies. In particular I hope it will be useful to young people of South Asian background who use English as their effective first language. In both India and Pakistan there are tens of thousands of people whose parents are Urdu speakers but whose own education has been through the medium of English, and who are likely to be considerably more fluent in English than in Urdu. I am very pleased to know that many of them regret that they have learnt less about Ghalib's poetry than about Wordsworth's, and would like to do something to change this situation. In India, many others who are not Urdu speakers have heard Urdu poetry recited or sung, and know that it has a rich literature. They look upon it as part of their wider South Asian heritage and would like to know more about it. In Britain, Canada, the USA and elsewhere where people from Urdu-speaking backgrounds have settled, many of their children and grandchildren have not had the chance to become confident speakers and readers of the language of their family and community. A growing number of them now feel a strong desire to learn more about the wealth of their literary heritage, and they have no choice but to do this through the medium of English.

How Urdu Became a Literary Language

Urdu is one of the fifteen or so major languages of the South Asian subcontinent. It was born out of the need of Muslim invaders of India from the tenth century onwards to create a language in which they could communicate with their Indian subjects. Its basic structure, and much of its everyday vocabulary is almost identical with that of Hindi, which in an earlier form had been the lingua franca of northern and central India. The Muslim invaders were men from different regions of what is now the Middle East and Central Asia, speaking different languages, but their common language of culture and administration was Persian. Gradually Persian words became more commonly used in the native Indian language framework, and the result was a new language, Urdu.

Like many other literatures, Urdu literature begins with poetry. But, like the modern languages of Europe, Urdu had to establish itself as a literary medium in the face of a convention that only a classical language could be a fit vehicle for poetry. In medieval Western Europe this language was Latin. In India it was Persian, and by comparison with Europe it was late in the day that the modern language won out. In northern India, it was not until the early decades of the eighteenth century that Urdu became accepted as the medium of poetry. The change came about because many Indians had begun to feel that they could not express themselves as adequately as they would wish in Persian, a language that was not their own; and major poets now appeared who made Urdu the medium of their work. Nevertheless, until well into the twentieth century there were Urdu-speaking poets who continued to write some of their verse in Persian as well, just as in England Milton wrote verse in Latin as well as English. All of them were completely familiar with the literary heritage of Persian, and followed Persian models in both genres and the established themes of classical poetry. Thus Urdu poetry represents, in a sense, a further development of a literature already centuries old, with only the language changed.

For a century after poets were writing in Urdu, Persian remained the only acceptable medium for serious writing in prose. It could be the vehicle of powerful feeling, but it was a highly stylized form of Persian which employed all manner of literary devices—wordplay, alliteration, antithesis, balancing rhythms and rhymes, and many more. What little Urdu prose there was, imitated this style of writing. Clearly, this could not be an all-purpose prose, able to meet all the varied needs of modern writing. For that it was necessary to establish the convention that the *spoken* language of educated people—Urdu—should be accepted as the medium of written literature, prose as well as poetry. When that change came about, it was partly as a response to a new colonizing presence, the British. This process is described in the section on 'The New Light'.

Urdu has predominantly been the language of Muslims. Its literature, like the *Thousand and One Nights,* is about people who profess the religion of Islam. A few non-Muslims have made major contributions to its literature, though until the 1920s those who did, wrote in the tradition which made the life and experiences of Muslims their theme. But its literature is not primarily a religious literature. Millions of non-Muslims have been able to read and write Urdu, and millions more have been able to understand and speak it. It is now the vehicle of one of the richest literatures of the subcontinent, in both poetry and prose. Its poetry has been made popular through song, and carries universal messages which have touched people of all backgrounds. Its prose offers a wealth of stories, and insights into a way of life.

How This Book is Organized

I have thought it best not to follow a chronological order, but to begin with a selection of twentieth century short stories and sketches. This is the part of Urdu literature which English-speaking readers will be able to relate to most easily, for twentieth-century writers are familiar with, and deeply influenced by Western literature, and so share a common background with the readers for whom this book is intended.

The next section is on popular literature, and mostly by anonymous writers. They write within a tradition that knows nothing of the literature of the West, in simple forms, and often on themes which are universal, which any modern reader can easily appreciate. Few histories or anthologies of Urdu literature would include them; but because their subject matter is drawn exclusively from their own tradition, you will learn from them things which will help you understand the society from which other forms of literature grew.

The third section is on poetry, which is without a doubt that part of literature which Urdu speakers most prize. Of the many genres of classical poetry, I have focused on the one that is most highly valued—the ghazal. To appreciate it you will need some explanation of its background and its form, though I have tried to present it in a way which makes only minimal comment necessary.

The last sections deal with prose literature of the late nineteenth century, when Urdu-speaking society was feeling the full impact of British rule and British ways.

Each section has an introduction of its own, and there are occasional explanations in footnotes. I have tried to keep these to a minimum and not stand in the way of your direct encounter with the literature.

Those who want to know more about the background of the literature can turn to my book *The Pursuit of Urdu Literature: A Select History*, which may be regarded as a companion to this volume.

A Note On the Selection

Those already acquainted with Urdu literature may be curious to know why I have chosen to include the writers that I have, and excluded others.

Every selection is bound to be determined by personal choice. I chose from the literature I know and have liked enough to want to translate. Urdu literature contains a great deal more than I have read, and I do not doubt that there are things which, if I had read them, I might have liked as much or more than the things I have included here.

Chronologically the selection ends in the early twentieth century, with the short story writers of the Progressive Writers Association. I decided not to go further, nor have I included any twentieth-century poetry, knowing that once readers' interest has been stimulated, it is twentieth-century writers that they will most easily find in good translations.

More importantly, my selection has been limited to work which is not only good, but is likely to appeal to an audience encountering Urdu literature for the first time. The tastes of such an audience are bound to be more circumscribed than of those who can read Urdu, who have grown up with its literature since childhood, and to whom its conventions present no problems. I have deliberately excluded those genres, and the work of those writers, which could only be made intelligible to English speakers by the introduction of an amount of explanatory matter so great as to scare them away. For these reasons I have not included the *marsiyas* of Anis, which I greatly admire, or extracts from the novels and other writings of Nazir Ahmad, whose vivid, magnificent Urdu prose far surpasses that of any other nineteenth-century writer and affords me some of my favourite reading.

I expect that most Muslim readers will particularly regret my omission of anything from the poet Iqbal. But Iqbal is above all a Muslim poet, and makes his most powerful appeal to his fellow Muslims. Many readers of this book may be non-Muslims, and though (as I have shown in *The Pursuit of Urdu Literature*) if his message is fully understood it can be valid for all humankind, the specifically Muslim form of its delivery is a barrier between him and the non-Muslim reader.

Other important writers have been omitted for a different reason. Readers who are encountering Urdu literature for the first time will be able to estimate its worth more easily if they are given substantial extracts from a relatively small number of the best writers than if they had been presented with a larger number in necessarily much smaller selections. That is why I present the ghazal through the poetry of Mir and Ghalib alone; it is not that I am unaware that there are other ghazal poets of the first rank. For similar reasons, I have chosen to represent the early novel by a long extract from Rusva's *Umrao Jan Ada* rather than by many shorter extracts from the work of other novelists. And those who compare my translations with the originals will see that I have occasionally abridged some passages, and transposed others where a different order is helpful to the English reader.

I hope that this selection will meet the needs and stimulate the interest of a wide variety of readers. The poet Ghalib talks, in one of his ghazals, about

> *… the music of His secrets*
> *Hidden no more than melody is hidden in the lute*

I like to think of the 'melody' as the charm of Urdu literature, and the 'lute' as the language in which it was written. I hope that in doing these translations I have played the lute in a way which reveals the melody and enables you to enjoy it.

RALPH RUSSELL

SHORT STORIES
AND SKETCHES

Short Stories and Sketches

The short story is one of the most common genres in modern Urdu literature. Its popularity was established in the early decades of the twentieth century, especially the 1920s and 1930s—a period of tremendous social and political upheaval which also resulted in vigorous cultural growth. All the stories and sketches in this section are products of this period, as indeed are the other genres represented here. It was a period in which the Indian struggle for independence first drew in a great mass of people, and the feeling rapidly grew that 'freedom' must mean 'freedom for all'—not just an end to British rule but an end also to the age-old exploitation of the poor, which had been a feature of Indian life long before the coming of the British.

Writers who held this view came together in 1936 to form the Progressive Writers' Association, and all the writers represented in this section except Shaukat Thanavi gave it their active support. The PWA, as it was known, included writers working in many Indian languages, but in no other language did it exert so great an influence as it did in Urdu. Its first conference was presided over by the forerunner of this approach to literature, Premchand (1880–1936), one of the greatest writers of twentieth-century India. A generation older than most of the PWA writers, he was a major figure in both Urdu and Hindi literature. He produced his own versions in both languages of almost everything he wrote—altogether nearly 300 short stories and twelve novels—and in them one finds an unparalleled picture of the life of Indian people. His first stories were published before the First World War, but it is those from the 1920s and early 1930s that are the basis of his fame. His outlook moved from that of a rather naïve nationalist, through being influenced by Gandhi's concern for the poor, to a many-sided realism about the social conflicts of his time. The story I have included here, *A Wife's Complaint* (in Urdu, *Shikva Shikayat*), shows some of his characteristic qualities—keen observation and sympathetic interest in the lives of ordinary people, and a wry, affectionate humour.

In Urdu a major challenge to traditional values in literature came in 1932 when a group of young writers published a collection of short stories entitled *Angaarey* (Burning Coals). It raised an uproar and was condemned by men who had never read it, because it was said to challenge traditional roles of women, write explicitly about intimate relationships, and satirize aspects of religion. It was banned by the British administration, and has only recently been republished. The only woman in the group was a remarkable young doctor, Rashid Jahan (1905–1952) whose intimate knowledge of the lives of Indian Muslim women is evident in her stories and one-act plays. Her short sketch included here, *Behind the Veil* (*Parde ke Peeche*), comes from *Angaarey*. For a modern reader it may be difficult to see why it was regarded as so shocking. For Urdu readers of the time, however, the dramatic impact derived from the fact that it was the kind of conversation among married women in purdah that they would commonly engage in in private, but would die rather than have it made public. Its authenticity is not in doubt. There had been women writers before her but none who portrayed so bluntly the callousness women suffer at the hands of their menfolk. Preoccupation with her medical practice and with the organization of the Progressive Writers' Association took up much of her time, and this along with her early death from cancer meant that her literary output was necessarily small.

Significantly, three of the stories here depict the lives of outcasts from respectable society, denied the same basic respect as any other human being. The first is by Ismat Chughtai (1915–1991), one of the most powerful of the PWA writers. She wrote short stories, sketches, essays, plays, novelettes and novels. Her work, like that of Rashid Jahan, whom she greatly admired, is at its most powerful when she portrays the life of women. Her frank handling of hitherto 'forbidden' themes stirred up much controversy when her work was first published in the 1930s. She went on writing all her life, and her place as a major figure in Urdu is assured. She depicts vividly, ruthlessly, and at the same time with the deepest sympathy the lives of women in Urdu-speaking society of the time, writing with an authenticity no male writer could have matched. These stories are told largely in the specific language of women, which since they lived in a world so largely separate from that of the men, has long had its own vocabulary and turns of phrase. The one included here is *Tiny's Granny* (*Nannhi ki Nani*), about a poor destitute woman who lives by her wits.

Saadat Hasan Manto (1912–1955) is, like Ismat Chughtai, distinguished by the skill with which he handles themes which had previously not been admitted to literature, though his range is wider. His stories have an appealing quality of a sort of informal, often ironic, yet sympathetic approach to his characters. He was provoked by what he saw as the dishonesty of many writers at the time in refusing to face reality. The story included here, *The Black Shalwar* (*Kali Shalwar*), about a prostitute, was shocking to his more conventional contemporaries because it did not sit in judgement on her or her lover. Some of his best stories treat bluntly, and with bitter irony, the terrible Hindu-Muslim riots which accompanied the coming of independence and the partitioning of the sub-continent in 1947. Afterwards, he became an alcoholic and virtually drank himself to death.

Krishan Chander (1914–1977) was the most prolific of all the progressive writers. He worked tirelessly to realize the PWA's aim of bringing the arts 'into the closest touch with the people,' and he gave readings to huge audiences made up of people who were mostly not literate. During the Hindu-Muslim riots around the time of Partition, he wrote story after story driving home the message that all decent people must abhor the communal killings

and do their best to stop them. Some estimates put the number
of his short stories at approximately 5000; he also wrote a few
novels and plays. Not surprisingly, many of his stories were of
indifferent quality, but the best are excellent and make a direct,
simple appeal to his readers' human sympathies. The story I have
selected is *Kalu Bhangi*.

The section ends with two extracts from personal memoirs,
which give different insights into family values of the time. *Love and
Prudence*, from the autobiography of Shaukat Thanavi (1904–1963)
illustrates the major features of marriage and love in traditional
South Asian societies, where marriages are seen as alliances between
families, and not as a partnership based upon the mutual free choice
of the boy and the girl. Falling in love, or imagining that one has
fallen in love, has all the romantic attraction of the illicit, and many
young people enjoy in fantasy an experience which they would
hesitate to risk in real life. The penalties of pursuing the course
which true love dictates—described more fully in the section on
love poetry—are sufficiently severe to deter young people from
embarking upon it, or at any rate from persevering in it.

The last piece is *Hellbound* (*Dozakhi*), Ismat Chughtai's vivid
and affectionate description of her older brother.

A significant feature of the writers in this section is that not
all are Muslim. I have explained in the Introduction that for the
most part, Urdu literature has been the literature of the Muslims
of South Asia: not in the sense that it was hostile to non-Muslim
communities—indeed classical Urdu poetry emphatically asserts
the right of all humankind to love and respect—but in the sense
that it was the product of Muslim writers portraying the life of
their own community. But in the twenties of the twentieth century
this situation changed. Of the seven writers presented in this
section two were Hindus: Premchand and Krishan Chander; yet
the Muslim-Hindu distinction is mostly irrelevant to their work.
All of them are concerned with human beings, not as Muslims or
Hindus, but simply *as* human beings, and the whole scope of Urdu
literature is thereby broadened.

A Wife's Complaint

PREMCHAND

I've spent the greater part of my life in this house, but I've never had any peace. I expect that in the eyes of the world my husband is a very good man—good, courteous, generous, and alert. But it's only when things happen to *you* that you know what they're really like. The world likes to praise people who make their homes a hell, but are willing to ruin themselves for outsiders. A man may be ready to die for his family, but the world doesn't praise *him;* instead it thinks him selfish, mean, narrow-minded, arrogant, and stupid. So why should a man's family praise him if he is ready to die for outsiders? Look at *him.* He is a trial to me from morning till night. Send him to get something and he'll get it from a shop where no one else would even dream of going. In shops like that there's nothing in good condition; and they don't give you full weight; and they don't charge reasonable prices. If there weren't all these things wrong with them, how could they have got a bad name? But with him it's like a disease. It's only in shops like these that he'll do the shopping. I've told him time and again, 'Go to a shop that's doing well. They have a faster turnover, and so the stuff that you get is fresh.' But no, he feels a sympathy for the little, struggling shopkeepers, and they take advantage of him. He'll bring home the worst wheat in the market, with weevils in it, and rice so coarse that an ox wouldn't look at it, and lentils full of grit, so hard that you can use any amount of firewood trying to cook them, but they won't soften. Ghee that is half oil, priced at only a fraction less than pure ghee. Hair oil that is adulterated; put it on, and your hair all sticks together—and he'll pay the same for it as you pay for the best quality jasmine oil. You'd think he was afraid to go to any shop that's thriving. Perhaps he goes by the saying 'Fine shop-front, tasteless food.' *My* experience tells me, 'Grubby shop, rotten food.'

If all this happened only occasionally you could put up with it. You can't put up with it when it happens day after day. I ask him *why* he goes to these wretched shops. Has he signed a contract to look after them? He says, 'When they see me they call out to me.' Wonderful! All they have to do is call him across and flatter him a little, and he feels wonderful and no longer notices what rubbishy stuff they're giving him. I ask him, 'Why do you go that way? Why don't you go some other way? Why do you encourage these thieves?' No answer. Silence fends off no end of troubles.

Once I had to have a piece of my jewellery repaired. I knew his lordship, and didn't see any need to ask *him* about it. I sent for a goldsmith I knew by sight. It so happened that *he* was there at the time. He said, 'You can't trust this lot. They'll swindle you. I know a goldsmith. He went to school with me and when we were little we used to play together all the time. He won't try any tricks with me.' I thought, 'Well, if he's his friend, and a childhood friend at that, he's bound to have some regard for that friendship.' So I handed over a gold ornament and 50 rupees—and God knows what rogue the good man gave it to. I had to pester him for years together, and when it came back the 'gold' was half copper and he'd made it into something so ugly that I couldn't bear the sight of it. Something I'd wanted for years was ruined, and all I could do was cry over it and then make the best of it. Such are his faithful friends who aren't ashamed to cut his throat for him. And he only *makes* friends with people who are half-starved, poor, penniless creatures whose trade it is to make friends with purblind people like him. Every day one or other of these gentlemen turns up to pester him; and they don't let go until he gives them something.

But I've never known any of them to pay back what they've borrowed. You lose once, and you learn your lesson—or lose *twice,* and learn your lesson; but *my* good man loses a thousand times and still never learns. When I tell him, 'You lent him the money. Why don't you ask him for it back? Has he gone off and died somewhere?' he just shrugs his shoulders. He can't bear to refuse anything to a friend. 'All right,' I tell him, 'don't then. I'm not telling you to be unsympathetic. But you can put them off a bit, can't you? Can't you make some excuse?' But he can't refuse anyone. A friend asks him for something and he feels it as a burden, and, poor fellow, he *can't* refuse. If he did people would think *he* was half-starved; and he wants the world to think him rich even if he has to pawn my jewellery to give that impression. There are times when we've been almost penniless, but this good man can't rest until he's as prodigal with his money to others as he is mean to us. Every day someone or other comes to pester us—a visitor from whom there's no escape. God knows where all these irresponsible friends of his come from. They come from all over the place. Our house is not so much a home as a refuge for the handicapped. It's only a small house; we can hardly muster four string-beds, and we haven't a lot of bedding. But *he's* always ready to invite people to stay. *He'll* be sharing a room with the guest, so he'll need a bed and bedding. Otherwise we can't keep up appearances. And it's me and the children who have to suffer for it and get through the night huddled together on the floor. In the summer it's not too bad, but in the winter it's torture. And in the summer too *they* occupy the open roof; the children and I are like birds trapped in a cage. He hasn't even got the sense to see that when this is how things are at home he shouldn't invite people to stay who've hardly got a rag to their name. By the grace of God, that's the kind of people *all* his friends are. There's not one of them who could even give him a penny if ever *he* should need help. He's had one or two bitter experiences—extremely bitter. But it's as if he's sworn never to open his eyes. It's penniless people like this that he takes to. He makes friends of people you're ashamed to speak of, people you wouldn't even open the door to. There are plenty of important, well-to-do people in the town, but he has no contact with any of them. He never goes to pay a call on them. These rich people are arrogant; they fancy themselves, and want you to flatter them. How *can* he go to them? No, he'll make friends with the sort of people who haven't even got anything to eat in the house.

Once we had a servant leave us and for some days we couldn't find another one. I was looking for a sensible, capable man, but he was anxious to get one as quickly as possible. The running of the house went on as usual, but to *him* it seemed that everything was being held up. One day he got hold of some yokel—God knows where from—and brought him along. You could tell simply by looking at him that he'd just come down from the trees, but *he* praised him to the skies. He's obedient; he's utterly honest; he's a real worker; he knows how to go about things; he's extremely well-mannered. Well, I took him on. I don't know why time after time I let him persuade me: it surprises even me. This man was a man only in the sense that he was something in human form. No sign of anything else human about him. He had no idea how to go about anything. He wasn't dishonest, but he was an idiot of the first order. If he'd been dishonest I'd at least have had the consolation of knowing that he was getting something out of it. But the wretched man was a prey to all the shopkeepers' tricks. He couldn't even count up to ten. I'd give him a rupee in the morning and send him off to the shops, and if you gave him till evening to work out how much he'd spent and how much change he should have he couldn't tell you. I'd just have to swallow my anger. My blood would begin to boil and I'd feel like tearing his ears off, the pig; but I never saw his lordship saying anything to him. After he'd bathed he'd be folding his loincloth, while the servant just sat there looking at him. It made my blood boil, but *he* wouldn't even notice it, and if the servant did offer to fold the loincloth, he wouldn't let him anywhere near it. He would present his faults as if they were virtues, and if he couldn't manage to do that, he'd conceal them. The wretched man didn't even know how to use a broom properly. The men's sitting room is the only decent room in the house. When he swept it, he'd put everything back in the wrong place. You'd think the room had been hit by an earthquake, and there'd be so much dust in the air that you could hardly breathe. But *he'd* sit there happily in the room as though nothing untoward was happening. One day I gave the man a good talking to. I told him, 'From tomorrow onwards if you don't sweep the room properly I'll dismiss you on the spot.' When I got up next morning I saw that the room had already been swept—everything in its proper place and not a trace of dust anywhere. My husband laughed and said, 'What are you staring at? Ghora got up very early to sweep the room. I explained to him how to do it. You explain nothing, and then you start scolding him.' So, you see? That too was *my* fault. Anyway I thought, 'Well that's *one* thing the useless man has learnt to do properly.' From that day forward I found every day that the room was clean and Ghora began to gain some respect in my eyes. Then for some reason I got up earlier than usual one day and as I went into the room what did I see? Ghora standing in the doorway and his majesty himself carefully sweeping the floor. I couldn't control myself. I snatched the broom from his hand, clouted Ghora on the head with it and told him to get out. My husband said, 'All right, but pay him what we owe him.' That's a good one! He doesn't do his work properly; he's insolent—and on top of all that I'm to pay him! I didn't pay him a penny. I'd given him a shirt to wear, and he took it with him when he went.

One day the sweeper asked me to give him our cast-off clothing. In these times of unemployment who has any clothes to spare? Maybe the rich do, but we don't even have all the clothes we need. You could pack up his majesty's complete wardrobe in a parcel and send it through the post. And that winter we hadn't been able to get new clothes made. I turned him down flat. It was extremely cold. I could feel that myself; and I knew very well what the poor must be suffering. But what can you or I do except feel sorry for them? When the rich and powerful have clothes enough to fill a goods wagon then of course the poor have to suffer the tortures of nakedness. Anyway, I refused. And what did *he* do? He took off his coat and gave it to him. I was furious. It was the only coat he had.

He didn't bother to think what *he* was going to wear. The sweeper salaamed him, called down God's blessings upon him, and was off. He put up with the cold for some days. Before that he used to go for a walk every morning, but now he gave up doing that. But it's a strange temperament God has given him. He's not ashamed to go about in rags. If people laugh at him, let them. *He* doesn't care. I could die of shame, but he doesn't even notice. In the end I couldn't bear it any longer and I got a coat made for him. It was the last thing I *wanted* to do. I felt like making him put up with the cold until he'd had a bellyfull, but I was afraid he might fall ill; and then we'd be in even worse trouble. After all, he's the breadwinner.

In all these years he's never of his own accord bought me a present. I grant you, when I've asked for something he's never once objected to going and buying it for me—provided that I give him the money for it. He's never felt inspired to pay for it himself. It's true that he never buys anything for himself either, poor fellow; he's quite content with what I get. But after all a man does sometimes fancy something. I see what other men do. They're always bringing something for their wives—jewellery, clothes, makeup.... But with us that practice is forbidden. I don't think he's even once in his life bought sweets, or toys, or a trumpet or anything like that for the children. It's as if he'd sworn not to. So I say he's mean, dried up—a man who has no enthusiasm for anything. And his generosity to others I put down to the fact that he's a simpleton; he's greedy for approval, and likes to show off. He's so weak and modest that he doesn't mix with any of the people who hold any position in the office where he works. It's against his rules to pay his respects to them, let alone give them presents. He doesn't even call on them at their homes. And it's he who reaps the consequences. Who else? Other people are given paid leave. *His* leave is unpaid. Other people get promoted. *He* is simply ignored. If he's even five minutes late for work he's asked for an explanation. The poor man works himself to death, and yet if anything difficult or complicated comes up it's him who's given the job of sorting it out, and he never objects. People in his office make fun of him and call him 'the drudge'. And no matter how difficult the task he's coped with, it's written in his fate that he'll get the same dry grass at the end of it. I don't call that modesty; it's a simple ignorance of the ways of the world. And why *should* anyone be pleased with him? It's tolerance and consideration that gets you by in this world. If you hold yourself aloof from people, then of course they'll hold themselves aloof from you. And once they take a dislike to you then of course that shows itself in office relationships. Subordinates who take care to keep their superiors happy, who make sure that their superiors get some personal advantage from them, and whom their superiors can depend upon are sure to win their superiors' regard. Why should they feel any sympathy for a man who wants nothing from them? After all they too are only human. How is their desire for respect and distinction to be satisfied if their subordinates are so independent? Everywhere he's worked, he's been dismissed. He's never lasted in any office for more than a year or two. He's either quarrelled with his superiors or gone and complained that they've given him too much work to do.

He claims that he looks after his relatives. He has several brothers and nephews. They never so much as ask after him, but he is always thinking of their needs. One of his brothers is a *tahsildar** now, and it is he who looks after all the family property. He lives in style. He's bought a car and has several servants, but it never even occurs to him to write to us. Once we were in desperate need of money. I said to him, 'Why don't you ask your munificent brother?' He said, 'Why should I bother him? He too has got to make ends meet, and he won't have much left over.' It was only because I kept pressing him that he wrote. I don't know what he said in the letter, but there was no money coming from *that* source, and we got none. After some days I asked him whether his illustrious brother had deigned to answer his letter. He was annoyed and said, 'It's still only a week since he'll have got it. How can you expect

* *Tahsildar:* Indian states are divided into districts and districts into *tahsils*. A *tahsil* usually comprises a town and an area of surrounding countryside, and the *tahsildar* is the administrative officer in charge of it.

a reply yet?' Another week went by, and *then* what? He never gave me the chance to say any more about it. He looked too happy for words. He'd go out and come back in great form, always with something amusing to tell me. He was constantly flattering me, and praising my family. I knew very well what he was up to. Saying all these things to please me so that I wouldn't have the chance to ask about his munificent brother. Expounding national, financial, moral and cultural questions, and in such detail, and with such a commentary that it would have astonished even a professor. And all this for no other reason than that he didn't want to give me a chance to ask about the matter. But *that* didn't stop me. When another two full weeks had passed and the date to send money to the insurance company was approaching as inexorably as death, I asked him, 'What's happened? Has your esteemed brother deigned to open his blessed lips? We've still heard nothing from him. After all, we too have a share in the family property, don't we? Or are you the son of one of the family's maidservants? It was earning a profit of five hundred rupees a year ten years ago. Now it must be earning at least a thousand. But we've never even got a bad penny of it. At a rough estimate we should have had two thousand. If not two thousand, one thousand; and if not one thousand, five hundred, or two hundred and fifty, or if nothing else at any rate the amount of the insurance premium. A tahsildar earns four times the amount we do. And he takes bribes. So why doesn't he pay us what he owes us?' He began humming and hawing. 'The poor man is having his house repaired. He has all the expense of entertaining his relations and friends.' Wonderful! As though the property's there for the sole purpose of earning the money for these things! And the good man is no good at making up excuses. If he'd asked me I could have provided him with a thousand. I'd have said that his house, and everything in it had been completely destroyed by fire; or that he'd been burgled, and the burglar had taken everything; or that he'd bought grain for 10,000 rupees, but had had to sell at a loss; or he'd been involved in a lawsuit, and it had bankrupted him. But the best excuses *he* can think up are really lame ones. That's the best his imagination can do for him—and he calls himself a writer and a poet. I bemoaned my fate and left it at that. I borrowed money from a neighbour's wife and that's how we got by. And even then he sings the praises of his brothers and his nephews. It makes me furious. God save us from brothers like his! They're as bad as Joseph's brothers.

By the grace of God we have two sons and two daughters. God's grace, or God's anger? They've all got too mischievous for words. But this good man will never so much as look disapprovingly at any of them. Eight o'clock at night and our eldest son is out somewhere and hasn't come back home. I'm worried. He's sitting there calmly reading the paper. I get cross, snatch the paper from his hand and say 'Why don't you go and look for him? See where he's got to, the brat? Don't *you* feel anxious? You don't deserve to *have* children. This time when he comes home give him a real dressing down.' Then he too gets angry. 'Isn't he back yet? He's really gone to the bad. This time I'll pull his ears off! I'll flay him!' He goes off in a real rage to look for him. But it so happens that he's only just gone out when the boy comes home. I ask him, 'Where have you been? Your father, poor man, has gone out to look for you. Just you see what he does to you when he gets back! You'll never do it again. He was gnashing his teeth. He'll be back any minute now. He's got his stick with him. You've got so unruly that you take no notice of anything we tell you. Well, today you'll learn to take notice. You'll learn what's good for you.' The boy is frightened. He lights the lamp and sits down to study.

It's almost two hours later when his father comes back, worried and distressed and not knowing what to do. The moment he gets in he says, 'Is he back?' I want to make him angry. I say, 'Yes he's back. *You* go and ask him where he's been. I've stopped asking him. He won't say anything.'

He thunders, 'Munna, come here!'

The boy goes out into the courtyard trembling in fear and stands there. The two girls go off and hide themselves inside the house, wondering what terrible thing is going to happen next.

The little boy is peeping out of the window like a mouse out of its hole. Their father is beside himself with rage, and his stick is in his hand. Even I, when I see his angry face, begin to regret having complained about the boy. He goes up to the boy—and then, instead of hitting him with his stick, he lays his hand gently on his shoulder and, pretending to be angry, says, 'Where did you get to, sir? You're forbidden to do things, and you take no notice. If ever you come home so late again, watch out! Boys who behave themselves come home in the evening, and don't go roaming about all over the place.'

I'm thinking, 'That's the preamble. Now he'll start on what he has to say. Not a bad preamble.' But it's both the preamble and the conclusion. He's calmed down. The boy goes off to his room and is probably jumping for joy there.

I raise my voice in protest. 'Anyone would think you're afraid of him. You might at least have given him a clout or two. This way you'll make him worse. Today he came in at eight. Tomorrow it'll be nine. What do you think he's thinking now?'

He says, 'Didn't you hear how I scolded him? He'll have been scared to death. You'll see, he won't come home late again.' 'Scold him? You didn't scold him. You dried his tears for him.' He's got hold of a new idea, that punishment is bad for a boy. He thinks boys should be free, and not subject to any kind of restriction or pressure. He thinks that restrictions hinder their development. That's why they get out of control. They won't sit still for a minute to open a book. Sometimes he's playing tip-cat, sometimes it's marbles, and sometimes it's kites. And his honour joins in. He's past forty now, but he's still a boy at heart. In *my* father's presence none of my brothers would have dared to fly kites or play tip-cat. He'd have had their blood. Every morning he'd sit down and start teaching them, and as soon as they were back from school he'd sit them down again. Half an hour's free time in the evening, and that was all. Then they'd again have to buckle to. That's how it was. He wouldn't be reading the newspaper while his sons roved around the backstreets.

Sometimes he plays the part of a youngster and sits down to play cards with the boys. How can a father like that inspire any awe in his children? Not like *my* dad. My brother wouldn't have dared to look him in the eye. We'd tremble at the sound of his voice. It was enough for him to set foot in the house for all of us to stop talking. The boys felt they were taking their lives in their hands when they faced him. And the result of this upbringing is that all of them now have good jobs. True, none of them has good health; but then daddy's health was not all that good either. Poor man, he was always falling ill. So how could his sons' health be good? Anyway, be that as it may, education and correction was something he never spared any of them.

One day I saw his honour teaching our elder son how to fly a kite—'Turn it like this, dip it like this, pull it like this, let it out like this.' He was putting all he had into his teaching, as if he were a guru teaching mantras. That day I gave him a telling off he's not likely to forget. I told him straight, 'Who do you think you are, ruining my children? If you've got no interest in our home, alright. But don't ruin my children; don't encourage them in idle pursuits. If you can't improve them, at any rate don't ruin them.' He tried to make excuses. My dad would never take any of his boys to any fair or to see any show. No matter how much fuss the boy created he would never relent. But *this* good man not only takes them but asks every one of them if they'd like to go. 'Come on! It'll be great there! There'll be fireworks, and balloons, and English big wheels. You'll enjoy going on them!' As though that were not enough he lets them play hockey. These English games frighten me. Cricket, football, hockey, each more fatal than the last. If the ball hits you it can practically kill you. But he thinks these games are great. When one of the boys comes home and tells him his side has won he's as happy as if they'd taken a fort. He's not in the least afraid—never thinks of what might happen if one of them gets hurt. If they break an arm or a leg, what sort of life will they have, poor boys?

Last year we got our daughter married. He was determined he wouldn't spend so much as a penny on a dowry, not even if the girl had to stay unmarried all her life. He sees every day how mean people are, but nothing gives him eyes to see. So long as our social system lasts and people point the finger at any girl who is left unmarried long after puberty, this convention won't disappear. You'll be lucky to find three or four people enlightened enough to forego a dowry. But the impact they make is very small, and the bad old ways continue as usual. It's only when the time comes when girls, like boys, can still be unmarried at twenty or twenty-five without getting a bad name, that this custom will disappear of its own accord. Wherever I tried to get a match for her the question of a dowry came up; and every time he dug his heels in. After this had gone on for a whole year, and the girl was nearly seventeen, I found someone who was willing. His honour too consented to it, because the people concerned hadn't made any formal agreement about it, although they felt sure in their own minds that they'd get a sizeable amount, and I too had made up my mind to do my very best to see to it that nothing was lacking. I felt sure that the wedding would go off without a hitch. But his holiness opposed me in everything. 'This custom is absurd, that custom is meaningless. Why need we spend money on that? Why do we need singers?' He got on my nerves. 'Why this? Why that? That's exactly the same as giving dowry. You've disgraced me. You've ruined my good name.' Just think of it, the bridegroom's party is waiting at the door and we're arguing over every little thing. The appointed time for the marriage was twelve o'clock at night. That day the girl's parents fast. I did, but he would have none of it. 'We don't need to fast. When the groom's parents don't fast why should the bride's parents fast?' Not only I, but the whole family tried to stop him, but no, he had his breakfast and his other meals as usual. Well, night came, and it was time for the kanyadan. He's always objected to this ceremony. 'A girl isn't something that you give away. Money you give away; animals you can give away, but "giving away" a girl is a lot of nonsense.' I did my utmost to persuade him. 'It's an ancient custom. The shastras clearly prescribe it.' His relatives and friends tried to persuade him, but he was absolutely unmoved. I said to him, 'What will people say?

They'll think we've abandoned our religion.' But he just wouldn't listen. I fell at his feet and pleaded with him—went so far as to say, 'All right, don't *you* do anything. All there is to do I'll do myself. But just come and sit in the pavilion next to the girl and give her your blessing.' But this man of God simply turned a deaf ear. In the end I burst out crying. I couldn't stomach the idea that when the girl's father was there his brother or my brother should give her away. So I did it all on my own. He never even glanced that way. And the best of it is that *he* was cross with *me*. For months after the bridegroom's party had left he wouldn't speak to me. And in the end it was I who had to climb down.

But it's a strange thing that in spite of all these things I can't bear to be parted from him for a single day. With all his faults, I love him. What there is about him that makes me crazy about him I don't know myself. But there's certainly *something* that makes me a slave to him. If ever he's a bit later than usual in coming home I get anxious. If he gets so much as a headache I go frantic. If fate today were to offer me in exchange for him a man who was the very embodiment of learning and intelligence and as rich and handsome as a god, I wouldn't so much as look at him. And it's not just that I'm doing my duty. Not at all. And it's not conventional loyalty either. It's just that something has happened to both of us, something that's given us an ability to adjust to, and harmonise with each other like the moving parts of a machine which long use has adapted to working together so perfectly that no new part, however well-formed and beautiful, could ever take their place. We walk along a familiar road, without fear, without looking, because our eyes have taken in all its ups and downs and twists and turns. Think how difficult it would be to walk along some *strange* road, afraid at every step of losing our way, afraid all the time of thieves and robbers. In fact, I think today that I wouldn't even want to exchange his faults for virtues.

Tiny's Granny

ISMAT CHUGHTAI

God knows what her real name was. No one had ever called her by it. When she was a little snotty-nosed girl roaming about the alleys, people used to call her 'Bafatan's kid'. Then she was 'Bashira's daughter-in-law,' and then 'Bismillah's mother'; and when Bismillah died in childbirth leaving Tiny an orphan, she become 'Tiny's Granny' to her dying day.

There was no occupation which Tiny's Granny had not tried at some stage of her life. From the time she was old enough to hold her own cup she had started working at odd jobs in people's houses in return for her two meals a day and cast-off clothes. Exactly what the words 'odd jobs' mean, only those know who have been kept at them at an age when they ought to have been laughing and playing with other children. Anything from the uninteresting duty of shaking the baby's rattle to massaging the master's head comes under the category of 'odd jobs'. As she grew older she learnt to do a bit of cooking, and she spent some years of her life as a cook. But when her sight began to fail and she began to cook lizards in the lentils and knead flies into the bread, she had to retire. All she was fit for after that was gossiping and tale-telling. But that also was a fairly paying trade. In every muhalla there is always some quarrel going on, and one who has the wit to carry information to the enemy camp can be sure of a hospitable reception. But it's a game that doesn't last. People began to call her tell-tale, and when she saw that there was no future there, she took up her last and most profitable profession: she became a polished and accomplished beggar.

At meal times Granny would dilate her nostrils to smell what was cooking, single out the smell she liked best and be off on its track until she reached the house it was coming from.

'Lady, are you cooking arbi with the meat?' she would ask with a disinterested air.

'No, Granny. The arbi you get these days doesn't get soft. I'm cooking potatoes with it.'

'Potatoes! What a lovely smell! Bismillah's father, God rest him, used to love meat and potatoes. Every day it was the same thing: "Let's have meat and potatoes," and now (she would heave a sigh), I don't see meat and potatoes for months together.' Then, suddenly getting anxious, 'Lady, have you put any coriander leaf in the meat?'

'No, Granny. All our coriander was ruined. The confounded water carrier's dog got into the garden and rolled all over it.'

'That's a pity. A bit of coriander leaf in with the meat and potatoes makes all the difference. *Hakimji's** got any amount in his garden.'

'That's no good to me, Granny. Yesterday his boy cut my Shabban Mian's kite string and I told him that if he showed his face again he'd better look out for himself.'

'Good heavens, I shan't say it's for you.' And Granny would gather her burqa around her and be off with slippers clacking to Hakimji's. She'd get into the garden on the plea of wanting to sit in the sun, and then edge towards the coriander bed. Then she'd pluck a leaf and crush it between her finger and thumb and savour the pleasant smell and, as soon as the Hakimji's daughter-in-law turned her back, Granny would make a grab. And obviously, when she had provided the coriander leaf, she could hardly be refused a bite to eat.

Granny was famed throughout the muhalla for her sleight of

---

* *Hakim:* A practitioner of the traditional Greek medicine, transmitted by the Arabs to the rest of the world.

hand. You couldn't leave food and drink lying unwatched when Granny was about. She would pick up the children's milk and drink it straight from the pan: two swallows and it would be gone. She'd put a little sugar in the palm of her hand and toss it straight into her mouth. Or press a lump of gur to her palate, and sit in the sun sucking it at her ease. She made good use of her waistband too. She would whip up an areca nut and tuck it in. Or stuff in a couple of chapatis, half in and half out, but with her thick kurta concealing them from view, and hobble away, groaning and grunting in her usual style. Everyone knew all about these things but no one had the courage to say anything, firstly because her old hands were as quick as lightning, and moreover when in a tight corner she had no objection to swallowing whole whatever was in her mouth; and secondly, because if anyone expressed the slightest suspicion of her she made such a fuss that they soon thought better of it. She would swear her innocence by all that was sacred, and threaten to take an oath on the Holy Quran. And who would disgrace himself in the next world by directly inviting her to swear a false oath on the Quran?

Granny was not only a tale-bearer, thief, and cheat. She was also a first-rate liar. And her biggest lie was her burqa which she always wore.

At one time it had had a veil, but when one by one the old men of the muhalla died off, or their eyesight failed, Granny said goodbye to her veil. But you never saw her without the cap of her burqa, with its fashionably serrated pattern on her head, as though it were stuck to her skull, and though she might leave it open down the front (even when she was wearing a transparent kurta with no vest underneath) it would billow out behind her like a king's robe. This burqa was not simply for keeping her head modestly covered. She put it to every possible and impossible use. It served her as bedclothes: bundled up, it became a pillow. On the rare occasions when she bathed, she used it as a towel. At the five times of prayer, it was her prayer mat. When the local dogs bared their teeth at her, it became a serviceable shield for her protection. As the dog leapt at her calves it would find the voluminous folds of Granny's burqa hissing in its face. Granny was exceedingly fond of her burqa, and in her spare moments would sit and lament with the keenest regret over its advancing old age. To forestall further wear and tear, she would patch it with any scrap of cloth that came her way, and she trembled at the very thought of the day when it would be no more. Where would she get eight yards of white cloth to make another one? She would be lucky if she could get as much together for her shroud.

Granny had no permanent headquarters. Like a soldier, she was always on the march—today in someone's verandah, tomorrow in someone else's back yard, the next day in some abandoned room. Wherever she spied a suitable site she would pitch camp and, when they turned her out, would move on. With half her burqa laid out under her and the other half wrapped over her, she would lie down and take her ease.

But even more than she worried about her burqa, she worried about her only grand-daughter Tiny. Like a broody old hen, she would always keep her safe under her sheltering wing, and never let her out of her sight. But a time came when Granny could no longer get about so easily, and when the people of the muhalla had got wise to her ways—as soon as they heard the shuffle of her slippers approaching they sounded the alert and took up positions of defence: and then all Granny's broad hints and suggestions would fall on deaf ears. So there was nothing that Granny could do except put Tiny to her ancestral trade, doing odd jobs in people's houses. She thought about it for a long time, and then got her a job at the Deputy Sahib's* for her food, clothing, and one and a half rupees a month. She was never far away though, and stuck to Tiny like a shadow. The moment Tiny was out of sight she would kick up a hullabaloo.

But a pair of old hands cannot wipe out what is inscribed in a person's fate. It was midday. The Deputy's wife had gone off to

---

* i.e. 'Deputy Collector', second in command to the 'Collector' (District Magistrate), the government officer in charge of one of the districts into which an Indian province was divided.

her brother's to discuss the possibility of marrying her son to his daughter. Granny was sitting at the edge of the garden taking a nap under the shade of a tree. The lord and master was taking his siesta in a room enclosed by water-cooled screens. And Tiny, who was supposed to be pulling the rope of the ceiling fan, was dozing with the rope in her hand. The fan stopped moving, the lord and master woke up, his animality was aroused, and Tiny's fate was sealed.

They say that to ward off the failing powers of old age the hakims and *vaids*,* besides all the medicine and ointments which they employ, also prescribe chicken broth—well, the nine-year-old Tiny was no more than a chicken herself.

When Tiny's Granny awoke from her nap, Tiny had disappeared. She searched the whole muhalla, but there was no sign of her anywhere. But when she returned tired out to her room at night, there was Tiny in a corner leaning up against the wall, staring about her with listless eyes like a wounded bird. Granny was almost too terrified to speak, but to conceal the weakness she felt she began swearing at Tiny. 'You little whore, so this is where you've got to! And I've been all over the place looking for you until my poor old legs are all swollen. Just wait till I tell the Master. I'll get you thrashed within an inch of your life!'

But Tiny couldn't conceal what had happened to her for long, and when Granny found out, she beat her head and shrieked. When the woman next door was told, she clutched her head in horror. If the Deputy's son had done it, then perhaps something might have been said. But the Deputy himself... one of the leading men in the muhalla, grandfather to three grandchildren, a religious man who regularly said his five daily prayers and had only recently provided mats and water-vessels to the local mosque—how could anyone raise a voice against him?

So Granny, who was used to being at the mercy of others, swallowed her sorrow, applied warm cloths to Tiny's back, gave her

---

* *Vaids*: Those who practice the ancient traditional (Indian) system of medicine.

sweets to comfort her, and bore her trouble as best she might. Tiny
spent a day or two in bed, and then was up and about again. And in
a few days she had forgotten all about it.

Not so the gentlewomen of the muhalla! They would send for
her on the quiet and ask her all about it.

'No, Granny will smack me,' Tiny would try to get out of it.

'Here take these bangles... Granny won't know anything about
it.' The eager ladies would coax her.

'What happened? How did it happen?' They would ask for all
details, and Tiny who was too young and innocent to understand
entirely what it all meant, would tell them as well as she could and
they would cover their faces and laugh delightedly.

Tiny might forget, but nature cannot. If you pluck a flower in the
bud and make it bloom before it is ready, its petals fall and only the
stump is left. Who knows how many innocent petals Tiny's face had
shed? It acquired a forward, brazen look, a look older than its years.
Tiny did not grow from a child into a girl, but at one leap became
a woman, and not a fully-fashioned woman moulded by nature's
skilled and practiced hands, but one like a figure on whom some
giant with feet two yards long had trodden—squat, fat, puffy, like a
clay toy which the potter had knelt on before it had hardened.

When a rag is all dirty and greasy, no one minds too much if
someone wipes his nose on it. The boys would pinch her playfully
in the open street, and give her sweets to eat. Tiny's eyes began
to dance with an evil light... And now Granny no longer stuffed
her with sweets: she beat her black and blue instead. But you can't
shake the dust off a greasy cloth. Tiny was like a rubber ball: hit it
and it comes bouncing back at you.

Within a few years Tiny's promiscuity had made her the pest of
the whole muhalla. It was rumoured that the Deputy Sahib and his
son had quarrelled over her...then that Rajva the palanquin-bearer
had given the *mullah** a thorough thrashing...then that she had

---

* *Mullah*: A Muslim divine, not generally highly educated, or highly
respected.

taken up regularly with the nephew of Siddiq the wrestler. Every day Tiny came near to losing her nose,* and there was fighting and brawling in the alleys.

The place became too hot to hold her. There was nowhere she could safely set foot any more. Thanks to Tiny's youthful charms and Siddiq's nephew's youthful strength, life in the muhalla became intolerable. They say that in places like Delhi and Bombay there is an abundant demand for their kind of commodity. Perhaps the two of them migrated there. The day Tiny ran away, Granny had not the slightest suspicion of what was afoot. For several days the little wretch had been unusually quiet. She hadn't sworn at Granny, but had spent a lot of time sitting quietly on her own, staring into space.

'Come and get your dinner, Tiny,' Granny would say.

'I'm not hungry, Granny.'

'Tiny, it's getting late. Go to bed.'

'I don't feel sleepy, Granny.'

That night she began to massage Granny's feet for her. 'Granny... Granny, just hear me recite the *Subhanakallahumma*† and see if I have got it right.' Granny heard it: Tiny had it off pat.

'All right, dear. Off you go now. It's time you were asleep.' And Granny turned over and tried to sleep.

A little later she could hear Tiny moving about in the yard.

'What the devil is she up to now?' she muttered. 'What b— has she brought home now? Little whore. She's got to use even the back yard now!' But when she peered down into the yard, Granny was filled with awe. Tiny was saying her *isha* prayer.‡ And in the morning she was gone.

People who return to this place from journeyings far afield sometimes bring news of her. One says that a great lord has made her his mistress and that she is living in fine style like a lady, with a

---

* Cutting off the nose was the traditional punishment inflicted on a loose woman. In this context, it would be the act of a jealous lover, punishing her for her promiscuity.

† Part of the words recited at each of the five times of prayer.

‡ *Isha:* Last of the five daily prayers prescribed by Islam.

carriage and any amount of gold. Another says she has seen her in the diamond market...others say she has been seen in Faras Road or in Sona Gachi.*

But Granny's story is that Tiny had had a sudden attack of cholera and was dead before anyone knew it.

After her period of mourning for Tiny, Granny's mind started to wander. People passing her in the street would tease her and make jokes at her expense.

'Granny, why don't you get married?' my sister would say.

Granny would get annoyed. 'Whom to? Your husband?'

'Why not marry the mullah? I tell you he's crazy about you. By God he is!'

Then the swearing would begin, and Granny's swearing was so novel and colourful that people could only stare aghast.

'That pimp! Just see what happens if I get hold of him! If I don't pull his beard out, you can call me what you like.' But whenever she met the mullah at the corner of the street, then, believe it or not, she would go all shy.

Apart from the urchins of the muhalla, Granny's lifelong memories were the monkeys—'the confounded, blasted monkeys'. They had been settled in the muhalla for generations and knew all about everyone who lived there. They knew that men were dangerous and children mischievous, but that only women were afraid of them. But then Granny too had spent all her life among them. She'd got hold of some child's catapult to frighten them with, and when she wound her burqa around her head like a great turban and pounced upon them with her catapult at the ready, the monkeys really did panic for a moment before returning to their usual attitude of indifference towards her.

Day in and day out, Granny and the monkeys used to fight over her bits and pieces of stale food. Whenever there was a wedding in the muhalla, or a funeral feast, or the celebrations that mark the fortieth day after childbirth, Granny would be there, gathering up the scraps

* Prostitutes' quarters in various Indian cities.

left over as though she were under contract to do so. Where free food was being distributed, she would contrive to come up for her share four times over. In this way she would pile up a regular stack of food, and then she would gaze at it regretfully, wishing that God had arranged her stomach like the camel's so that she could tuck away four days' supply. Why should He be so utterly haphazard? Why had He provided her with a machine for eating so defective that if she had more than two meals' supply at any one time, it simply couldn't cope with it? So, what she used to do was to spread out the food to dry on bits of sacking and then put them in a pitcher. When she felt hungry she would take some out and crumble it up, add a dash of water and a pinch of chillies and salt, and there was a tasty mash all ready to eat. But during the summer and during the rains this recipe had often given her severe diarrhoea. So when her bits of food got stale and began to smell she would, with the greatest reluctance sell them to people for whatever price she could get to feed to their dogs and goats. The trouble was that generally the stomachs of the dogs and the goats proved less brazen than Granny's and people would not take her dainties as a gift, let alone buy them. And yet these bits and pieces were dearer to Granny than life itself; she put up with countless kicks and curses to get them and dry them in the sun even though this meant waging holy war against the whole monkey race. She would no sooner spread them out than the news would, as though by wireless, reach the monkey tribes, and band upon band of them would come and take up their positions on the wall or frisk about on the tiles raising a din. They would pull out the straws from the thatch and chatter and scold the passers-by. Granny would take the field against them. Swathing her burqa around her head and taking her catapult in her hand, she would take her stand. The battle would rage all day, Granny scaring the monkeys off again and again. And when evening came she would gather up what was left after their depredations, and cursing them from the bottom of her heart, creep exhausted into her little room to sleep.

The monkeys must have acquired a personal grudge against Granny. How else can you explain the fact that they turned their backs on everything else the world had to offer and concentrated all their attacks on Granny's scraps of food? And how else can you explain the fact that a big rascally, red-behinded monkey ran off with her pillow, which she loved more than her life? Once Tiny had gone, this pillow was the only thing left in the world that was near and dear to her. She fussed and worried over it as much as she did over her burqa. She was forever repairing its seams with stout stitches. Time and again she would sit herself down in some secluded corner and start playing with it as if it were a doll. She had none but the pillow now to tell all her troubles to and so lighten her burden. And the greater the love she felt for her pillow, the stouter the stitches she would put into it to strengthen its seams.

And now see what trick Fate played on her. She was sitting leaning against the parapet with her burqa wrapped around her, picking the lice out of her waistband, when suddenly a monkey flopped down, whipped up her pillow, and was off. You would have thought that someone had plucked Granny's heart out of her breast. She wept and screamed and carried on so much that the whole muhalla came flocking.

You know what monkeys are like. They wait until no one is looking and then run off with a glass or a katora, go and sit on the parapet, and taking it in both hands start rubbing it against the wall. The person it belongs to stands there looking up and making coaxing noises, and holding out bread, or an onion: but the monkey takes his time, and when he has had his bellyful of fun, throws the thing down and goes his own way. Granny poured out the whole contents of a pitcher, but the bastard monkey had set his heart on the pillow, and that was that. She did all she could to coax him, but his heart would not melt and he proceeded with the greatest enjoyment to peel the manifold coverings off the pillow as though he were peeling the successive skins off an onion—those same coverings over which Granny had pored with her weak and watering eyes, trying to hold them together with stitching. As every fresh cover came off, Granny's hysterical wailing grew louder. And now the last covering was off, and the monkey began bit by bit to throw down the contents...not cotton wadding but... Shabban's quilted jacket...Bannu the water carrier's waistcloth... Hasina's bodice...the baggy trousers belonging to little Munni's doll...Rahmat's little dupatta...and Khairati's knickers...Khairan's little boy's pistol...Munshiji's muffler...the sleeve (with cuff) of Ibrahim's shirt...a piece of Siddiq's loin cloth... Amina's collyrium bottle and Bafatan's kajal-box...Sakina's box of tinsel clippings... the big bead of Mullan's rosary and Baqir Mian's prayer board... Bismillah's dried navel string, the knob of turmeric in its satchet from Tiny's first birthday, some lucky grass, and a silver ring... and Bashir Khan's gilt medal conferred on him by the government for having returned safe and sound from the war.

But it was not Granny's own trinkets that interested the onlookers. What they had their eyes on was her precious stock of stolen goods which Granny had got together by years of raiding.

'Thief!... Swindler!... Old hag!...Turn the old devil out!... Hand her over to the police! Search her bedding: you might find a lot more stuff in it!' In short, they came straight out with anything they felt like saying.

Granny's shrieking suddenly stopped. Her tears dried up, her head drooped, and she stood there stunned and speechless... She passed that night sitting on her haunches, her hands grasping her knees, rocking backwards and forwards, her body shaken by dry sobbing, lamenting and calling now the names of her mother and father, now her husband, now her daughter Bismillah, and her granddaughter Tiny. Every now and then, just for a moment, she would doze, then wake with a cry, as though ants were stinging an old sore. At times she would laugh and cry hysterically, at times talk to herself, then suddenly, for no reason, break into a smile. Then out of the darkness some old recollection would hurl its spear at her, and like a sick dog howling in a half-human voice, she would rouse the whole muhalla with her cries. Two days passed in this way, and the people of the muhalla gradually began to feel sorry for what they had done. After all, no one had the slightest need for any of these things. They had disappeared years ago, and though there had been weeping and wailing over them at the time, they had long since been forgotten. It was just that they themselves were no millionaires, and sometimes on such occasions a mere straw weighs down upon you like a great beam. But the loss of these things had not killed them. Shabban's quilted jacket had long since lost any ability to grapple with the cold, and he couldn't stop himself growing up while he waited for it to be found. Hasina had long felt she was past the age for wearing a bodice. Of what use to Munni were her doll's baggy trousers? She had long passed the stage of playing with dolls and graduated to toy cooking pots. And none of the people of the muhalla were out for Granny's blood.

In the old days there lived a giant. This giant's life was in a big black bee. Across the seven seas in a cave there was a big chest, and in it another chest, and inside that was a little box, in which there was a big black bee. A brave prince came...and first he tore off the bee's legs and, by the power of the spell, one of the giant's legs broke. Then the prince broke another leg, and the giant's other leg broke. And then he crushed the bee, and the giant died.

Granny's life was in the pillow, and the monkey had torn the enchanted pillow with his teeth, and so thrust a red-hot iron bar into Granny's heart.

There was no sorrow in the world, no humiliation, no disgrace, which Fate had not brought to Granny. When her husband died and her bangles were broken, Granny had thought she had not many more days to live; when Bismillah was wrapped in her shroud, she felt certain that this was the last straw on the camel's back. And when Tiny brought disgrace upon her and ran away, Granny had thought that this was the death-blow.

From the day of her birth onwards, every conceivable illness had assailed her. Small pox had left its marks upon her face. Every year at some festival she would contract severe diarrhoea.

Her fingers were worn to the bone by years of cleaning up other people's filth, and she had scoured pots and pans until her hands were all pitted and marked. Some time every year she would fall down the stairs in the dark, take to bed for a day or two and then start dragging herself about again. In her last birth Granny surely must have been a dog-tick; that's why she was so hard to kill. It seemed as though death always gave her a wide berth. She'd wander about with her clothes hanging in tatters, but she would never accept the clothes of anyone who had died, nor even let them come into contact with her. The dead person might have hidden death in the seams to jump out and grab the delicately nurtured Granny. Who could have imagined that in the end it would be the monkeys who would settle her account? Early in the morning, when the water carrier came with his water skin, he saw that Granny was sitting on her haunches on the steps. Her mouth was open and flies were crawling in the corners of her half-closed eyes.

People had often seen Granny asleep just like this, and had feared she was dead. But Granny had always started up, cleared her throat and spat out the phlegm, and poured out a shower of abuse on the person who had disturbed her. But that day Granny remained sitting on her haunches on the stairs. Fixed in death, she showered continuous abuse upon the world. Through her whole life she had never known a moment's ease and wherever she had laid herself down there had been thorns. Granny was shrouded just as she was, squatting on her haunches. Her body had set fast, and no amount of pulling and tugging could straighten it.

On Judgement Day the trumpet sounded, and Granny woke with a start and got up coughing and clearing her throat, as though her ears had caught the sound of free food being doled out... Cursing and swearing at the angels, she dragged herself somehow or other, doubled up as she was over the Bridge of Sirat* and burst into the presence of God the All Powerful and All Kind... And God, beholding the degradation of humanity, bowed His head in shame and wept tears, and those divine tears of blood fell upon Granny's rough grave, and bright red poppies sprang up there and began to dance in the breeze.

---

* In Islamic belief, a bridge thin as a hair and sharp as a sword, over which the true believer must pass to enter paradise.

Behind the Veil

RASHID JAHAN

Translator's Note:

This is described as 'a one-act play'. Western readers may perhaps regard it as a play only in the sense that it is dialogue, with an occasional stage direction. The description of the room where the conversation takes place would at once tell an Urdu speaking reader what kind of women the participants are. They belong to the traditional, respectable Muslim population of Old Delhi, families pride themselves on being *sharif*—'of good family'—and on maintaining the old-fashioned standards. In families of this kind elder relatives are not referred to by name but by relationship names, and English doesn't have the range of words for these that Urdu does. For example, Urdu has different words for 'uncle' showing specifically the relationship: father's younger brother is 'chacha', mother's brother is 'mamu', etc. In a traditional joint family household there may be the parents with all the grown-up sons and their families, so cousins grow up virtually as brothers and sisters. So someone referred to as a 'brother' may well be a cousin. Terms such as these recur in the dialogue, and in translating I have had to find other means to make clear who is who.

The setting: a house of this kind is enclosed on all sides, with one or more small courtyard. There are separate parts for the men and the women so that purdah can be observed, and they have several servants attending them. The living room floors are carpeted, and over the carpets, lighter carpets, often embroidered, are laid which keep the heavier carpet clean. There are no chairs and tables. People sit on the floor, and lean on a rather hard bolster. There may be beds in the room so that people can lie down when they want to. Both men and women habitually chew *paan*—betel leaf, wrapped around other ingredients often including betel nut and tobacco—and spittoons are at hand because the liquor from the paan is not swallowed but spat out. There are earthenware pitchers of water, each covered with a lid and with a drinking bowl on top of it. Shelves are not common; small arch-shaped recesses in the wall serve the same purpose. The fan is a long piece of heavy cloth, often with a fringe, fastened to a long piece of wood, hung from the ceiling and one of the servants is there to pull the rope to and fro when needed.

~

A lady [Muhammadi Begum] is tired and depressed. An older lady [Aftab Begum], about forty years of age, is sitting facing her, slicing betel nut into a small draw-string bag. On one side of her is a small box and on the other side a spittoon. There are doors in front, and niches and shelves with pans and lids arranged on them on the other walls. In the middle of the room a fan with a pink fringe hangs from the ceiling. In one corner of the room is a bed with a bedspread on it. On the other side of the room is a small embroidered carpet, a bolster, and a spittoon.

Muhammadi: Oh, sister. I've nothing left to live for. Much of my life has passed, and God will get me through the rest somehow. I'm so tired of life that if it weren't for the little ones I swear by God I'd have taken poison.

Aftab: Have you gone mad? You're no age yet. Why talk of taking poison? These are the best days of your life. The children, bless them, are growing up, and *now* you want to take poison! Look at me...

Muhammadi: Why should I look at you? It's not a question of age. Is it only old people that get tired of life? I've seen more zest for life in old people than in young ones. Everyone's dying. Why don't *I* die? And children soon forget; after a few days everything's all right again.

Aftab: Come to your senses, girl, come to your senses. You're no age at all and here you are wanting to die. You're ten to twelve years younger than me. The year you were born they were talking about getting me married. That was the year that the queen [Victoria] died. I remember it well. Aunty, God bless her—as pleased as if you'd been a boy. It was all of thirty years after she was married that you were born. A feast, and dancing to watch, and *domnis.** And how happy she was when you were married! How she'd longed for that day! All Delhi welcomed it! No one can match your luck. And look at *me,* how unlucky *I* am. You, God keep you, have everything—husband, children, home, everything...

Muhammadi: You're right; husband, children, home, everything. But young? Who would think me young? I look like an old woman of seventy—always ill, always under the hakim or the doctor, and every year a baby. Yes, no one can match *my* luck!

> *Her eyes fill with tears. She wipes them with her handkerchief, spits into the spittoon, and goes on.*

It's only two months ago—I'm talking of the time before my last miscarriage—that they decided to send for the lady doctor. Dr Ghiyas too had said that there might be something wrong inside that made me run a temperature so often, and that the lady doctor ought to look at my insides. I'll tell you what she said about my age. She asked me how old I was. I said, 'Thirty-two.' She smiled as if she didn't believe me. I said to her, 'Miss, what are you smiling at? Let me tell you I was married when I was eighteen, and I've had a baby

---

* *Domnis:* A low caste of singers and dancers who regularly provide entertainment on festive occasions.

every year since then—except for one year when my husband was in England for a year, and another year when we'd quarrelled. And these missing teeth that you can see—Dr Ghiyas pulled them out. Paria [pyorrhea] or something—I don't know what it was called. It was all because when my husband came back from England he said my breath smelt.' Poor woman, she had a good laugh at that.

Aftab: When you talk like that who can help laughing?

Muhammadi: Anyway the poor woman looked at my chest, and looked at my belly; and when she looked inside me she was alarmed and said, 'Begum Sahiba, it looks as though you're two months pregnant.' My heart sank, and I thought, 'More trouble.'

> *At this point the sound of children crying, and of shouting and bawling comes from the other room. Muhammadi gets up and shouts:*

You wretches! You don't give me a chance to rest and sleep, or any time to talk. A houseful of maidservants, and *still* there's the children making a din. Better if God strike me dead. I'd be rid of all the troubles of this world.

> *The door opens, and two wet nurses come in in clean dress—striped paijama, muslin shirts and dupattas. They bring in with them two children, who are crying. Other children, older than these two, can be seen standing in the doorway. All of them are thin, pale and weak. Beyond the door the courtyard can be seen.*

A wet nurse: Begum Sahiba, the little master won't do as he's told. He comes into the room and teases the little ones and won't let them play. He's run off with Miss Nanni's doll and the little boy's ball, and gone straight into the men's quarters.

Muhammadi (furiously): Blast him! He doesn't give any of us a moment's peace. Takes after his father.

> *She picks up the child and cuddles him, takes something out of the box and gives it to the two children to eat, and sends the wet nurse away again.*

Go! for God's sake go. Shouting and bawling from morning to night...

She pauses when the servants leave the door open.

Hey! Shut the door! I've told you several times this morning already to shut the door when you go out.

Aftab: Sister, in your house, God bless you, there's always some wretched doctor there. But look at your children—poor wretches they look thin and pale and miserable and half-starved.

Muhammadi: They're bound to be when they've not had their mother's milk. We take on any wet nurse that's going—fat, thin, pock-marked, one-eyed—anyone. Husband's orders. 'When God has given us money why should *you* be troubled?' he says. But it's his own pleasure he's thinking about. If the baby was with me *he'd* be inconvenienced. Doesn't matter whether it's day or night, he wants his wife. And not only his wife. He goes the rounds to other women too.

Aftab: Muhammadi Begum, you blame your husband for everything, poor man. If he gets you a wet nurse, that's wrong. And if he hadn't, *that* would've been wrong. Sister, remember what God commands you!

Muhammadi: Oh dear, sister. You weren't here when Nasir died. Poor little chap, he was only four months old. I wouldn't wish on my worst enemy all that *he* had to suffer. Even strangers couldn't bear to look at him. His wet nurse was quite a strapping girl. She looked quite healthy. But she had VD, and no one had the least suspicion of it. The baby caught it. He got huge blisters all over his body, and when they burst the flesh was all raw and there was pus oozing from everywhere. The same doctor, Dr Ghiyas, used to draw off whole basinfuls of it. I used to watch him from behind the curtain. They say, 'Don't complain; give thanks to God.' Anyway, he rotted away for two months and then died. After him I've had three more babies. I've said again and again, 'I'll breastfeed them,' but he takes no notice of me. And he threatens that if I breast feed he'll take another wife. 'I need a woman all the time,' he says. 'I'm not going to stand for you spending your time fussing around children.'

Aftab: Oh, *so that's it!* I never knew. God save us from men like that. Even animals shrink from that. They're worse than animals. God save a woman from falling into the clutches of men like that. Things used not to be like that. But now every wretched man you hear about is like this. Now my husband—well, he's an old man now, but even when he was young he never went too far. (Smiling) By God, I used to keep him on tenterhooks for hours...!

Muhammadi (sighing): We all have our own fate. What you've just said reminds me I didn't finish telling you about the lady doctor. We went off onto other things. When she said I was two months pregnant, she looked at me in astonishment and said, 'Begum Sahiba, you were telling me that you've been confined to bed for the last four months, and getting a temperature every evening. And Dr Ghiyas was telling me the same thing—that you've been running a temperature of 100 to 101 every evening. And you mean to tell me that in spite of that your husband...?' I said, 'Oh, miss *you're* all right. You earn your living, you eat well and sleep soundly. It's not like that with us. These fellows don't care whether they go to heaven or to hell when they die. They know what they want here. They don't care whether their wives, poor wretches, live or die. Men want their satisfaction.' The poor woman had nothing to say to that. She said, 'You're seriously ill...' Poor woman—and don't *all* the doctors say this?—'How can your children be strong and healthy when, for one thing, *you're* so weak, and then you have children so quickly—one after another.' What can we do? We'd have been better off if we'd been Christians.

Aftab: Don't! Don't say such wicked things! May God destroy those unbelievers! I've only one son and he's gone and married a Christian. I can't tell you how I was looking forward to arranging his marriage. I'd wanted to marry him to my brother's daughter Vahida. I'd planned their marriage when they were children. And now my brother has got fed up and he's got Vahida engaged. It's agony to think that my son's married a stranger. Better he'd never been born. As far as I'm concerned he's dead already.

Muhammadi: How can you have the heart to curse him like that? He's the one who'll support you when you're old. He'll come round and be all right one day.

Aftab: Oh no, he won't. It's two years now, and I haven't set eyes on him. I long to see him. He lives here in the city and he never even comes my way. I hear now that he's getting 150 a month. I thank God that at any rate there are no children yet. My one prayer to God is that even if there is no one to light a lamp on my grave when I'm dead, He'll see to it that this bastard Christian woman— may she die young!—never bears him a child. Anyway, sister, what's the point of telling people your troubles? Everyone's got troubles of their own... And, Muhammadi Begum, have you heard? Mirza* Maqbul Ali Shah has married again. Two of his wives have died. He's even got grandchildren who have children of their own. And this new wife—how innocent she looks!—is quite a young woman, quite young; not more than twenty at the most. What rotten luck for her! But the poor girl still has six sisters not yet married. That's why her parents, poor people....

> *At this point a boy of about twelve, his paijama bottoms caked with mud, bursts open the door and runs into the room. He has a cotton reel in one hand and scissors in the other. A sturdy-looking young girl, the boy's elder sister Sabira, in tight paijama, grubby clothes and trailing dupatta runs in after him.*

Sabira: Mummy, Mi won't let me alone. Look (she raises her kurta), he's cut my new paijama. I wasn't even saying anything to him. I

---

* *Mirza* is a form of address (or reference) to a person of Turkish Mughal descent. It is used not only in formal contexts but in quite informal ones too, where in English one would use the person's name.

was sitting there quietly sewing the buttons on daddy's *achkan.**
And look, he's torn the end of my dupatta.

She turns her face to the wall and starts crying with frustration.

Mirza (mimicking his sister): Boo hoo! You don't tell her what
you were doing. Sewing, were you? Shall I tell mummy you were
reading trashy books? *The Loving Friend,* or *The Lively Lad.* I didn't
see properly what it was.

Sabira (turning quickly towards him): For God's sake don't tell
such big lies. Mummy, I swear by God I was reading Maulvi Ashraf
Ali Thanavi's *Bahishti Zewar.†* He pestered me to show him, and I
wouldn't, so he cut my paijama. You never say anything to *him.*

Muhammadi: (Beating her forehead in exasperation, and speaking
sarcastically) Well done, daughter, well done! It's all the same to
you whether your mother lives or dies. Let alone helping her, you
quarrel with your young brothers and sisters. (Turning to the boy)
And this pest is pestering one or other of them all day long. Get
out of here!

Aftab: Give the scissors to me, son. Look at you, pestering your big
sister. How much longer will she be here with you? In a year or
two she'll be married and off to her in-laws. Then you'll be longing
to see her.

Sabira feels shy and bows her head at this and quietly creeps away.
Mirza makes a horse out of his mother's bolster, sits astride it a few
minutes and then begins to jump about on it.

Mirza: Well, why wouldn't she show me the book, then?

Muhammadi: For God's sake Mirza have mercy on me and don't
shake me up like this. You're making my whole body shake. My

---

* *Achkan*: A long coat that buttons up the front to the neck.
† A famous book written around 1901-1903 to teach Muslim women
their religious duties. It is still very widely read.

heart's beating fast. For God's sake go out. Go to your dad. And the *maulvi* sahib* will be coming. Have you learnt the lesson he set you?

Aftab: You've got too many children. Bless you, the house is full of them. But all this noise wears you out. And me, I sit in the house all day like someone hired to scare the crows. He comes home to say his prayers, sits with me a few minutes and goes off to the sitting room. God shouldn't make anyone so lonely. And all the hopes I had....

The door opens and a maidservant comes in carrying a dish.

Servant: Salaam, Begum Sahiba. (Turning to Aftab) Salaam, I was just on my way to your house with your share. (Turning again to Muhammadi) How are you, Begum Sahiba? And the children, God keep them, how are they?

Muhammadi: Oh, just as usual. Is your mistress well? Are all the children well? Congratulations on the birth of the grandchild.

That'll be *panjeri.*† (Turning to her own maidservant) Here, Rahiman, take the dish and empty it. (She opens a box) Sister [Aftab], give her a paan.

Aftab: Rahiman, I'll take my share here too. (She begins to make up a paan. Muhammadi gives two annas to the servant who has brought the dish.)

Muhammadi: My best greetings and best wishes to everyone. One day if I feel well enough I'll come. I'm longing to see you all again. I very much want to see the children. And tell your mistress from me, 'It seems you've sworn not to come and see me.'

* *Maulvi:* A Muslim divine, one of whose regular employments is to teach children to read the Quran—'read' in the sense of pronouncing the words correctly. The child does not learn what the words mean. Those who can afford it have the maulvi come to the child's home to do this.

† *Panjeri:* A sweetmeat made of five ingredients—almonds, cashews, pistachios, semolina and raisins. When anyone has good news to impart to relations and friends the custom is to send sweets to them.

Aftab gives her a paan and takes two annas from her waistband to give her.

Servant: Begum Sahiba, my mistress too often thinks of you. She just doesn't have time to come and see you. And these days, of course, the house is full of people. Everyone has come.

Aftab: Give my blessing to Sultan Dulhan, and my congratulations on the birth of her grandson. God willing, I'll come on Friday.

The servant takes both the dishes and leaves.

Muhammadi: Sultan is a really good manager. Her husband's never earned more than forty rupees a month, but, God bless her, she manages so well that she's done everything necessary—arranged the marriages of her sons, and her daughters. And now her son's got a good job—about a hundred and twenty rupees. And prospects of promotion too.

Aftab: Yes, he's got a good wife too. (Sighing deeply) We all have what's coming to us. Here's me...Well, never mind about that now. Tell me, is there any news of your cousin Razia? Your uncle was in such a hurry to get her first engaged and then married that he didn't even invite anyone.

Muhammadi: No, he didn't, but what of it? He had double and triple portions of food sent to every house. And the poor girl was married like that in a hurry, because he was afraid for his family's good name. And God bless him for it!

Aftab: Oh, so *that* was it. I'd no idea. What happened, then?

Muhammadi: You don't know? Well, everyone knows now. The poor girl's no age at all—only two and a bit years older than my Sabira. It was after I was married that she was born, when my younger uncle came back from Calcutta. He'd been there for years. We were all there to welcome him back. Granny, poor woman—she had the palsy—was happier than any of us. When Razia was born I took her home with me for a while. Her mother went off to her parents and Razia stayed on with me for three or four months. And after that too she often stayed for long periods in my house. She loved us—her father's people—and didn't like her mother's people at all. And it was quite natural that she should stay on. I was like an elder sister to her. I had no idea it would lead to any trouble.

Well, eventually she went back to her mother's house. Then one day, not long ago, she sent me a note begging me to come quickly. I don't know how to tell you what happened next. When I got there her grandmother—you've seen her; you know what she's like, how big she talks. Well, she gave me a grand welcome. Razia gave me a note when she wasn't looking, and said quietly 'Uncle* comes to see us every day and mummy makes a great fuss of him and talks secretly with him.' She's a young, unmarried girl. How could she say more than that? Poor girl, it took courage to say even that much. When I looked at the note it was one from my husband to Razia—a more passionate love letter than the ones you read in novels. I was furious. I warned her not to say anything to anyone and said I wouldn't mention her name to anyone. I got home burning with rage. I spoke to him about it. Sister, I swear to you he looked me straight in the eye and said, 'What's wrong with it? I'm going to marry Razia even if I have to divorce you.' I said, 'Are you in your right mind? Or have you completely lost your senses? She comes from a respectable family. If you so much as mention her name her father and his brother will make mincemeat of you. Don't even think of it!'

Aftab: That means her mother must have fixed it all up secretly. That's why he came out with it so boldly.

Muhammadi: Of course! God forgive her, she's always hated mummy and me. Even when mummy was ill she'd tell her to her face, and swear to it, that she wouldn't rest until she'd ruined me. And it wasn't only us. She had the same grudge against mummy's

---

* Muhammadi's husband.

elder brother. And since Razia's engagement had been fixed with a boy in her father's family—our side of the family—there were quarrels every day, with her mother insisting that she wouldn't marry her daughter to anyone in her enemies' family.

Aftab (laughing): And, sister, what makes your husband such a wonderful catch? He's got a wife and children. Granted, he has money. But the family she was to be married into isn't badly off either. Have respectable families ever done this? Those wretched Punjabis will marry off two of their daughters—two sisters—to the same man, but *we* never do that. Well, in these days *anything* can happen...

Well, what happened then?

Muhammadi: When I got angry and swore at him he began to implore me. 'I've fallen in love with her. For God's sake help me. It's your *duty* to help me.' He'd sit down and open the Holy Quran and read out verses telling me all that would happen to me in the next world if I didn't help him. But could hell fire be any worse than *this* fire that I burn in all the time? Well, he kept telling me all the time that he'd go mad. He'd shut himself in his room and lie face down and cry 'Razia! Razia!' And I'd sit there listening to it all. By God, I was in such a state that I thought, 'All this money is a curse. I wish we had only dry bread, and happiness.' Sister, give me a paan. All this talking's made my mouth dry.

> *She pours water from the pitcher and drinks it. Aftab eats a paan and gives Muhammadi one.*

Anyway, things went on like this, with him using lovers' language about that poor innocent girl and me listening to it all and feeling all choked by it. And the girl's mother's still making the same fuss of him. 'Razia, your uncle has come to see you. Give him a paan. Give him some cardamoms.'

Aftab: So all this was *her* doing.

Muhammadi: Of course. The girl would cry for hours together, and if I chanced to see her she'd pour out her heart to me. For a month I said nothing. Then one day both my uncles came to see me and I said, 'Well uncle, has Razia's engagement fallen through?' They both panicked. I'd restrained myself all this time and now I told them the whole story. They must have talked to each other about it, because three days later Razia was married.

Aftab: My God!

Muhammadi: But for six months after that he never came near me—was off in Chawri all the time. That suited me fine. As God's my witness, the day he goes off somewhere I sleep soundly at night. But every day it's, 'You're always ill. How long am I to put up with it? I'm going to marry again.' And on top of that, 'You must arrange a marriage for me. The *shariat** allows a man four wives; so why shouldn't I marry again?' I told him, 'Go ahead. Sabira's due to be married in a year's time. You can get married at the same time. You'll be able to take your grandchild and your new wife's baby on your knee at the same time.' Then he starts to row with me. 'What do women know about it? God didn't give them feelings.' I said, 'And it seems to me that He gave you the feelings of all men put together for your share.'

Aftab (flaring up): Muhammadi Begum, wherever you look these days you see this going on everywhere. The men win either way, every time. It's too much! He not only wants to marry again: on top of that his wife, poor wretch, is to arrange it for him.

Muhammadi: And that's what burns me up and makes me pray for death. I'm ill all the time. Then the children are always falling ill. Well, the eldest boy, bless him, is quite strong; but the little ones are always ailing. And all this means that there's no longer any joy in living. And I know that he'll marry again. No doubt about it. And I live in fear all the time. God take me away before I have to see the

---

* *Shariat*: Muslim law.

face of a co-wife. And I can't tell you all the things I've done from fear of that. I've had myself operated on twice.

Aftab: Yes, I'd heard that you'd had something done so that you couldn't have any more children.

Muhammadi: Who told you that? It wasn't that at all. My womb and all my lower parts had fallen. I got it put right so that he could get the same pleasure again as he'd got from a newly-married wife. But when a woman has a baby every year how *can* she stay in good shape? It slipped down again. And then he went at me and threatened me until he got me butchered again. And even then he wasn't satisfied.

    The call to prayer is heard from the mosque nearby.

Aftab: Good heavens, it's time now for the *zuhr*[*] prayer. I was so busy talking that I forgot everything else. (She closes the drawstring bag.) Now I'll have to say the prayer here before I go. My husband will be expecting me, poor man.

Muhammadi: Well sister, because of you coming I've got a lot of things off my chest. You must come a bit more often. *I'm* ill, I can't get about any more.

(Calling her servants.) Rahiman! Rahiman! Gulshabo!

    Rahiman enters.

Go and see to Badi Begum's ablutions.[†] And put down the prayer mat in the little room.

---

  [*] *Zuhr.* One of the five daily prayers prescribed by Islam; *zuhr* is recited just after midday.

  [†] *Badi Begum*: 'The elder lady'—a polite way of referring to Aftab.

Kalu Bhangi

KRISHAN CHANDER

I have often wanted to write about Kalu Bhangi, but what *can* one write about him? I have looked at his life from all sorts of angles and tried to assess and understand it, but I could never find anything out of the ordinary on which I could base a story, or even a plain, uninteresting, photographic sketch of him. And yet, I don't know why, every time I start to write a story I see Kalu Bhangi standing there in my imagination. He smiles at me and asks: 'Chhote Sahib, won't you write a story about *me*? How many years is it since you started writing?'

'Eight years.'

'And how many stories have you written?'

'Sixty—sixty-two. Sixty-two.'

'Then what's wrong? Can't you write one about me, Chhote Sahib? Look how long I've waited for you to write about me. I have been a good servant to you all these years—your old sweeper Kalu Bhangi. *Why* can't you write about me?'

There is nothing I can say in reply. His life has been so dull and uninteresting that there is simply nothing I can write about it. It's not that I don't want to write about him; for ages I've really wanted to write about him, but I could never do it, try as I might. And so today too, Kalu Bhangi is standing there in the corner of my mind, holding his old broom, and his big bare knees, his rough, cracked, ungainly feet, his varicose veins standing out on his dried-up legs, his hip-bones sticking out, his hungry belly, his dry, creased, black skin, the dusty hair on his sunken chest, his wizened lips, wide nostrils, wrinkled cheeks, and bald head shining above the dark hollows of his eyes. Many characters have told me their life stories, asserted their importance, impressed upon me their dramatic quality, and disappeared. But Kalu Bhangi is in his old place, standing there in just the same way, holding his old broom. He has seen every character that has come into my mind, watched them weeping and beseeching, loving and hating, sleeping and waking, laughing, making speeches—seen them in every aspect of life, on every level, at every stage from childhood to old age and from old age to death. He has seen every stranger who has peeped through the door, and, seeing that they were coming in, swept their path before them, himself moved to one side as a sweeper should, and stood respectfully by until the story has begun to be written, until it has ended, until both the characters and spectators have taken their leave. But even then Kalu Bhangi has gone on standing there; and now he has simply taken a step forward and come into the centre of my imagination, so that I may see him clearly. His bald plate is shining and an unspoken question is on his lips. I have been looking at him a long time, and I just can't think what I can write about him. But today this apparition is not to be put off...

I was only seven years old when I first saw Kalu Bhangi. Twenty years later when he died he looked exactly the same. Not the slightest change. The same knees, same feet, same complexion, same face, same bald head, same broken teeth, same broom. His broom always looked as though he had been born with it in his hand, as though it were a part of him. Every day he used to empty the patients' commodes, sprinkle disinfectant in the dispensary, and then go and sweep out the Doctor Sahib's and the Compounder* Sahib's bungalows, after which he would take the Doctor Sahib's cow and the Compounder Sahib's goat out to graze. Towards evening he would bring them back to the hospital, tie them up in

*The man who made up the medicine from the prescriptions.

the cattle-shed, go off to prepare his food, eat it, and go to bed. I watched him at these tasks every day for twenty years—every day without fail. During this whole time he was never ill for so much as a single day, which was something to wonder at—but still not so wonderful that you can write a story about it. Well, I'm writing this story under pressure. I've been fobbing him off for eight years, but the old man wouldn't let me alone. He kept on pressing me to write a story, and that was unfair both to me and to you—to me because now I'm having to write it, and to you because you're having to read it—this in spite of the fact that there is nothing much in him to justify all this labour. But what can I do? I am compelled to go on writing, though even as I write I keep on thinking, 'What *can* I write about a life such as his?' He's kept cropping up in my imagination continually for the last eight years— God knows why. I can't see what that proves, except his obstinacy. Even in the days when I was writing romantic stories, painting scenes of silvery moonlight, when my outlook on the world was a very milk-and-watery one—even then Kalu Bhangi was standing there. When I got beyond romanticism, and seeing both the beauty of life and its bestial passions, began to see its falling stars, then too he was there. When I looked down from my balcony and saw the poverty of those who give us our food, and when I saw rivers of blood flowing on the soil of the Punjab and realized that we are savages, then too he was standing on the threshold of my mind, silent and mute. But now I shall surely get rid of him; now he'll *have* to go; now I'm writing about him. Please, listen to his dull, flat, uninteresting story, so that I can send him packing and be rid of his unclean presence. If I don't write about him today and you don't read about him, he'll still be there another eight years hence— perhaps, indeed, for as long as I live.

But what bothers me is the difficulty of knowing what to write. Kalu Bhangi's father and mother were sweepers, and I should think that all his ancestors were sweepers too and lived in this same place for hundreds of years just like him. Kalu Bhangi never got married, never fell in love, never travelled very far—in fact, believe it or not, he never even went out of his own village. All day he would work, and at night he would sleep, and next morning get up again to busy himself with the same tasks. And from his very childhood this is what he had done. Oh yes, there is one quite interesting thing about him. He used to love to get some animal, a cow or a buffalo for example, to lick his bald head. I have often seen him at midday under the blue sky, sitting on his heels on the low earthen wall of some field near the hospital in the bright sunshine, with the green velvet carpet of grass behind him, and a cow licking his head, again and again, until the soothing feeling has sent him off to sleep. I used to feel a curious thrill of pleasure whenever I saw him sleeping like this, as though I had caught a glimpse of the drowsy, languid, all-pervading beauty of the universe. Why I don't know, but never in any other scene have I felt such innocence, such beauty and tranquillity, as I used to feel when I was seven years old and that field used to seem so huge and the sky so blue and clear, and Kalu Bhangi's bald head shone like glass, and the cow's tongue, gently licking his head as though to soothe him, made a dreamy rustling sound. I used to feel like getting my own head shaved like his, so that I could sit beneath the cow's tongue and drop off to sleep like him. In fact once I tried it out, and what a thrashing I got from my father! And Kalu Bhangi got it even worse. My father thrashed him so hard that I was afraid he would be kicked to death, and cried out in alarm. But he suffered no ill effects at all, and next day turned up as usual, broom in hand, to sweep our bungalow.

Kalu Bhangi was very fond of animals. Our cow was devoted to him, and so was the Compounder Sahib's goat, although goats are very fickle creatures, worse even than women. But Kalu Bhangi was a special case. It was he who watered them, fed them, took them to graze, and tethered them in the cattle-shed at night. They could understand his every sign as well as a man understands a child. On several occasions I have followed him. Whether in the open or on the road, he used to let them loose, but they would still walk along beside him, suiting their pace to his, as though they were three friends out for a walk. If the cow stopped to take a mouthful of green grass, the goat would stop too and begin to nibble the leaves of some bush; and as for Kalu Bhangi, he would pluck a leaf and start eating it—eating it himself and feeding it to the goat too, and talking to himself. Not only to himself; talking to them too. And the two animals would join in the conversation, grumbling, flapping their ears, shuffling their feet, lowering their tails, curvetting—in all sorts of ways. I'm sure *I* couldn't understand what they used to talk about. Then after a few moments, Kalu Bhangi would start off again, and the cow too would leave off grazing, and the goat would leave his bush and go along with him. If they came to some little stream or spring, Kalu Bhangi would sit down there and then, or rather lie down, and put his lips to the surface of the water and begin to drink, just like an animal does. And the two animals would begin to drink in just the same way, because after all they weren't human and didn't know how to drink from their hand.

Then if Kalu Bhangi lay down on the grass, the goat too would lie down by his legs, drawing her legs in and going down on her knees as though she were saying her prayers; and the cow would sit down near him with such an air that you would think she were his wife and had just finished cooking the dinner. A sort of tranquil, homely air showed itself in every expression which passed over her face, and when she began to chew the cud she looked to me for all the world like some capable housewife settling down to her crotchet or to knitting Kalu Bhangi a pullover.

Besides this cow and goat there was a lame dog with whom Kalu Bhangi was very friendly. Because of his lameness he couldn't roam about much with other dogs and would usually get the worst of it in a fight. He was always hungry and always getting hurt. Kalu Bhangi was always busy tending his wounds and generally dancing attendance upon him—bathing him in soap and water or getting the ticks out of his coat, or putting ointment on his wounds, or feeding him on bits of dried maize bread. But the dog was a very selfish creature. He'd only show up twice a day, once at midday and once in the evening, when he would eat his meal, get his wounds dressed, and be off again. His visits were always very brief and would absorb all of Kalu Bhangi's attention. I didn't like the animal at all, but Kalu Bhangi always received him with great affection.

And then, Kalu Bhangi knew every living creature of the forest. If he saw an insect at his feet his would pick it up and put it on a bush. He would answer the mongoose with its own cry. He knew the call of every bird—the partridge, the wood-pigeon, the parra-keet, the sparrow, and many more. In this respect he was more learned than Rahul Sankrityayan* and, at any rate to a seven-year-old like myself, the superior even of my own parents.

He used to roast corn on the cob beautifully, parching it carefully over a low fire so that every grain would gleam like gold and taste like honey and smell as fragrant and sweet as the fragrance of earth itself. He would roast the cob slowly, calmly, expertly, looking at it repeatedly on every side as though he had known that particular cob for years; he would talk to it like a friend, treat it as gently and kindly and affectionately as though it were some kinsman, as though it were his own brother. Of course other people used to roast cobs, but who could compare with him? Their cobs used to be so half-baked, so tasteless, so altogether ordinary, that they scarcely deserved the name. And yet the self-same cob in Kalu Bhangi's hands became completely transformed, and would come off the fire like a new bride gleaming with gold in her wedding dress. I think that the cob itself would get an inkling of the great love which Kalu Bhangi bore it, otherwise where could a lifeless thing acquire such charm? I used to thoroughly enjoy the cobs which he prepared, and would eat them secretly with great delight. Once I was caught and got a real good thrashing. So did Kalu Bhangi, poor fellow, but the next day there he was at our bungalow as usual.

Well, that's all; there's nothing else of interest to be said about him that I can recollect. I grew up from boyhood to youth and Kalu Bhangi stayed just the same. Now he was of less interest to me; in fact you may say of no interest at all. True, his character

* A celebrated Indian scholar of Sanskrit and Pali.

occasionally attracted my attention. Those were the days when I had just begun to write, and to help my study of character I would sometimes question him, keeping a fountain-pen and pad by me to take notes.

'Kalu Bhangi, is there anything special about your life?'

'How do you mean, Chhote Sahib?'

'Anything special, out of the ordinary, unusual?'

'No, Chhote Sahib.'

(A blank so far. Well, never mind. Let's persevere. Perhaps something may emerge.)

'All right, tell me then, what do you do with your pay?'

'What do I do with my pay?' He would think. I get eight rupees. I spend four rupees on atta, one rupee on salt—one rupee on tobacco—eight annas on tea—four annas on molasses—four annas on spices. How much is that, Chhote Sahib?'

'Seven rupees.'

'Yes, seven rupees. And every month I pay the money-lender one rupee. I borrow the money from him to get my clothes made, don't I? I need two sets a year; a blanket I've already got, but still, I need two lots of clothes, don't I? And Chhote Sahib, if the Bade Sahib would raise my pay to nine rupees, I'd really be in clover.'

'How so?'

'I'd get a rupee's worth of ghee and make maize parathas. I've never had maize parathas, master. I'd love to try them.'

Now, I ask you, how can I write a story about his eight rupees?

Then when I got married, when the nights seemed starry and full of joy, and the fragrance of honey and musk and the wild rose came in from the nearby jungle, and you could see the deer leaping and the stars seemed to bend down and whisper in your ear, and someone's full lips would begin to tremble at the thought of kisses to come— then too I would want to write something about Kalu Bhangi, and I would take a pencil and paper and go and look for him.

'Kalu Bhangi, haven't you got married?'

'No, Chhote Sahib.'

'Why?'

'I'm the only sweeper in this district, Chhote Sahib. There's no other for miles around. So how *could* I get married?'

Another blind alley. I tried again. 'And don't you wish you could have done?' I hoped this might lead to something.

'Done what, Sahib?'

'Don't you *want* to be in love with somebody? Perhaps you've been in love with someone and that's why you don't marry?'

'What do you mean—been in love with someone, Chhote Sahib?'

'Well, people fall in love with women.'

Fall in love, Chhote Sahib? They get married, and maybe big people fall in love too, but I've never heard of anyone like me falling in love. And as for not getting married, well I've told you why I never got married. How *could* I get married?'

How could I answer that?

'Don't you feel sorry, Kalu Bhangi?'

'What about, Chhote Sahib?'

After that I gave up, and abandoned the idea of writing about him. Eight years ago Kalu Bhangi died. He who had never been ill suddenly fell so seriously ill that he never rose from his sick bed again. He was admitted to the hospital and put in a ward of his own. The compounder would stand as far away as he could when he administered his medicine. An orderly would put his food inside the room and come away. He would clean his own dishes, make his own bed, and dispose of his own stools. And when he died the police saw to the disposal of his body, because he left no heir. He had been with us for twenty years, but of course he was not related to us. And so his last pay-packet too went to the government because there was no one to inherit it. Even on the day he died nothing out of the ordinary happened; the hospital opened, the doctor wrote his prescriptions, the compounder made them up, the patients received their medicine and returned home—a day just like any other day. And just like any other day the hospital closed and we all went home, took our meals in peace, listened to the radio, got into bed and went to sleep. When we got up next morning we heard the police had kindly disposed of Kalu Bhangi's body, whereupon the Doctor Sahib's cow and the Compounder Sahib's goat would neither eat nor drink for two days, but stood outside the ward lowing and bleating uselessly. Well, animals are like that, aren't they?

What! You here again with your broom? Well? What do you want? Come now! I've written down everything about you, haven't I? What are you still standing there for? Why do you still pester me? For God's sake go away! Have I forgotten anything? Have I missed anything out? Your name: Kalu Bhangi; Occupation: sweeper. Never left this district. Never married. Never been in love. No momentous events in your life. Nothing to thrill you—as your beloved's lips, or the kisses of your child, or the poems of Ghalib* thrill you. An absolutely uneventful life. What *can* I write? What else *can* I write? Pay: eight rupees. Four rupees atta, four annas spices, one rupee salt, one rupee tobacco, eight annas tea, four annas molasses. That's seven rupees. And one rupee for the moneylender, eight. But eight rupees don't make a story. These days even people earning twenty, fifty, even a hundred rupees aren't interesting enough to write stories about, so it's quite certain that you can't write about someone who only earns eight. So what can I write about you? Now take Khilji. He's the compounder at the hospital. He gets thirty-two rupees a month. He was born in a lower middle-class family and his parents gave him a fair education up to middle.† Then he passed the qualifying examination to be a compounder. He is young and full of life, with all that that implies. He can wear a clean white shalwar, have his shirt starched, use brilliantine on his hair and keep it well combed. The government provides him with quarters, like a little bungalow. If the doctor makes a slip he can pocket the fees, and he can make love to the good-looking patients. Remember that business about Nuran? Nuran came from Bhita. A silly young creature of about sixteen to

---

* Ghalib was a celebrated Urdu poet of the nineteenth century. See section on Love Poetry.

† i.e. education such as an English child received to the age of 14.

seventeen. She'd be sure to catch your eyes even if she were four miles away, like a cinema poster. She was a complete fool. She had accepted the attentions of two young men of her village. When the headman's son was with her she was his. And when the *patwari's** boy turned up she would feel attracted to him. And she couldn't decide between them. Generally people think of love as being a very clear-cut, certain, definite thing; but the fact is that it is usually a very unstable, vacillating, uncertain sort of condition. You feel that you love one person and also another person, or perhaps no one at all. And even if you are in love, it's such a temporary, fickle, passing feeling, that no sooner is the object of your affection out of sight than it evaporates. Your feeling is quite sincere, but it doesn't last. And that's why Nuran couldn't make up her mind. Her heart throbbed for the headman's son, and yet no sooner had she looked into the eyes of the patwari's boy than her heart would begin to beat fast and she would feel as though she were alone in a little boat in the midst of a vast ocean, and rolling waves on all sides, holding a fragile oar in her hand; and the boat would begin to rock, and go on gently rocking, and she would grab the fragile oar with her fragile hands just as it was slipping from her grasp, and gently catch her breath, and slowly lower her eyes, and let her hair fall in disorder; and the sea would seem to whirl around her, and ever-widening circles would spread over its surface and a deathly stillness would descend on all sides and her heart would suddenly stop beating in alarm, and then someone would hold her tight in his arms. Ah! When she gazed at the patwari's boy that was just how she felt. And she just couldn't decide between the two. Headman's son, patwari's son... patwari's son, headman's son... She had pledged herself to both of them, promised to marry both of them, was dying of love for both of them. The result was that they fought each other till the blood streamed down, and when enough young blood had been let, they got angry with themselves for being such

---

* *Patwari*: The village official responsible for keeping the records relating to land tenure etc.

fools. And first of all the headman's son arrived on the scene with a knife and tried to kill Nuran, and she was wounded in the arm. And then the patwari's boy came, determined to take her life, and she was wounded in the foot. But she survived because she was taken to hospital in time and got proper treatment.

Well, even hospital people are human. Beauty affects the heart—like an injection. The effect may be slight or it may be considerable, but there will certainly be some effect. In this case the effect on the doctor was slight; on the compounder it was considerable. Khilji gave himself up heart and soul to looking after Nuran. Exactly the same thing had happened before. Before Nuran it had been Beguman, and before her, Reshman, and before her, Janaki. But these were Khilji's unsuccessful love affairs, because these three were all married women. In fact Reshman was the mother of a child too. Yes, there were not only children, but parents, and husbands and the husbands' hostile glares which seemed to Khilji to pierce right into his heart, seeking to find out and explore every corner of his hidden desires. What could poor Khilji do? Circumstances had defeated him. He loved them all in turn—Beguman, and Reshman, and Janaki too. He used to give sweets to Beguman's brother every day; he used to carry Reshman's little boy about with him all day long. Janaki was very fond of flowers; Khilji would get up and go out very early every morning, before it was properly light, and pick bunches of beautiful red poppies to bring her. He gave them the very best medicine, the very best food, and the very best of his attention. But when the time came and Beguman was cured she went away with her husband, weeping; and when Reshman was cured she took her son and departed. And when Janaki was cured and it was time to go, she took the flowers which Khilji had given her and pressed them to her heart, and her eyes were brimming with tears as she gave her husband her hand and went off with him, until they at last disappeared beneath the crest of the hill. When they reached the farthest edge of the valley, she turned and looked in Khilji's direction, and Khilji turned his face to the wall and began to weep. When Reshman had left he had wept too, and when Beguman went he again wept, in the same unrestrained way, with the same sincerity, overwhelmed by the same agonized feelings. But neither Reshman nor Beguman nor Janaki stayed for him. And now, after I don't know how many years, Nuran had come, and his heart had begun to beat faster, in just the same way; and every day it throbbed for her more and more. At first Nuran's condition was critical, and there was very little hope for her, but as a result of Khilji's unflagging efforts, her wounds gradually began to heal; they began to discharge less, and the bad smell went away, and the swelling subsided. The lustre gradually returned to her eyes and the healthy colour to her wan face; and on the day when Khilji removed the bandages from her arm, then Nuran on a sudden impulse of gratitude threw herself into his arms and burst into tears. And when the bandages were removed from her foot she put henna on her feet and hands and lampblack on her eyelids, and arranged the long tresses of her hair. And Khilji's heart leapt for joy to see her. Now Nuran had given her heart to him and promised to marry him. The headman's son and the patwari's son had on several occasions come to see her, and to ask her forgiveness and to promise to marry her; every time they came Nuran would take fright and begin to tremble, and look this way and that to avoid their glances; and she would not feel at ease until they had gone and Khilji would take her hand in his. And when she was quite recovered the whole village turned out to see her. Thanks to the kindness of the Doctor Sahib and the Compounder Sahib, their lass was better, and her mother's and father's gratitude knew no bounds. Today even the headman had come, and the patwari too, and those two conceited asses—their sons, who every time they looked at Nuran felt sorry for what they had done; then Nuran went to her mother and leaning upon her, looked towards Khilji, her eyes swimming with tears and lampblack, and without a word left for her village. The whole village had come to meet her, and the headman's son and the patwari's son were following at her heels. Khilji felt their steps, and more steps, and more steps—hundreds of steps passing across his breast as they went on their way taking Nuran with them, and leaving behind them a cloud of dust hanging over the road. And turning his face to the wall of one of the wards he began to sob.

Yes, Khilji's life was a beautiful and romantic one—Khilji, who had passed his middle, whose pay was thirty-two rupees a month and who could earn fifteen to twenty rupees over and above; Khilji who was young, who knew what it is to love, who lived in a little bungalow, read the stories of reputable authors, and wept for his love. What an interesting, and romantic, and imaginative life Khilji's was! But what can you say about Kalu Bhangi? Except the following:

1. That Kalu Bhangi washed the blood and pus from Beguman's bandages.
2. That Kalu Bhangi emptied Beguman's commode.
3. That Kalu Bhangi cleaned Reshman's dirty bandages.
4. That Kalu Bhangi used to give Reshman's boy corn-on-the-cob to eat.
5. That Kalu Bhangi washed Janaki's dirty bandages and every day sprinkled disinfectant in her room, and every day towards evening closed the window of the ward and lit the wood in the fireplace so that Janaki shouldn't feel cold.
6. That Kalu Bhangi for three months and ten days regularly emptied Nuran's commode.

Kalu Bhangi saw Reshman departing; he saw Beguman departing; he saw Janaki departing; he saw Nuran departing. But he never turned his face to the wall and wept. At first he would look a bit perplexed for a minute or two and would scratch his head. And then when he couldn't account for what was going on, he would go off into the fields below the hospital and let the cow lick his bald head. But I've already told you about that.

Well, what more am I to write about you, Kalu Bhangi? I've said all there is to say, told all there is to tell about you. If *your* pay had been thirty-two rupees, if *you'd* passed your middle—or even failed it—if *you* had inherited a little culture, a little refinement, a little human joy and the exaltation which it brings, I'd have written something about *you*. But as it is what can I write about your eight rupees? Time and again I pick up your eight rupees and study them from all angles—four rupees atta, one rupee salt, one rupee tobacco, eight annas tea, four annas molasses, four annas spices—that's seven—and one rupee for the moneylender—that makes eight. How can I make a story out of that, Kalu Bhangi? No, it can't be done. Go away. *Please* go away. See, I implore you with folded hands. But he still stands there, showing his dirty yellow, uneven teeth and laughing his cracked laugh.

I see I can't get rid of you so easily. Very well, then. Let me rake over the embers of my memory once more. Perhaps for your benefit I'll have to come down a bit below the thirty-two rupees level. Let's see what help I can get from Bakhtyar the orderly. Bakhtyar the orderly gets fifteen rupees a month. And whenever he goes out on tour with the doctor or the compounder or the vaccinator he gets double allowance and travelling expenses too. Then he has some land of his own in the village, and a small house, surrounded on three sides by lofty pine trees, and with a beautiful little garden on the fourth side laid out by his wife. He has sown it with all sorts of vegetables—spinach and radishes, and turnips and green chillies, and pumpkins, which are dried in the summer sun and eaten in the winter when snow falls and there are no greens to be had. Bakhtyar's wife knows all about these things. Bakhtyar has three children, and his old mother, who is always quarrelling with her daughter-in-law. Once Bakhtyar's mother quarrelled with her daughter-in-law and left home. The sky was overcast with thick clouds and the bitter cold made your teeth chatter. Bakhtyar's eldest boy came running to the hospital to tell him what had happened, and Bakhtyar set out there and then to bring his mother back, taking Kalu Bhangi with him. They spent the whole day in the forest looking for her—Bakhtyar and Kalu Bhangi, and Bakhtyar's wife, who was now sorry for what she had done and kept on weeping and calling out to her mother-in-law. Their hands and feet were getting numb with the cold, and the dry pine twigs were slippery underfoot; and then it began to rain. And the rain turned to sleet and a deep stillness descended all round, as though the gate to the abyss of death had opened. The snowflakes kept falling, still, silent, voiceless, and a layer of white velvet spread over valley and hill and dale.

'Mother!' shouted Bakhtyar's wife at the top of her voice.

'Mother!' shouted Bakhtyar.

'Mother!' called Kalu Bhangi.

The forest re-echoed and was quiet.

Then Kalu Bhangi said, 'I think she must have gone to your uncle's at Nakkar.'

Four miles this side of Nakkar they found her. Snow was falling, and she was making her way along falling and stumbling, panting and out of breath. When Bakhtyar caught hold of her, for a moment she resisted, and then fell senseless into his arms, and Bakhtyar's wife held her up. All the way back Bakhtyar and Kalu Bhangi carried her turn by turn and by the time they reached home it was pitch dark and when the children saw them coming they began to cry. Kalu Bhangi withdrew to one side, and looking about him, began to scratch his head. Then he quietly opened the door and came away.

Well, after all this rummaging around in my memory I'm at a loss. What can I do? Go away now, for God's sake. You've pestered me too much already.

But I know that he won't go. I shan't be able to get him out of my mind, and in all my stories he'll be standing there with his filthy broom in his hand. Now I know what it is you want. You want to hear the story of something which never happened, but which *could* have happened. I will begin with your feet. Listen. You want your dirty rough feet to be washed clean, washed until all the filth has been washed away. You want ointment to be rubbed on their cracks. You want your bony knees to be covered with flesh, your thighs to be strong and firm, the creases on your withered belly to disappear, the dust and grime to be washed from the hair on your weak chest. You want your thin lips to become full and to receive the power of speech. You want someone to put lustre in your eyes, blood in your cheeks, give you clean clothes to wear, to raise the four walls of a little home about you, pretty and neat and clean, a home over which your wife will rule and in which your laughing children will run about.

I cannot do what you want. I know your broken teeth and your half-weeping laugh. I know that when you get the cow to lick your head, in your imagination you see your wife passing her fingers through your hair and stroking your head until your eyes close and your head nods and you fall asleep in her kindly embrace. And when you roast the cob for me so gently over the fire and look at me so kindly and affectionately as you give it to me to eat, in your mind's eye you are seeing that little boy who is not your son, who has not yet come into the world, and while you live never will come, and yet whom you have fondled like a loving father, and held in your lap while he played, and kissed on the face, and carried about on your shoulder saying, 'Look! This is my son!' And when you could have none of these things, then you stood aside and scratched your head in perplexity and all unconsciously began to count on your fingers: one, two, three, four, five, six, seven, eight—eight rupees. I know the story of what could have happened. But it didn't happen. I am a writer, and I can fashion a new story, but not a new man. For that I alone am not enough. For that the writer, and his reader, and the doctor, and the compounder, and Bakhtyar and the village patwari and headman, and the shopkeeper, and the man in authority, and the politician, and the worker, and the peasant toiling in his fields, are all needed—the united efforts of every one of those thousands and millions and hundreds of millions of people. Until all of us join hands to help one another, this task cannot be carried out and you will go on standing there on the threshold of my mind, just the same with your broom in your hand; and I shall not be able to write a really great story, in which the splendour of the complete happiness of the human spirit will shine; and the builders will not be able to build that great building in which the greatness of our people will reach its highest achievement; and no one will be able to sing a song in whose depths will be mirrored all the greatness of the universe.

The Black Shalwar

SAADAT HASAN MANTO

Before they came to Delhi she had lived in Ambala Cantonment, where she had several whites among her clients. From being with them she'd learnt ten to fifteen sentences of English. She didn't use them in ordinary conversation with them. But when after coming here to Delhi she couldn't make a go of things she said to her neighbour Tamancha Jan one day, 'This life...very bad,' adding that you couldn't earn enough even for your food.

In Ambala Cantonment she'd done very well. The British Tommies used to come to her when they were drunk, and within three to four hours she could handle nine or ten of them and make twenty to thirty rupees. These Tommies were better than her own countrymen. True, they spoke a language Sultana didn't understand, but her ignorance of their language proved very useful to her. If any of them wanted anything extra from her she would say, 'Sahib, I don't understand what you're saying.' And if they pestered her too much she would begin to swear at them in her own language. They would stare at her, completely nonplussed, and she would say in Urdu, 'Sahib, you're a real bloody fool, a real bastard. Do you understand?' And when she said this she would not speak harshly, but on the contrary in a very affectionate tone. The Tommies would laugh, and when they laughed they did look real bloody fools.

But since she'd been in Delhi not a single Tommy had visited her. She'd been three months now in this city, a city where she'd heard

that the Big Lord Sahib* lived. But only six men had visited her—
only six; that is two a month. And as God was her witness she'd
made only eighteen and a half rupees out of these six customers.
No one would pay more than three rupees. She'd told five of them
that her charge was ten rupees—and was surprised when every one
of them said, 'Not a penny more than three.' God knows why, but
not one of them thought her worth more than three. So when the
sixth one came she herself said, 'Listen, I charge three rupees a time.
Not a farthing less. Now it's up to you. You can stay or you can go.'
He didn't argue, and stayed. When they went into the other room
and he took off his coat she said, 'And one rupee for milk.' He
didn't give her one rupee, but took a shiny new four-anna piece
out of his pocket, with the head of the new king† on it, and gave
it to her. She too didn't argue and took it without saying anything,
thinking, 'Well, it's better than nothing.'

Eighteen and a half rupees in three months—and the rent of
her place alone was twenty a month. Her landlord called it a 'flat',
using the English word. In this flat there was a toilet in which when
you pulled a chain the water immediately carried all the filth away
into the sewer. It made a tremendous noise, and at first she'd felt
very scared at this noise. On the first day there when she'd gone to
the toilet she'd felt a sharp pain in her waist, and when she stood up
she'd got hold of this hanging chain to help her up. She'd noticed
this chain and had thought that since the flat had been specially
fitted out for them‡ it had been put there to make it easier for them
and give them some support when they got up from the toilet.
But no sooner had she taken hold of the chain to get up than she
heard a sort of clanking sound above her and all of a sudden water
came out with a rush, and she was so frightened that she let out
a shriek. Khuda Bakhsh had been in the next room seeing to his
photographic equipment and pouring hydroquinine into a clean
bottle when he heard Sultana shriek. He came running and asked

---

* The Viceroy.
† George VI.
‡ i.e. for prostitutes.

her, 'What's the matter? Was that you shrieking?' Sultana's heart was beating fast. 'What's this wretched toilet up to?' she said. 'What's this chain hanging down like the chain in a railway carriage? I had a pain in my waist and I thought I'd support myself by it, but I'd no sooner touched it than there was a sort of great explosion, so loud that...'

Khuda Bakhsh had laughed his head off. Then he'd told Sultana all about it. 'It's a new-style toilet. You pull the chain and all the filth goes down into the ground.'

How Khuda Bakhsh and Sultana had got together is a long story. He came from Rawalpindi. After he'd passed his entrance exam he'd learnt to drive a lorry, and for four years worked as a lorry driver on the Rawalpindi-Kashmir run. Then he took up with a woman in Kashmir and carried her off with him to Lahore. He couldn't get work in Lahore, so he set this woman to work as a prostitute. This went on for two or three years, and then the woman ran off with someone else. Khuda Bakhsh learnt that she was in Ambala and went there to look for her. There he met Sultana. Sultana liked him, and that's how they got together.

From the time when Khuda Bakhsh joined her, trade began to look up. She was a superstitious woman and concluded that Khuda Bakhsh was a man of great spiritual power, and that this was why things had improved so much with his arrival. And this enhanced Khuda Bakhsh's standing in her eyes even more.

Khuda Bakhsh was a hard worker. He didn't like sitting about all day doing nothing. So he made friends with a photographer who used to take photos with a polaroid camera outside the railway station. This man taught Khuda Bakhsh how to take photos, and then he took sixty rupees from Sultana and bought a camera. Gradually he got together a screen, two chairs, and equipment for developing film, and set up on his own. He did well, and in no time at all had established himself in Ambala Cantonment. There he'd take photos of the British Tommies. Within a month he had a wide circle of acquaintances in the cantonment. So he moved Sultana there too, and thanks to him a number of British Tommies became

Sultana's regular clients and she made twice as much as she'd been making before.

Sultana bought herself earrings and got eight gold bracelets made, each weighing five and a half tolas. She accumulated ten to fifteen good quality sarees, and furniture for their home. In short, in Ambala she was very well off. Then suddenly—God knows why—Khuda Bakhsh took it into his head to move to Delhi. How could Sultana refuse? She thought that Khuda Bakhsh brought her good luck. She gladly agreed. She thought that in a big city like that, where the Big Lord Sahib lived, her trade would prosper even more. She'd heard her friends singing the praises of Delhi. And the shrine of Nizam-ud-Din was there, and he was a saint for whom she felt a great devotion. So she quickly sold off all her heavy possessions and went off with Khuda Bakhsh to Delhi. Here he got a flat for twenty rupees a month and both of them moved into it.

It was one in a long line of new houses lining the road. The municipal committee had designated this part of the city as the prostitutes' quarter so that they would not establish themselves all over the city. On the ground floor were shops, and the two storeys above the shops were flats. Because all were built to the same design Sultana at first had great difficulty in working out which flat was hers. But then a laundryman took the shop on the floor below and put up his signboard above it, and that gave her a sure landmark. 'Clothes Washed Here', it said, and she at once located her flat. In the same way she established many other landmarks for herself. For example, her friend Hira Bai, who sometimes sang on the radio, lived above the shop which announced in great big letters that it sold coal. Above 'Excellent Cuisine for Gentlemen' another friend, Mukhtar, lived. Above the workshop that made the broad tape for beds, Nuri lived. She was in the regular service of the man who owned the workshop, and since he needed to keep an eye on it at nights he used to spend the nights with her.

When you first set up shop you can't expect customers to start coming right away, and when for the first month Sultana had no customers she comforted herself with this thought. But when two months had gone by and no one had approached her she got very worried. She said to Khuda Bakhsh, 'Why is it, Khuda Bakhsh? Today we've been here a full two months and no one has come our way. I know that trade is slack these days, but it's not so slack that throughout the month no one even looks at you.' Khuda Bakhsh too had been getting troubled about this for a long time, but he hadn't said anything. But now that Sultana herself had raised the matter he said, 'I've been thinking about it for some days. All that I can think is that people have taken up war work and can't think of anything else. Or maybe it's that...' But before he could say any more they heard someone coming up the stairs. Khuda Bakhsh and Sultana both pricked up their ears. Shortly there was a knock at the door. Khuda Bakhsh rushed to open it and a man came in. This was their first customer and they settled for three rupees. After that five more came—that meant six in three months; and Sultana got eighteen and a half rupees from them.

Twenty a month went in rent for the flat. Water rates and electricity bill on top of that. And all the other household expenses— food, drink, clothes and medicines. And no income. You can't call it income when all you get in three months is eighteen and a half rupees. Sultana was worried. One by one, the eight bracelets of five tolas each that she'd had made in Ambala were sold off. When only one was left she said to Khuda Bakhsh, 'Listen to me. Let's go back to Ambala. There's nothing here for us. And even if there is, I don't like it here. You too used to do well there. Come on, let's go back, and cut our losses. This is my last bracelet. Go and sell it. Meanwhile I'll pack, and we'll leave by tonight's train.'

Khuda Bakhsh took the bracelet from her and said, 'No, my love. We're not going back to Ambala. We'll make our living here in Delhi. You'll get back all your bracelets right here. Trust in God. He provides, and here too He'll provide us with some means.'

Sultana said nothing, and took the last bracelet off her arm. It made her sad when she looked at her bare arm, but what could she do? They had to find *some* way to fill their bellies.

When five months had gone by and income still didn't cover even a quarter of their expenditure, Sultana grew all the more anxious. And now Khuda Bakhsh was out all day, and this upset her all the more. True, there were two or three of her neighbours she could go to see, and she could pass the time with them. But she didn't like going there every day to sit with them for hours together; so gradually she stopped going altogether. She would sit all day in her empty house, sometimes slicing betel nut and sometimes mending her old clothes. And sometimes she would go out onto the balcony and stand by the railings and aimlessly watch the moving and stationary engines in the railway sheds opposite.

On the other side of the road there was a warehouse, reaching from one corner to the other. To the right, under the metal roof lay some big bales, along with piles of all sorts of goods. To the left there was an open space, criss-crossed by innumerable railway lines. When Sultana saw how these iron rails shone in the sun she would look at her hands, on which the blue veins stood out just like the railway lines. In this long, open space engines and trucks were moving all the time this way and that, puffing and clattering. When she got up early in the morning and went out onto the balcony a strange sight confronted her. Thick smoke rising from the engines through the mist, rising to the overcast sky like fat, burly men. Great clouds of steam too, rising noisily from the rails, and gradually dispersing into the air. Sometimes when she saw a carriage shunted and left to run on its own along the line she thought of herself, thought how she too had been shunted onto a line and left to run on her own. Others would change the points and she would move on, not knowing where she was going. And a day would come when the impetus would gradually exhaust itself and she would come to a halt somewhere, in some place she had never before seen.

She would stand for hours, aimlessly watching these vivid, lively railway lines and the engines standing on them or moving along them. But all sorts of thoughts would come and go in her mind. When she had lived in Ambala, there too her house had been quite near the station, but thoughts like these had never occurred to her. Now she sometimes thought of this network of railway lines, from which steam and smoke were always rising, as a huge brothel—lots of trucks being shunted hither and thither by a few fat engines. Sometimes she felt that these engines were like the businessmen who sometimes used to visit her in Ambala. And sometimes when she watched an engine moving slowly past the lines of trucks she thought it was like a man walking slowly through the red light quarter looking up at the balconies where the prostitutes sat.

Sultana thought that thoughts like these would lead to some sort of mental disorder. So when she began to think like this she stopped going out onto the balcony.

She asked Khuda Bakhsh repeatedly to take pity on her and stay at home, and not leave her alone in the house lying there like someone ill. But every time she did he would tell her, 'My love, I go out to try and earn something. God willing, in a little while all our problems will be solved.' But five full months had gone by and both Sultana's problems and his were still unsolved.

The month of *Muharram** was drawing near, and Sultana had no means of getting black clothes made for herself. Her friend Mukhtar had had a fashionable Lady Hamilton *qamis* made, with black georgette sleeves. And to match it she had a black satin shalwar that shone like black eyeliner. Anwari had bought herself a fine silk georgette saree. She told Sultana she would wear a white petticoat underneath it. This was the latest fashion, she said. And she had got herself black velvet shoes to wear with it—very dainty ones. When Sultana saw all these things it grieved her very much that she couldn't afford clothes like these for Muharram.

When she got back home after being shown Anwari's and Mukhtar's clothes she felt extremely depressed—as though a boil had begun to swell up inside her. The house was empty. Khuda Bakhsh, as usual, was out. She put a bolster under her head and lay

---

* *Muharram*: The month of the year in which Muslims mourn the martyrdom of Husain, the grandson of the Prophet.

down on the carpet. She lay there until the height of the bolster began to make her neck stiff. Then she got up and went out onto the balcony, hoping to get these painful thoughts out of her head.

There were carriages standing on the rails, but not a single engine. It was evening. Water had already been sprinkled in the street and there was no dust in the air. People had begun to pass along the street, people who looked about them as they went silently home. One of them raised his head and looked at Sultana. She smiled at him and then forgot about him, because an engine had appeared on the lines opposite and she had begun to give it all her attention. Gradually the idea came into her head that the engine too was wearing black. To banish this weird idea from her mind she looked down again at the street, and saw that the same man was standing there by an ox-cart, the one who had been staring at her greedily. She beckoned to him. He looked around him and gestured to ask her the way up to her flat. She showed him. He stood there for a moment, but then quickly came upstairs.

Sultana invited him to sit down on the carpet, and when he had sat down, she said, to get the conversation going, 'You were afraid to come up.' He smiled. 'What made you think that?—what is there to be afraid of?' Whereupon Sultana said, 'I thought that because you waited there a little while before you decided you would come up.' He smiled again and said, 'You were mistaken. I was looking at the flat above you. There was a woman standing there taunting some man. I was interested. Then a green light went on on the balcony, and I waited a bit longer, because I like green light.' He began to size up the room. Then he got up. Sultana said, 'Are you going?' 'No,' he said. 'I want to see your flat. Come on, show me all the rooms.'

Sultana showed him all three rooms, and he looked over them without saying a word. When they went back into the room where they had been sitting he said, 'My name is Shankar.'

Now for the first time Sultana looked at him attentively. He was of medium height, and nothing special to look at. But his eyes were unusually clear and bright, with an occasional strange twinkle in

them. A well-knit, little body. Hair greying at the temples. Trousers
of warm cloth. A white shirt, with a stand-up collar.

He sat there on the carpet as though not he but Sultana was
the client, and this worried her a little. So she said, 'What can I do
for you?'

He lay back and said, 'What can you do for me? What can I do
for you? It was you who invited me up.' When Sultana made no
reply he sat up again.

'Oh, I see,' he said. 'Now listen to me. Whatever you were
thinking, you thought wrong. I'm not one of those who come up
here, give you something and go away again. I expect a fee, like a
doctor does. When people send for me they have to pay a fee.'

Sultana was flabbergasted, but she couldn't help laughing. 'What
do you do?' she asked him.

'I do what you lot do,' he replied.

'What's that?'

'What do *you* do?'

'I... I... I don't do anything.'

'I too don't do anything.'

Sultana said crossly, 'That doesn't make sense. There must be
something you do.'

'And there must be something *you* do,' Shankar calmly replied.

'Yes, I waste my time.'

'I too waste my time.'

'Come on then, let's waste time together.'

'I'm at your service. But I never *pay* to waste time.'

'Use your head...This isn't a charity.'

'No, and I'm not a volunteer.'

Sultana hesitated. 'Who are these volunteers?' she said.

'Bloody fools,' said Shankar.

'Well, *I'm* not a bloody fool.'

'No; but that Khuda Bakhsh who lives with you—he's a bloody
fool.'

'Why?'

'Because he's been going for days to a holy man, hoping that he'll change his fortunes—when he hasn't a hope of changing even his own...like trying to open a lock that's rusted fast.' And he laughed.

Sultana said, 'You're a Hindu. That's why you ridicule our holy men.'

He smiled, 'In places like this the Hindu-Muslim question doesn't arise. If Pandit Malaviya and Mr Jinnah were to come here they'd both behave like gentlemen.'

'I don't know what you're talking about... Well, then, are you staying or not?'

'Only on the condition I told you.'

Sultana got up. 'On your way, then,' she said.

Shankar got up, entirely at ease, and thrusting his hands in his trouser pockets said as he left, 'I come this way every now and then. Whenever you need me, call me. I can do a lot for you.'

Shankar went off and Sultana forgot all about her black dress and thought about all this for a long time. What he had said had lightened her grief considerably. If he'd come to her in Ambala, when she was well off, she'd have looked at him in quite another light, and would probably have pushed him out. But here she was depressed, and she had liked the way he talked.

When Khuda Bakhsh got home in the evening Sultana asked where he'd been all day. Khuda Bakhsh was exhausted. He said, 'I've been to the Old Fort. There's a holy man who's been staying there some days. It's him I'm going to every day, so that our fortunes may change.'

'Has he said anything to you?'

'No, so far he hasn't deigned to. But Sultana, my waiting upon him won't be for nothing. If God is gracious we'll be in clover.'

Sultana's head was full of Muharram. She said in a mournful voice, 'You're out all day and every day. And I'm here like a prisoner in a cage. I can't go anywhere. And Muharram will soon be here. Have you thought about that? Has it occurred to you that I need black clothes? We haven't got a farthing in the house, I had my bracelets, but one by one we've sold them. How much longer are you going to be trailing behind these holy men? It looks to me as if God Himself has turned His back on us since we came to Delhi. If you take my advice you'll get started on your work here. It'll bring in something at any rate.'

Khuda Bakhsh lay down on the carpet. 'But to get started I need a bit of capital,' he said. 'For God's sake don't say such painful things. I can't bear it. You're right; it was a really bad mistake to leave Ambala. But everything that happens happens by God's will, and happens for our good. Who knows? We'll have to put up with all this for a while, and then...'

Sultana interrupted him. 'For God's sake do something. Steal. Commit armed robbery. But no matter what else you do, bring me the material for a black shalwar. I've got a qamis of white material. I'll get it dyed black. And I've got a white muslin dupatta—the one you brought me for Diwali. I'll get that dyed along with the shirt. All I need is the black shalwar, and some way or other you've got to produce it. Look, I'm putting you on oath. Some way or other you've *got* to get it.'

Khuda Bakhsh sat up. 'What's the point of going on and on about it? Where am I going to get it? I haven't even the money for opium.'

'I don't care what you do. You're to bring me four and a half yards of cloth for a black shalwar.'

'Pray that God sends you two or three clients this very night.'

'But *you* won't do anything. You can get together enough money if you want to. Before the war you could get satin for twelve to fourteen annas a yard. Now they charge one and a quarter rupees a yard. What will four and a half yards cost?'

'Alright, if you say so, I'll find some way.' He got up. 'And now forget it. I'm going to bring in some food.'

Food arrived. They sat together and somehow got it down, and then went to bed. In the morning Khuda Bakhsh went off to the holy man in the Old Fort. Sultana was left alone. She lay down for a while, slept, and wandered from room to room. After her midday meal she got out her muslin dupatta and her white qamis and took them to the laundryman downstairs to get them dyed. He did dyeing as well as washing.

Having done that she came back and read film magazines. These published the stories and songs of the films she had seen. She fell asleep while she was reading, and when she woke up she could see that it was already four o'clock because the sun had reached the drain in the yard. She took a bath, wrapped a warm sheet around her and went out onto the balcony. She stood there for the best part of an hour. It was evening now and the lamps were being lit. The road below began to look quite splendid. It grew cold, but Sultana didn't mind. For a long time she watched the tongas and the cars going by. Suddenly she caught sight of Shankar. When he reached the point in the street beneath her flat he raised his head, looked at her and smiled. Sultana, without meaning to, beckoned to him to come up.

When he came up she felt very worried. She didn't know what to say to him. Actually she'd beckoned to him without thinking. Shankar was completely at ease, as though he were in his own home. He put a bolster under his head and lay down, just as he had done on the occasion when he had first come. When after quite a long time Sultana had still not said anything he said, 'You can invite me up a hundred times and send me away again a hundred times. Things like that never upset me.'

Sultana didn't know what to do. 'No,' she said. 'Sit down; no one's telling you to go.'

Shankar smiled. 'Does that mean you accept my conditions?'

She laughed. 'What conditions? Are you marrying me then?'

'Marriage? Neither you nor I will ever get married. These conventions are not for us. Don't talk such nonsense. Say something to the point.'

'What do you want me to say?'

'You're a woman. Say something to keep me happy for a while. There's more to life in this world than buying and selling.'

In her heart of hearts Sultana had now accepted him. 'Speak plainly,' she said. 'What do you want of me?'

'The same as the others want.' He sat up.

'Then what's the difference between you and them?'

'There's no difference between me and you. But there's all the difference in the world between me and them. There are plenty of questions you shouldn't ask; you should know the answers without asking.'

Sultana did her best for a while to understand what he'd said, and then said, 'I understand.'

'Tell me then. What are you going to do?'

'You've won. I've lost. But I tell you to this day no one else has ever accepted a condition like that.'

'You're wrong... In this very quarter you'll find women who are so simple that they won't believe that any woman can accept the degradation that you regularly accept without even feeling it. They don't believe it, but there are thousands of you... Your name's Sultana, isn't it?'

He got up and started laughing. 'And mine's Shankar. What ridiculous names! Come on, let's go in.'

When they came back they were both laughing—God knows what at. When he was about to go Sultana said to him, 'Shankar, will you do something for me?'

'First tell me what it is,' he said.

She felt a bit embarrassed. 'You'll say I'm trying to make you pay, but...'

'Go on, tell me. What are you stopping for?'

Sultana plucked up courage and said, 'The thing is that Muharram is coming and I haven't got enough money to get myself a black shalwar made. You know all about the trouble we're in. I had a qamis and a dupatta, and I've taken them only today to be dyed.'

Shankar said, 'You want me to give you money so that you can get this black shalwar made?'

'No,' she said quickly. 'What I mean is that if you can, you should get one made for me.'

He smiled. 'It's only by luck that I ever have anything in my pocket. But anyway I'll do what I can. You'll get your shalwar on the first day of Muharram. So? Are you happy now?' Then he looked at Sultana's earrings and said, 'Can you give me those earrings?'

Sultana laughed. 'What do you want with them?' she said. 'They're ordinary silver earrings. Worth five rupees at the most.'

Shankar laughed and said, I asked you for the earrings. I didn't ask you what they cost. Are you going to give me them or not?'

'Take them,' she said, and she took them off and gave them to him. She regretted it afterwards, but Shankar had already gone.

Sultana didn't believe for a moment that Shankar would fulfil his promise, but eight days later the first day of Muharram came, and at nine in the morning there was a knock at the door. Sultana opened it to find Shankar standing there. He gave her something wrapped in newspaper and said, 'It's a black satin shalwar. Just take a look at it. It might be a bit too long. I'm off.'

And without saying anything else to her he went. His trousers were creased and his hair dishevelled. It looked as though he had just got up and come straight here. Sultana opened the package. It *was* a black shalwar, exactly like the one she'd seen Mukhtar wearing. Sultana was delighted. She had the shalwar, Shankar had kept his promise, and all the regret that she'd felt at the loss of her earrings and the 'bargain' she'd made was banished.

At midday she went down to get her dyed qamis and dupatta from the laundryman. She had just put on all three things when there was a knock at the door. Sultana opened it and Mukhtar came in. She looked at Sultana's clothes and said, 'It looks as though your qamis and dupatta have been dyed; but the shalwar looks new. When did you get it made?'

Sultana said, 'The tailor has just brought it.' And as she said the words she noticed Mukhtar's earrings. 'Where did you get the earrings?' she said.

'I got them only today,' said Mukhtar.

And for a little while neither of them could say anything.

Love and Prudence

SHAUKAT THANAVI

It was about this time that Cupid must needs select me as a target on which to practice his skills. As a matter of fact strange feelings had been developing in my heart about a girl who was closely related to me; and now I declared them, and told my cousin Arshad Thanavi, who had now also become my brother-in-law— my sister's husband—of my choice. Actually the girl was his sister. Arshad did not evince any deep interest in the matter, probably because he did not think I was serious about it; he thought it was perhaps a passing, childish emotion which would not last. But the strength of my feeling grew from day to day. I don't know about *her,* poor girl, but I had reached the conviction that, more likely than not, this feeling which had arisen in my heart was what they call love, and that if the outcome should not be what I wanted it to be, then God alone knew what would become of me. What had really happened was this: most of my friends were already in love, and were always telling one another about it. One would show us a love letter proving how his beloved was restless with longing for him. Another would read out the letter he was writing to his beloved or to his fiancée. Another used to carry around with him a dried flower—'My beloved fixed this to my coat with her own hands as a memento of her love for me.' One of my friends was so deeply in love that he was looking after an extremely repulsive, emaciated cat, and when he was asked to explain this manifestation of his sound taste, would explain that it had belonged to his kind beloved, but that when she had moved from the neighbourhood she had entrusted its care to him, so that he might experience the love Majnu felt for his beloved Laila's dog.* In such circumstances how could *I* be content not to be in love? I already felt on friendly and affectionate terms with my cousin and my regard for her was completely sincere, but when these feelings took the form of love, it was undoubtedly under the influence of fashion that they did. Accordingly, I informed my friends of my love, and they showed an interest in it, because we would get together to sigh and weep over our sad state.

> The nightingale laments the rose's coldness
> And we lament the wounds upon our heart.†

My cousin, poor girl, is dead now, and may God grant me His forgiveness and not put her soul to shame, because she was absolutely without blame in the matter. All the foolishness was mine. I didn't want to be seen to be outrun by any of my friends in this race, and so I forged letters in disguised handwriting in reply to mine, and showed them to my bosom friends, whose love letters I had seen. My object was simply to show that I too could hold up my head among them, that they must understand that I too was someone with whom beautiful girls could be infatuated—though the fact is that only a beautiful girl whose eyesight was seriously defective could be infatuated with me. The poor girl of whom I am speaking had not the remotest idea that her promising young cousin and candidate for marriage was composing forged letters as documentary proof of her passion for him. The most she knew was that I wanted to be married to her. So I went on forging these letters, and at the same time pestering my elder sister and her husband Arshad to see to it that our marriage was arranged.

In due course my father came to know of this. He refused

---

* Majnu and Laila were the two most famous lovers in Arabic legend.

† In Persian and Urdu poetry, the nightingale is the symbol of the lover, who pours out his love for the rose in beautiful song. The rose is the beloved—beautiful, but totally unmoved by the nightingale's love.

outright to agree to the match. But, I ask you, do we true lovers succumb to such threats? I had decided once and for all that I should be married, and married to *her;* and if I could not marry her then I would never marry anyone. Things reached a stage where my mother tried to reason with me, and I summoned up all my courage and said that if they would not arrange my marriage with this girl then I would commit suicide. Now my resolution was at its highest pitch. I was a lover, and not afraid of anything. If one is not prepared to face disaster, if one is intimidated by opposition, then one should not fall in love. In the end I wrote a letter to my father, saying that if my marriage to this girl were not arranged I would commit suicide. My father took his revolver, loaded it with six bullets and said to the servant, 'Take this to your young master and tell him to go ahead.' This was not at all the response I had expected. The sight of the revolver took my breath away. Meanwhile my mother was frantic. 'What are you doing?' she said to my father. 'He'll kill himself!' But my father, experienced police officer and old hand that he was, replied with the utmost indifference, 'Be quiet and don't worry. People who say they'll kill themselves never do; and if he does commit suicide then you can rest assured that he'll have done the right thing. In the long run, people like that either come to their senses or go on until they hang for murder.' Anyway I picked up the revolver with trembling hands, summoned up my courage, put the barrel to my temple, recited the *kalima,** fingered the trigger—and then suggested to Cupid that it would be well if he would reconsider his decision. He agreed. I lowered the revolver from my temple, laid it on the table, and at once realized that love is a pleasant pastime until such time as it puts one's life in danger. The revolver went back to my father, and I went to fall at his feet and ask his forgiveness....

Some time later my cousin was married to a much better man than I was...but she had not been married long when she caught pneumonia, poor girl, and departed from this world where love,

---

* The Muslim profession of faith.

like wild animals, runs away from revolvers. It was I who had threatened to die, and she who died. Truly, it takes a man to face the trials of love, and I probably do not need to throw any further light on *my* manhood.

Hellbound

ISMAT CHUGHTAI

The first part of this piece is extracted from a brief autobiographical essay, included here because it forms a good introduction to the rest. Ismat's elder brother, Azim Beg Chughtai, was a well-known writer.

It was after we'd come to Aligarh that I became day by day more aware of Azim's presence. God knows why he suddenly became interested in me. I'd always preferred my older brother, Nasim. Even when he hit me there was still pleasure in it because he'd also give me money and sweets. Azim gave me neither money nor slaps; he talked to me seriously. And then he began to teach me History and English. I don't remember how it started; all I remember is that in the evenings when he came back exhausted from the day's work, he'd go and lie on the string bed on his verandah and say to me, 'Come on, read. Loudly.' Then he would correct my translation, and give me dictation, and after that we would talk. I don't remember what it was we began talking about. Later on he used to tell me things about the Traditions* and the Quran. His teaching method was an odd one. He'd give me a novel and say, 'Go and translate it. From English into Urdu, and from Urdu into English.' Ten pages at a time he'd set for me to translate. For me, there were several advantages in this approach—one was that before I could translate the novel I had to finish reading it, and it's from that time that I

---

* Traditions: Accounts of the words and deeds of the Prophet in which Muslims find guidance for their own conduct.

became so intensely absorbed in reading novels. I would lie awake the entire night reading stories and novels. But in those days they were all wasted on me—I hadn't a clue what they meant. So I've had to read them all again. Hardy was the first novelist that, as Azim said, I drank to the last drop.

In those days Azim made such an impression on me that I became just an echo of him. 'It's Mansur's voice,* but God who speaks.' Whenever I opened my mouth the others in the family would tease me that it wasn't me but Azim speaking, and Azim himself took advantage of my naivete. When there was something he didn't want to say himself he would carefully instill it into my head, and I would immediately blurt it out. In those days the family used to say that he put me up to all sorts of things. Even before, I had already been headstrong and obstinate; and now under his encouragement I became even more uncontrollable.

At that time he was studying law, and along with that had a job in a factory. He was also writing articles. And after all that he would go on to teach me for several hours. Sometimes he had a temperature, sometimes a pain in his chest; sometimes he'd get cramps in his arms and legs. His wife and daughter would rub his chest, and he would go on teaching me. He never asked me to massage his head or feet, nor did I ever think it necessary to do anything for him. He was my older brother, after all, so it was his job to teach me. On one occasion he had a long fit of intense coughing. Two hours passed, and we hadn't even managed to finish a few pages of translation. I got cross. 'I'm not studying with you, you cough far too much,' I said angrily.

'You stupid child, do you think I'm coughing on purpose?' he laughed, and then promised that from now on he wouldn't cough.

I don't know why he came to take such an interest in my future. When I passed matric I think he was even more delighted than when his son was born.

During the holidays he invited me to his house—by now he had

* Mansur: See p. 221.

started practising law in Jodhpur. That was the time he helped me to read the translation of the Quran and the Traditions. And perhaps—no, not 'perhaps', but without doubt—it was from reading the stories that he gave me that I too began secretly to write.

As long as college dominated my life, reading and writing took up all my time, and I couldn't give any attention to literature; and as soon as I left college I got it into my head that anything written two years ago was rotten stuff—false and uninteresting. 'The new literature' was the literature of today or yesterday. And this 'new literature' made such an impact on me that God knows how many books there were that I dismissed when I'd done no more than look at their titles and written them off as worthless. And the books that seemed most worthless of all were those of Azim Beg Chughtai. 'A prophet is not without honour....' It was a case of that.

His books were scattered all over the house, but no one except my mother and a few of my old-fashioned sisters-in-law paid the least attention to them. I used to think, 'What's the point in reading *them*? They're not literature—nothing but clowning and buffoonery, rotten, old-fashioned love stories and the sort of stuff that it makes you cross to read.' In other words, I'd made up my mind about them without even reading them. I myself didn't really know why I'd not read my brother's stories. There may have been a bit of arrogance in my attitude, priding myself that I was a 'new' writer and he an old one.

One day in a moment of idleness my eye lighted on his essay *Ekka*.* [My brother] Nasim and I began to read it. God knows what mood we were in, but we began to laugh, and we laughed so much that we could hardly go on reading. While we were reading it Azim came in. He saw that we were reading his book and was very pleased. But we were annoyed at this and made a face. He knew what he was about. 'Give it to me,' he said, 'I'll read to you.' He read two or three of his pieces and had us literally rolling about. All our pretence was gone. It was not only what he was reading

* *Ekka*: A horse-drawn vehicle that plies for hire in poor areas.

but the fact that it was he who was reading it. It was as though
there was laughter everywhere, like sparks flying. When he'd made
us look properly foolish he said, 'You lot say that there's nothing
in my writings,' and started teasing us. We were crestfallen, but we
gradually recovered and got really cross with him. God knows what
absurd things we said to him. We were very put out, and began to
dislike his books even more than before.

While he was alive I never praised his writings, though when
he read what *I* wrote he was more pleased with them than words
can say, and very loving in his praise. But I'd got into the habit of
taking offence at everything he said. I thought he was making fun
of me—and, by God, when he *did* make fun of people, his sarcasm,
and bitter smile and cutting remarks would make them feel like
getting down on the floor and kicking and crying like a child. I
was always afraid that he'd make fun of me and I'd swear at him.
Sometimes he'd say, 'I'm afraid, in case you start writing better than
I do.' And that too when I'd only written a few things. And that's
why I got angry and thought he was making fun of me.

After he died, for some reason I began to feel an attachment to
all his things. Every word he had written began to make an impact
on me, and now, for the first time in my life I got down to reading
his books. Got down to! That's absurd. I didn't need to 'get down
to' it. I positively wanted to. 'Good God!' I would think, 'That's
how he wrote!'

When I began to read his books every word in them evoked the
picture of how he looked in his last years. Within moments I would
see his eyes, struggling to smile through all the pain that racked
him all the time. I saw his dense hair falling over his dark, wasted,
melancholy face, over which it seemed as if dark rain clouds had
gathered, his bluish-yellow high forehead, his shrunken, purple
lips, his uneven, prematurely broken teeth, his dried up, emaciated
hands, with their long delicate fingers like a girl's, impregnated
with the medicines he was taking. And then the swelling attacked
his hands. I saw his thin matchstick legs, ending in ugly, swollen
feet which we felt afraid to look at, and so always went to the head

of his bed. I saw his cage-like chest, working like a bellows, and the clothes piled on his body, and vests in layer upon layer. And that breast held an ever lively, ever high-spirited heart. God, how that man could laugh! Like a demon or a jinn, ready to grapple with every power in the universe. Never defeated, always smiling. A wrathful and tyrannical God visited upon him every torture that his constant coughing and asthma could bring him, and he responded to all of them with a laugh. No pain that this world or the next could produce was spared him, but nothing could reduce him to tears. One would have thought it beyond the power of any human being to laugh in all this pain and distress, let alone to make others laugh too. My uncle used to say, 'He's a living corpse.' Well, by God, if corpses can be so lively, so restless, so ever-active one could wish that everyone on earth was a corpse.

When I looked at him not with a sister's eyes but simply with the detached eyes of a fellow human being, it made me reel. What a stubborn heart he had! How full of life he was! There was almost no flesh on his face, but soon after it had begun to swell he began to look quite handsome. His temples and his sunken cheeks began to fill out. A death-like radiance came to his face, and a sort of magical greenness like that of an embalmed mummy. But his eyes were the eyes of a mischievous boy, dancing in response to every little thing, or sometimes the merry eyes of a youngster. And these eyes, when an attack of severe pain was upon him, would scream out, and the clear bluish surface of his skin would turn a muddy yellow, and his helpless hands would tremble and it seemed as though his breast would burst. And when the attack was over, the same radiance, the same dancing brightness.

Only a few days ago I read his *Khanam* [Lady] for the first time. He is not its hero. Its hero is someone much stronger and healthier than he was, the embodiment of the hero he could imagine that he might have been, like the active vigorous youngster in whom a lame man would like to see himself; not him, but his *hamzad*,*

---

* *Hamzad:* A jinn (genie) said to be born at the same time as a child and to stay with him/her for life, often playing malevolent tricks on him/her and others.

whom he watched getting up to all the tricks that he, lying there a helpless prey to illness, could not get up to. Others may think that *Khanam* is nothing much. But all its characters except his hero are accurately portrayed, living characters—all exactly like the people who made up, and still do make up, a family. At any rate that's what my family was like, and every word is true to life. Azim watched all of us in action in the home and when he wrote he portrayed accurately all that he saw… Everyone is there—and always will be. It is as though when he wrote all of us acted parts for him, all of us were moving puppets in his hands, and he produced a faithful picture of it all.

He loved talking to people, and would make friends with absolutely anyone. There was an old *mirasan*.* He would sit for hours and talk nonesense with her. People were astonished. They'd think 'Good God! What have *those* two got to talk about?' But everything in his story *Khurpa Bahadur* is what this old mirasan told him. He would even stop the sweeper or the water carrier or anyone passing in the street to talk to them. Once he had to go to hospital for some days, and at nights, when everything was quiet he'd secretly gather all the patients together to chat with them. He and they would tell each other innumerable stories, and these were the basis of things he wrote. It used to give him great pleasure to encounter liars and cheats. He'd say 'Tricking people and deceiving them is no joke. You need intelligence for things like that.' Everything he wrote he took from life, including all the lies in which life abounds. He wrote many improbable things, because his poetic imagination could accept all of them.

He used to love watching singing and dancing—but the kind of dancing he liked was the kind that wandering holy men would perform. He'd often give them money and then watch them dancing to the beat of the drum, watching so intently that you'd envy him his enjoyment. God knows what he could see in their naked, hungry dancing.

* *Mirasan*: One of a caste of women singers.

He had been opposed to purdah for ages, but in the end he used to say, 'All that's out of date. They can't preserve purdah now, no matter how hard they try. We've finished with that now. Now there are fresh things to worry about.'

He did not take much interest in politics. He used to say, 'I can't be a leader, so what's the point? People would say "Show us some results" but this wretched cough and asthma plagues me all the time.' Many years ago he wrote some articles on politics and economics that were published in *Riyasat*. God knows what became of them.

His writings cut no ice with us present-day writers. The world has changed and people's ideas have changed. We're outspoken, and abusive. When we feel pain, we cry. Capitalism, socialism, unemployment—these things have seared us with their flames. We grind our teeth as we write and spit out the poison we brew from our secret griefs and our crushed emotions. He too felt pain—he was poor, ill and destitute. He too was oppressed by capitalism, and yet with all that he had the courage to make faces at life and to joke at his distress. It was not only in his stories that he laughed; in every department of life he defeated distress with laughter.

One of the reasons that Azim is not popular with contemporary, that is, *completely* contemporary readers, is that he did not write as openly and directly as the new writers do. He could see women's beauty, but he hardly saw their bodies. In the old *masnavis** like *Zahr-e-Ishq*, the description of women's physical form is quite prominent. Then such writing came to be called old-fashioned. And now this old fashion has revived and the new literature is full of rising and falling breasts, shapely calves and soft thighs. He used to think such 'naked' writing pornographic, and fought shy of it, though his writing abounds in the portrayal of naked emotions and he would write without hesitation of really filthy things. He would portray a woman's naked emotions, but the woman would always

---

* *Masnavis*: Romantic verse narratives. *Zahr-e-Ishq* (The Poison of Love), written in the mid-nineteenth century, is one of the most popular.

be fully clothed. He never spoke very freely with me, because he looked upon me as a child. And he never discussed sexual problems with anyone at all. The most he said, speaking to a friend, was 'The new writers are all very spirited, but they're hungry, and very much under the influence of sex. In everything they write you feel as though they're saying, "Mummy, I'm hungry."' He used to say too that in every age Indian literature has borne the clear imprint of sex. 'Our people are much affected by it. Our poetry, our painting and even our ancient styles of worship all express our sexual hunger. If they forget love and sex even for a moment they lose their popularity.' And that is why *his* way of writing was soon abandoned and the old *Thousand and One Nights* style of writing prevailed again.

He was especially fond of Hijab Imtiyaz Ali's stories. (I must say, with apologies to the lady, that the secret of why he liked them has died with him.) He used to complain to me that I wrote the kind of lies that have no head or tail to them, that *my* lies were the cry of a hungry man, while *his* lies were the smiles of a hungry man. God knows what he meant by that.

We generally used to tell him his stories were 'all lies'. Whenever he started talking my father would say to him, 'Have you started your castles in the air again?'... Azim would tell him, 'My dear Sir, it's lies that give colour to life. If you want to make what you say interesting you must mix lies with truth.' And he would say, 'The descriptions of Heaven and Hell too are no more than castles in the air.' At this my uncle would say, 'Stop this living corpse saying such things. It's blasphemy.' And Azim would mock him and his in-laws, and tell them that they were a superstitious lot.

I never saw him saying his prayers. He used to read the Holy Quran lying down. He showed no respect for it and would fall asleep as he read. When he was rebuked for this he put it in paper covers and would tell people he was reading a law book. He used to study the Traditions a lot, and look out and memorize very strange ones so that he could argue with people about them. He would read them out and argue about them. People were at a loss to cope with them. He used to memorise verses of the Quran too, and never tire of referring to them; and if you cast doubt upon them he would take the Quran out by the head of his bed and show you them.

He was a great admirer of Yazid,* and talked a lot of nonsense about Imam Husain. He would argue for hours on this theme. He used to say, 'I dreamt that Hazrat Imam Husain was standing somewhere when Yazid the accursed came along, fell at his feet, humbled himself and joined hands in supplication to him. At this Husain was deeply moved. He raised him up and embraced him. From that day I too began to revere Yazid. In Paradise they were reconciled. So why should we fight over them?'

He used to think that *piri muridi*† was a hoax. But he would say, 'All hoaxes are attractive lies; and lies are in themselves attractive.' He used to say, 'If my health had permitted, I'd have got people to worship at my father's grave. I'd have arranged qawwalis for two years, and got people to donate coverings for his tomb. It would have been a fine and enjoyable way to earn an income.'

He was addicted to religious controversy, but in the end he stopped arguing so much. He would say, 'You lot are strong and healthy, and I'm dying. And if by any chance it turns out that there is a heaven and a hell what shall I do? Best keep quiet.' When people used to tell him he would go to hell he used to say, 'And what sort of paradise has the Good Lord given me here that threats of hell should deter me? I don't care. I'm used to hell. If the Good Lord burns me in hell he'll be wasting his sticks and coal, because there's no suffering I haven't got used to.' Sometimes he said, 'If I go to hell then at any rate these germs will be killed. If I go to heaven I'll infect all the maulvis with my T.B.'

---

* The ruler who encompassed the death of Husain, the grandson of the Prophet. He is execrated by all Muslims.

† The practice of giving allegiance to a *pir* (spiritual guide) whose guidance one trusts and follows implicitly. Commonly, a long-dead saint would be regarded as a *pir* and a devotee (*murid*) would go to his tomb and seek guidance from its guardians.

And that's why everybody called him a hellbound rebel.

It seems as though he was *born* crying, and he was reared with all care and attention. People saw how weak he was and forgave him everything. He would hit his big stalwart brother, who would just bow his head and take it. Because he was so weak, my father would excuse him no matter what he did. Everyone tried all the time to please him, but when you're forever telling someone who is ill that he's ill, how *can* you please him? All our kindnesses to him only made him feel his weakness more. He got more and more rebellious, more and more angry; but he was helpless. All of us began to adopt Gandhi's policy of non-violence, but what *he* wanted was to be counted with others as a member of the human race, to be scolded as others are scolded, to be numbered among the living. And he worked out that the way to achieve this was to be a troublemaker. Whenever he felt like it he could get any two people to quarrel with each other. God had given him a good brain, an astonishing imagination and a sharp tongue, which he would ply with great enjoyment and to great effect. His brothers and sisters and our mother and father all began to loathe him. Our home became a fair old battlefield, and it was he who caused it all. What more could he want? All his self-regarding emotions were satisfied, and the weak, helpless, ever-ailing villain of the piece became a hero. He made all his weaknesses his weapons.

But he didn't really want people to abandon him. The more his family avoided him, the tighter he clung to them. In the end, may God forgive us, we all came to loathe the very sight of him, and, for all his pleadings, to regard him as our enemy. His wife didn't look upon him as a husband, nor his children as a father. His sisters told him, 'You're no brother to me,' and his brothers would turn away in disgust at the sound of his voice. My mother would say, 'I gave birth to a snake, not a child.'

Before he died he was in a pitiable state. Not as his sister but simply as a human being I tell you that I wished he would die and get it over with. But even then he never stopped hurting people. He was like the torments of hell. The hero of a thousand stories had become a villain and his ambition was satisfied. Yet even now he wanted people to love him, wanted his wife to worship him, and his children to look affectionately upon him, and his sisters to feel ready to do everything for him, and his mother to take him to her bosom.

And his mother *did* that, returning to the path from which she'd strayed. She was his mother, after all. But the others still hated him, until the time came when his lungs packed up, the swelling got worse, his eyesight failed and he would grope his way like a blind man and still not find it. He had made himself a hero, but in the end he was defeated. He never got what he had wanted. What he got instead was hatred, revulsion, and contempt... Such was the man who, with ulcers in his lungs and legs that had been stiff for ages, and arms pierced with innumerable injections, and boils on his hips the size of apples, laughed as he lay there dying. The ants had begun to crawl over his body, and he looked at one of them and said, 'How impatient my lady ant is! She's here before time to claim her portion.' This was two days before he died. What a heart he must have had to joke like this when he was dying!

At four o'clock one morning he who had been born forty-two years earlier as a weak little child had played his role in the drama of life. At six in the morning on 20th August Shamim came and told me to get up, because Azim was dying.

'He'll never die,' I said crossly. 'Don't wake me up for nothing.' And I tried to get to sleep again in the cool of the morning.

Shamim got worried, and shook me, 'Get up, you wretch. He's asking for you.'

'Tell him I'll see him on Judgement Day,' I said. 'I tell you, Shamim, he *can't* be dying.'

But when I went down he could no longer speak. All the furniture, all the junk, all the books had been cleared from the room. Medicine bottles were rolling uselessly about. Two of the little children were staring anxiously at the door. My sister-in-law was making them drink their tea. There were no tears in her eyes.

I leant over him, 'Munne bhai,' I said. For a moment his eyes focussed, and he compressed his lips. Then he again lapsed into a coma. We all sat waiting outside his room, and for four hours watched the struggle that his dried up, lifeless hands were waging. It looked as though even Azrail, the Angel of Death, was losing the unending battle.

'He's dead.' I don't know who it was who told us. I thought to myself, 'He isn't. He can never die.' And today I look at his books and say, 'Impossible! He can never die. He's still fighting. What difference does death make?' For me it was his death that brought him to life, and God knows how many more there will be—how many there will go on being—for whom he will be born after his death.

His message was, 'Fight pain, fight hatred, and go on fighting even after you're dead.' He'll never die. No one can kill his rebellious spirit. He was not a virtuous man. If his health had been good he would not have been an abstemious man either. He was a liar. His life was a lie—the biggest lie of all. His tears were a lie, and his laughter was a lie. People say, 'He caused nothing but pain to his mother and father, and to his wife, and to his children, and to the whole of creation. He was a malevolent spirit sent into the world to plague it, and now the only proper place for him is hell.'

Wherever he is, whether it's in heaven or in hell, I want to see him. I'm certain that he's laughing even now. Worms will be eating his body, and his bones will be crumbling to dust and his neck will be bowed under the burden of the *fatwas* of the mullahs, and the saw will be tearing at his body. But he'll still be laughing. His mischievous eyes will still be dancing, his blue, dead lips will be moving in bitterness, but no one will be able to reduce him to tears. Wherever he is, I want to see him, to see if his sharp tongue is at work there too, to see whether he's making love to the *houris* in heaven or laughing as he angers the angels in hell, whether he's quarrelling with the maulvis or whether in the leaping flames of hell his cough resounds and he's breathing with difficulty, and the angels are giving him his injections. What difference does it make to go from one hell into another? Where else would the hellbound be?

POPULAR LITERATURE

Popular Literature

I call this section 'popular' for want of a better word. The literature presented in the other sections in this book is also popular, that is, widely read and appreciated; but the literature in this section is popular in another sense, in that it appeals primarily to a plebeian audience, and is generally the written record, by anonymous writers, of stories that were current long before anyone wrote them down. At bus stations and on railway platforms all over North India and Pakistan you can buy cheap booklets, printed on newsprint, with these kinds of stories.

The first group I have called *Outwitting the Powerful*—a popular type of anecdote that celebrates, with great satisfaction, situations in which ordinary people have kept their end up, or even scored against those who exercise autocratic and arbitrary powers over them. Another popular theme is mocking the purveyors of superstition.

Next come stories of *Akbar and Birbal*, traditional stories of the great Mughal Emperor Akbar (1556–1605) and one of his ministers Birbal, a Hindu. The punch line of almost all of these stories shows Birbal turning the tables on the emperor whenever Akbar tries to present him with insoluble problems or ask him what he thinks will be unanswerable questions. These are sometimes put to him at the instigation of other courtiers who hope to score against him. Though Birbal was indeed one of Akbar's ministers, there is nothing in the historical record which testifies to his having played this kind of role.

Less common but essentially of the same genre are humorous

stories of other kinds, often included in the Akbar and Birbal
booklets, even when Akbar and Birbal do not figure in them.
Among these are stories of *Mullah Dopiaza*, Birbal's rival. His real
name is said to have been Abul Hasan, and though he is counted
with Birbal and others as one of the 'Nine Jewels' of Akbar's court,
no one knows whether he was a historical personage or not. He is
said to have got his nickname because of his inordinate fondness
for the dish so named—a meat dish in which two onions ('do piaz')
form part of the ingredients, and his fame under this nickname is so
great that most people have never known his real name. As his title
tells us, he was a Muslim. Birbal was a Hindu, and Hindu–Muslim
rivalry is reflected in many of the stories told of the two men.

Another group of stories are those of *Shaikh Chilli*. His name
is said to mean 'the shaikh of Chilla', Chilla being a village in the
present Indian state of Uttar Pradesh; but there is no evidence that
any such person existed. The root meaning of 'shaikh' is an old
man, and hence an elder, one whose age commands respect. It
may be used of Shaikh Chilli ironically—he is proverbial for his
stupidity, naivete and occasionally for an unexpected sharpness.

In all of these anecdotes, where you might need terms explained,
I have given these before the story rather than in a footnote.

Tales of Famous Men are short anecdotes with a punchline, some
traditionally associated with particular prophets in Islam (some also
known in Jewish and Christian traditions by another name). Others
are linked to historical figures in the Greek tradition, which must
have become familiar in Muslim lands after the Muslim conquest
of parts of the Byzantine empire.

Then follow two extracts from a book called *Stories of the
Prophets* (*Qasas ul Anbiya*) written by Ghulam Nabi but based on
much older, anonymous Persian originals. They are addressed to
the same sort of audience as the anecdotes above, but concern
themselves for the most part with serious questions of religion and
morality. The book has long been famous and continues to be very
popular. Muslim divines regard it as a morally sound book, but
stress that its stories have no basis in anything but popular tradition;

and because it is popular above all with readers who are not highly educated, it is not usually judged as a work of literature. Modern English readers would put it in the same class of literature as the *Thousand and One Nights*. It is in fact a very interesting book— not, as it stands, a work of folk literature, but clearly bearing the marks of folk influences. Many of the stories add vivid detail to the outlined versions which one finds in the Quran, and supply answers to questions which the Quran's references may have given rise to in the ordinary Muslim's mind.

The first extract is about the creation of Adam and the loss of Paradise. A central concept in Islamic belief is that Adam was created by God to be his *khalifa*—a word generally translated by the rather unusual English word 'vicegerent', one who 'acts for' the authority that appoints him. Neither 'representative' nor 'deputy' nor 'plenipotentiary' convey the exact sense. This extract gives the story of how this happened, and the consequences.

The second is about Sikandar, the Muslim name for Alexander the Great. Traditionally, he is identified with the ruler whom the Quran calls 'Dhool Karnain' but these stories add much that is not found there, especially the best-known of all the Sikandar stories, that of his search for the water of life with someone called 'Khizar'. Khizar is generally identified with an unnamed person who appears in a passage in the Quran immediately before the account of Sikandar, and who explained certain of God's actions to Moses.

Both of these stories were well known to classical poets, and allusions to them are common in their work, as you will see in the section on the ghazals of Mir and Ghalib.

The last piece in this section, *Guests are Pests*, is 'popular literature' in another sense. It is the text of a radio broadcast made in 1932 by a spiritual leader—a pir—Khwaja Hasan Nizami (1878–1955). He was the spiritual successor of the medieval saint Nizam-ud-Din, and the incumbent of his famous shrine on the outskirts of Delhi. His devotees (*murid*) numbered hundreds of thousands from all walks of life, and they looked unquestioningly to him for guidance in every aspect of their lives. He provided this in a stream of pamphlets on an enormous range of subjects. In a letter he wrote to me a few years before his death, he said, 'I am now 74 years old, but even now...I write a book of 16 pages every day, and...have announced that before I die I will write 100,000 books'. In view of the immense number he had already written this did not seem too unrealistic an aim. He always bore in mind that he needed to reach a mass audience, and he expressed himself forthrightly in simple, but extremely effective language in the pure idiom of Delhi.

Outwitting the Powerful

Crows for Good Luck

A nobleman had been told by a Brahmin that anyone who saw a pair of crows sitting together early in the morning, before the sun was up, would have very good luck. So he ordered one of his servants to look out for this, and when he saw a pair to call him at once. The servant kept a lookout and one day saw a pair sitting there. He told his master at once, who got up and came out of the house, tying his loincloth. But meanwhile one crow had flown off. He was very annoyed and told his servant, 'You useless wretch, you're dismissed. Get out!' The servant replied, 'I saw the two crows, and look what has happened to me! You should be glad that *you* did not see them.' His master laughed, and kept him on.

The King and the Slave

[In Urdu, the Knave in a set of playing cards is called the Slave.]

A king once asked one of his slaves who was a jester if he could play cards. 'No,' he said, 'I can't even tell the difference between a King and a Slave.'

Bringing the Dead to Life

A nobleman was having sexual intercourse with his maidservant, but could not maintain an erection. He told her to take his penis in her hand and help him. As she did so he farted. The maidservant laughed. He said, 'What's there to laugh about? I'm not Sulaiman [Solomon] that I can command the wind.' 'No,' she said, 'and I'm not Isa [Jesus] that I can bring the dead to life.'

'He has all the gear'

[Jami was a famous Persian poet.]

One day an officer of the law was leading a prisoner, seated on an ass and with arms pinioned, through the streets of the city. It so happened that he encountered Jami. When he saw what was happening he told the officer to release the man. 'I shall not release him', the officer said. 'He drinks wine, and sells wine, and has all the gear for making wine.' Jami replied, 'Then execute me too. I have all the gear for committing adultery.' The officer felt ashamed and let his prisoner go.

True or False

[A 'qazi' is a Muslim magistrate]

A king once summoned a learned man and said, 'I wish to make you qazi of this city.' The man replied, 'Your majesty, I am not fit for this post.' The king said, 'Why?' The man said, 'Consider whether what I have just said is true or false. If it is true, then accept it. And if it is a lie then reflect that it is not permissible to make a liar a qazi.'

Onions for the Emperor

Some hillmen who lived on the slopes of the Himalayas far from the capital, heard of the greatness of the Mughal Emperor Akbar and decided to go to his court and to take him a gift. They picked some walnuts for this purpose, but on their way down from the hills they came to a town where they saw some onions in someone's house. They had never seen an onion before and concluded that this must be some very rare and precious fruit, and a gift much more fit for a king than walnuts. So they exchanged their walnuts for onions, and on arriving at Akbar's court presented them to him. Akbar was furious and gave orders that one onion at a time should be placed on their bare heads and beaten with a shoe until it was crushed. As his men carried out the order one of the hillmen glanced at another and said, 'It's a good thing we changed our walnuts for these!' The king overheard this and at once understood what must have happened. He laughed and let the hillmen go.

Questions for a Holy Man

['Holy men' were revered because they had turned their back on material things to live the spiritual life.]

A man went to a holy man and put three questions to him. First he said, 'God is everywhere, but I can't see him anywhere. Why not?' The second question was, 'No one can do anything except by God's command. So where's the justice in their being punished for their sins and faults? They have no power to do otherwise.' And the third question was, 'We are told that Satan is made of fire. So how can he feel any pain in the fires of hell? It was from this same fire that he was made.'

The holy man made no reply but picked up a brick and hit him on the head with it. At this, crying with pain, the man went to the qazi and laid a complaint before him, telling him that he had put three questions to the holy man, and that instead of replying to them he had hit him on the head with a brick and caused him pain. The qazi sent for the holy man and called upon him to explain why he had not replied to the man's questions. He said, 'The blow I gave him *was* a reply. He says he feels pain. If he can show me his pain I'll show him God. And his complaining to you is useless, because no man can act except by God's command. I hit him, and had no power to do otherwise. And the brick is made of clay and man is made of clay. So how can he feel any pain?' The qazi was pleased with his reply and dismissed the complaint.

A Fair Trial?

[A mufti is an expert on Muslim law.]

A man was dissatisfied with a junior magistrate's decision. The junior magistrate said, 'Go and appeal to the qazi.' He replied, 'He's your brother, he won't listen to me.' The magistrate said, 'Go to the mufti.' The man replied, 'He's your uncle.' The magistrate said, 'Go to the minister.' The man said, 'He's your grandfather.' The magistrate said, 'Go to the king.' The man said, 'Your niece is engaged to him.' The magistrate said, 'Go to hell then.' The man said, 'That's where your esteemed father is. He'll see to it that I get no satisfaction there.'

The Ass and the Ox

A Muslim had a neighbour whose donkey never stopped braying. He prayed to God night and day, 'O God, destroy this donkey!' A little later one of his brothers' oxen died. He called out to God, 'Glory be! You've been God all these years, and you don't yet know the difference between an ass and an ox.'

A Prophecy

[Astrologers were consulted by rulers to advise on, for example, an auspicious day for undertaking important projects.]

A king went to an astrologer and asked him, 'How much longer have I got to live?' He replied, 'Ten years.' The king was so depressed and worried by this that he fell ill. His minister was a wise man. He summoned the astrologer into the king's presence and said to him, 'Tell me, how much longer have *you* got to live?' The astrologer said, 'Twenty years.' The minister at once drew his sword and cut off the astrologer's head. The king was much relieved and thereafter paid no attention to astrologers' prophecies.

The Mullah's Chapatis

A mullah used to fetch six chapatis from the bazaar every day. One day a friend of his asked him, 'My friend, what do you do with these six chapatis?' He replied, 'One I keep for myself; one I throw away; two I lend; and with the other two I repay a debt.'

His friend said, 'I don't understand. Tell me plainly what you mean.'

The mullah said, 'I eat one myself. One I give to my mother-in-law [*'thrown away' because it brings me no benefit*]. One each I give to my son and my daughter [*'lent' because in my old age they will repay me by taking care of me*]. And two I give to my mother and father' [*i.e. I repay the debt I owe them for bringing me up*].

Akbar and Birbal

'The first person you see'

In Akbar's time there lived in Delhi a merchant of whom it was said that if he was the first person you saw in the morning it would bring you bad luck and you would get nothing to eat for the rest of the day. Akbar heard of this and had him brought to the palace where he was to be kept overnight and presented to the Emperor first thing in the morning. And this was done. Akbar then went to take his breakfast, but no sooner had he sat down than a maidservant came running to tell him that his queen had suddenly fallen ill and was asking him to come to her. Akbar at once went to her. The royal physician was summoned and he gave the queen medicine which made her feel better. Two hours had passed and he ordered a fresh breakfast to be prepared. But before it was ready he felt a severe pain in his stomach. The royal physician was again summoned. He told the Emperor he must fast for a complete day, as his breakfast must have given him indigestion. Akbar said he had *had* no breakfast, and it soon emerged that the first person he had seen that day was the unlucky merchant.

Akbar reflected that this man was a pest not only to him but to any of his subjects, and gave orders that he should be executed. When he mounted the scaffold he asked the hangman why he had been sentenced to death, and the hangman told him.

The man then burst into such floods of tears that even the hangman felt sorry for him. He said, 'If there is one man who can help you it is Birbal. Come, I'll take you to him.' Birbal listened to his story and then whispered something in his ear. The man then said that before he died he would wish to see the king once more. His request was granted. When he was brought before the king he asked permission to say something, and this request too was granted. He said, 'I was the first person you saw in the morning and you had to go hungry all day. The first person I saw was you, and I have to forfeit my life for it. So, which of us brings the worse bad luck?'

The king realized that he had been too harsh, and not only revoked his sentence but gave him gifts as well.

As he left, Akbar asked him, 'Who told you to say this to me? Was it Birbal?'

'Yes', said the man, 'it was.'

The Marriage of the River

On one occasion Birbal so displeased Akbar that he banished him from his kingdom. After some time he began to regret his action, but no one knew where Birbal had gone. Akbar had a search called for him far and wide, but without success. Then he thought of a plan. He had messages sent to the kings of many kingdoms. It said, 'I am going to celebrate the marriage of my river. The rivers of your kingdom are invited.' Most of the kings did not know what to reply, but one sent this response: 'I accept your invitation to our rivers, but please send your well so that we may send you our rivers in it.' Akbar realized that only Birbal could have suggested this reply, and he sent for him to come back to his court.

King of Vegetables

Akbar was dining one day in Birbal's presence, and began to sing the praises of the aubergine. 'Birbal,' he said, 'the aubergine is the king of vegetables.' Birbal enthusiastically agreed. Some days later when he was again dining in Birbal's presence he began to disparage the aubergine as a rotten, worthless vegetable. Birbal echoed his views at once. 'None worse,' he said. 'The moment you eat it it gives you a stomach ache. It really is the worst!' Akbar burst out laughing and said, 'Only a day or two ago you were praising it to the skies, and now you're condemning it.' Birbal said, 'Yes, your majesty. And whose servant am I? Yours or the aubergine's?'

Giving and Taking

Akbar once asked Birbal, 'Why are there no hairs on the palms of my hands?' Birbal said, 'Your constant giving of bounty has worn them away.' Akbar said, 'And people who never give anything, why are there no hairs on *their* palms?' Birbal said, 'Because constantly taking has worn them away.' Akbar said, 'And those who neither give nor take? Why are there no hairs on *their* palms?' Birbal said, 'Because they are always wringing their hands with regret that they live in a world where they can neither give nor take.'

An Appetite for Stones

One day the Emperor Akbar and his queen were sitting together eating mangoes. Birbal too was present. As he ate, the Emperor put the stones down in front of the queen. When he had finished he said to her, 'What an appetite you have! Look at all the mangoes you have eaten!' The queen was very embarrassed. Birbal said, 'Your majesty, there's no limit to *your* appetite. You haven't even left the stones.' It was Akbar's turn to feel embarrassed.

A Pit of Honey

One morning Akbar said to Birbal, 'Birbal, last night I dreamt that I had fallen into a pit filled with honey and you into one filled with refuse.' Birbal at once replied, 'Lord of the World, I too had just such a dream, but in my dream I was licking you and you were licking me.'

The Eunuch's Questions

Akbar once showed his pleasure with Birbal's services by promising to award him a large grant of land. But he soon forgot his promise. One day he and Birbal were taking the air when they saw a camel standing there with its head turned away. Akbar said, 'Birbal, why is he standing with his head turned away like that?' Birbal replied, 'Your majesty, he too has promised someone a grant of land.' Akbar was put to shame and at once fulfilled his promise.

One of Akbar's eunuchs said to him, 'Your Majesty, Birbal always has a ready answer for every question, but he should be asked questions that he cannot answer.' The king replied, 'He shall be asked whatever you say.' The eunuch said, 'Let him be asked where the centre of the earth is, and how many stars there are in the sky, and how many men and how many women there are in the world.' The king said, 'Very well, let him be sent for.' But before the words were out of his mouth Birbal appeared. The king thereupon asked him the questions the eunuch had proposed. Birbal listened to them and said he would give his answers the next day. Early the next morning he appeared with a hammer and a large iron pin and came into the king's presence. The king, as soon as he saw him, asked if he had brought the answer to the questions he had been asked. He replied that he had, and taking the iron pin to the centre of the palace, he drove it into the floor and said, 'The centre of the earth is here. If you do not believe it, have measurements taken.' The king made no response to this but asked him for the answer to the second question. Birbal had a ram brought in and said, 'Your Majesty, the number of stars in the sky is exactly the same as the number of hairs on this ram's body. If you doubt it, you may count them. And I have also brought the correct answer to the third question except that one thing makes me uncertain. These eunuchs—they are neither men nor women, so which category should I count them in?'

The Portrait in the Toilet

[Rajahs were princes who ruled over territories of varying size in different parts of India. Many were unwillingly obliged to recognize the Mughal emperor as their overlord.]

A rajah who had heard Birbal's praises sung invited him to his court. Akbar granted him leave to accept. He was greeted there with great pomp and ceremony. The rajah had planned to insult the Emperor, and for this reason had had the Emperor's portrait put up in the lavatory. When Birbal had occasion to go there he saw it and at once understood what the rajah intended. When he came out he went straight to the rajah and said, 'Do you suffer from constipation? I imagine you do, because I see you have had the Emperor's portrait hung there. When you see it you are so frightened that your bowels open. Am I right?' The rajah felt very ashamed. Birbal returned to Delhi and related the whole thing to Akbar, who was very pleased with him.

Mullah Dopiaza

Who is the Fool?

One day a merchant came to Akbar's court bringing several fine horses for sale. Akbar greatly admired them and asked him to bring more of the same kind. The man asked for an advance payment, and Akbar had him paid a hundred thousand rupees.

Some time later Akbar ordered Mullah Dopiaza to make him a list of all the fools in his court. When he brought him this list Akbar saw to his astonishment that his own name topped the list. He asked Mullah Dopiaza to explain. Mullah Dopiaza said, 'Without even thinking about it you gave that merchant a hundred thousand rupees. Do you think he'll bring the horses? Do you think you'll ever see his face again?' Akbar said, 'And what if he does bring them?' Mullah Dopiaza said, 'In that case I'll cross out your name and put his in its place.'

Cloths Stained in Blood

[*Sunnis and Shias are the two major sects of the Muslim community. Akbar and the ruling family of India were Sunnis, while the kings of Iran were Shias. Shias hold in especial veneration the family of the Prophet, including his grandson Husain who was martyred at Karbala. 'Istinja' is earth used after urinating or defecating to clean oneself when water is not available.*]

One day the Emperor Akbar handed over a number of locked boxes to Birbal with instructions to take them as a gift to the King of Iran. Birbal took the boxes home, broke the locks and opened them. He took out all the contents and filled them instead with earth that had been used for *istinja* and clothes stained with menstrual blood. He then re-locked the boxes and returned with them to the Emperor asking him to hand over this task to Mullah Dopiaza. He calculated that when the King of Iran opened the boxes and saw what was in them he would have the Mullah executed, and thus Birbal would be rid of him. The Emperor granted his request, and handed over the boxes to the Mullah. He, suspecting nothing, and knowing nothing of what was in them, at once set out for Iran, and on the very day of his arrival presented himself at the King's court and conveyed Akbar's greetings. Two or three days later he presented the boxes he had brought from India. The King ordered them to be opened in his presence, and when this was done he saw the things which Birbal in his malice had put in them. The Mullah was astonished, anxious and deeply embarrassed, but his quick mind came to his aid at once and he said, 'This is the gift His Majesty sent, but he also gave me a verbal message to deliver along with it. May I do so?'

'Yes,' said the king, 'do so.'

The Mullah said, 'My King had obtained from Exalted Karbala this cleansing earth and these clothes stained with the blood of martyrs. But knowing that in India they would not be accorded the respect which is due to such precious things, he dispatched them to Your Majesty.'

The King and his courtiers were delighted, and the King said to the Mullah, 'If all the wealth of the world had been sent me I would not have been so pleased as I am with this gift.'

The Full Moon and the Crescent Moon

While Mullah Dopiaza was in Iran he worsted many of Iran's learned men in religious controversy, and they laid a plan for his downfall. They proposed to the King of Iran that he should be asked, in the presence of the King and all his courtiers, to say who was the greater king—Akbar or the King of Iran. They reckoned that if he said 'Akbar' the King of Iran would be insulted and have him put to death; and if he gave precedence to the King of Iran, then Akbar would hear of it, and on his return his life would be forfeit there too. The King warmly approved of this plan, had him summoned to court and had this question put to him. Mullah Dopiaza was silent for a moment and the whole court waited in silence. Then the King himself spoke, 'Mullah Sahib, why are you silent? Give your reply.'

Mullah Dopiaza had by now recovered himself. He said, 'Your Majesty, I am your humblest servant. By God's grace you are the full moon and he is the cresent moon.' The King was greatly pleased. Along with other gifts, he conferred on him a costly ceremonial robe. And at the same time he sent word to Akbar of what Mullah Dopiaza had said.

Akbar was exceedingly angry. He sent for Mullah Dopiaza and said, 'Tell me, sir, how is it that you abuse me before foreigners, breaking the vessel from which you eat your food? You must pay the penalty. Tomorrow you will be executed.' Mullah Dopiaza, joining his hands in supplication, asked to be told for what fault he was to be punished. The King then told him of the report he had received from Iran. Mullah Dopiaza kissed the ground at Akbar's feet and said, 'First, Your Majesty, ponder the meaning of what I said.'

Akbar replied angrily, '*You* tell me what it meant.'

Mullah Dopiaza replied, 'When your humble servant described Your Majesty as a crescent moon, he spoke the truth. Your Majesty grows in lustre every day. And the King of Iran, like the full moon of the fourteenth day, is at the beginning of daily decline. What comparison can there be between him and you—between the atom and the sun that lights the world?'

The king was pleased with this answer. He conferred on him more gifts and more favour than the King of Iran had done and gave orders that he should never leave him.

Shaikh Chilli

'She Told Me Herself'

One day when Shaikh Chilli was away from home some mischief-maker went to his wife and told her that he had died. His wife and children began to cry, and his wife took off her ornaments and began to wail in lamentation, 'Alas! I am widowed. Alas! my children are orphaned.'

While this was happening Shaikh Chilli returned home. Seeing that his whole family was crying he too began to cry. The sound of their crying brought all the neighbours round to ask what had happened. Shaikh Chilli did not know, so he asked his wife. She said, 'Someone told me that you had died and I was a widow.' He, still weeping, repeated these words to the neighbours. 'My wife has been widowed!' One of them said, 'What nonsense are you talking? You're here—alive and well, fit and strong. How can your wife be a widow?' He said, 'I may be well and strong, but my wife told me herself that she was a widow. How can I doubt her word?'

The Barber's Clothes

One day Shaikh Chilli went to visit his in-laws, and a barber went with him. When they got near his father-in-law's village it occurred to him that the barber was better dressed than he was, and that people might think the barber was him and he was the barber's servant. So he at once had the barber exchange clothes with him. When he got to his father-in-law's house his father-in-law asked him, 'Who is this man with you?' Shaikh Chilli said, 'He's the man whose clothes I'm wearing.'

His father-in-law was greatly surprised at this answer and said to him, 'When anyone else asks you don't say that. Let them think that they're *your* clothes.'

Shaikh Chilli took due note of what his father-in-law had said, and now when anyone came to see him he would say, 'These clothes I'm wearing are mine; they're not my companion's.' This upset his father-in-law even more and he said to him, 'Why mention your clothes at all?'

Next day when some more people came to see him he said, pointing to the barber, 'This is my companion', and then, pointing to his clothes, 'but I won't say anything about these clothes because my father-in-law has forbidden me to say whether they're mine or his.'

Guarding the Horse

Once when Shaikh Chilli was employed as a servant he went on a journey with his master. They stopped for the night at an inn. When night came his master said to him, 'You go to sleep; I'll keep an eye on the horse so that no one can steal it.' He said, 'Impossible! Can a servant sleep in peace while his master stays awake? Don't worry; I'll stay awake all night. No one will dare even to look at the horse.' His master was reassured by this speech, and Shaikh Chilli was soon lost in his own thoughts.

After some hours his master awoke and asked him what he was doing. He said, 'I was wondering how God keeps the sky above us without a pillar to hold it up.' His master said, 'If that's the state you're in, it's goodbye to the horse. I'll stay awake.' But Shaikh Chilli again reassured him, and he went to sleep again.

About midnight he again awoke and asked Shaikh Chilli what he was doing. He said, 'I was wondering why God made some people rich and others poor. For instance, why did He make you the master and me the servant? Why didn't He make everybody equal?' His master was alarmed and said, 'That's it! You sleep and I'll keep awake. Otherwise it'll be goodbye to the horse.' But Shaikh Chilli again reassured him and he went to sleep.

Some hours before dawn he awoke again and asked Shaikh Chilli what he was doing. He said, 'I'm thinking God *has* made us equal in one thing. You and I will both have to walk; and I'm wondering who'll carry the saddle—you or me?'

'Your turn'

One night it was raining, and Shaikh Chilli and his master, each on his own bed, were reclining indoors. After a while the master said, 'Just take a look outside and see if it's still raining.' He said, 'No need for that. The cat has just come in and her fur's dry. I stroked her to see.' Some time later his master told him to put out the lamp. He said, 'Close your eyes and you'll think I *have* put it out.'

A little later his master said, 'All right, get up and shut the door.' He said, 'Sir, I've already done two things. This time it's *your* turn.'

'I don't know how to'

On one occasion Shaikh Chilli went on a journey with someone. When they stopped for the night his companion lit a fire and asked Shaikh Chilli to knead the dough. Shaikh Chilli said, 'I'm sorry, I've never done that before.' So his companion had to do it. Then he said, 'I'll clean the plates. You cook the bread.' Shaikh Chilli said, 'I'm sorry, I don't know how to.' So he cooked it himself. After a while he said, 'I'll be serving the food. You go and fetch some water.' Shaikh Chilli said, 'I don't know where the well is. Besides, there might be no water in it.' So the poor man went for water himself.

When the food was on the table he said, 'Come on then. Have something to eat.' Shaikh Chilli said, 'I feel ashamed that all those times I didn't do what you wanted me to. This time I'll do as you tell me.'

Tales of Famous Men

Ibrahim [Abraham]

Ibrahim was famous for his hospitality. Anyone who was passing at mealtimes would be invited to join him. One day an old man came to Ibrahim's house. When he sat down to eat he did so without offering thanks to God, and Ibrahim, seeing that he must be an idolater or a fire-worshipper ordered his servant to turn him out of his house. At this a voice from the unseen said, 'I have fed him all his life, though he opposes Me. Are you afraid to feed him even once? If he worships fire, why should that affect your generosity?'

Yusuf [Joseph]

In the days when Yusuf governed Egypt he never ate his fill of food. People would ask him why and he would reply, 'If I eat my fill I shall forget the plight of the hungry.'

Musa [Moses]

Musa complained to God, 'People tell lies about me. Do something to ensure that they tell nothing but the truth.' God replied, 'I cannot make them do that even about Me.'

Idris [a prophet]

Idris expressed a wish to visit paradise. The angels made him promise that he would return, but when he reached paradise he refused to go back. The angels said, 'Sir, you must keep the promise you gave us to return.' He replied, 'One keeps promises in order to go to paradise, not in order to be expelled from it.' The voice of God came saying, 'Let him stay.'

Luqman [a wise man whom some considered a prophet]

The ruler of Aden gave Luqman a goat, telling him to slaughter it and bring the best parts to him. Luqman brought him its heart and its tongue. The next day the ruler gave him another goat and told him to bring him the worst parts. He again brought the heart and the tongue. The ruler said, 'You're a strange man! You think that "best" and "worst" mean the same thing.' Luqman replied, 'No. When the heart and the tongue are good there is nothing better, and when they are bad there is nothing worse.'

Buqrat [Hippocrates]

Buqrat once told a chatterbox, 'There is pleasure in speech when for every one thing you say you listen to two.' He said, 'How so?' Buqrat replied, 'Because you have one tongue and two ears.'

Sikandar [Alexander the Great]

Sikandar once confided an important secret to one of his officers, telling him he must not tell anyone else. The officer did tell someone else. Sikandar was very angry and asked a wise man what punishment such a person should be given. 'None,' said the wise man. 'When you could not keep a secret, why should he?'

Aqlidas [Euclid]

The ruling king sent for Aqlidas. He refused to go and sent a message to him saying, 'I can't come to you for the same reason that you can't come to me. You must excuse me.'

Isa [Jesus]

Isa was walking with his disciples when they came upon a dead dog. It lay there and the stench was overpowering. The disciples all complained of it. Isa said, 'How beautiful its white teeth are!'

Ardeshir [a legendary king of Iran]

Ardeshir asked, 'Who is that man who fears no one?' The reply was, 'That man whom no one fears.'

Qabad

During Qabad's reign an innocent man was condemned to death for the murder of a woman. He was about to be executed when the real murderer confessed. The king pardoned them both. Qabad was asked why. He replied, 'One was innocent, and the other had both taken a life and saved a life. He has squared the account, so why should he be hanged?'

A Slave of Khusrau [king of Iran]

A slave came into Khusrau's presence carrying a dish of food, but he felt in such awe of him that his hands trembled and he spilt some of it. Khusrau was angry and gave orders that he should be put to death. At this the slave emptied the whole dish into Khusrau's lap. Khusrau asked him, 'Why have you done that?' He replied, 'O king, mine was a trifling fault, not one that deserved a death sentence. Now I deserve to die. If you had put me to death before, people would have called you cruel. Now no one will.' Khusrau pardoned him.

The Creation of Adam and the Loss of Paradise

['Khalifa' is usually translated as 'Vicegerent'—see note in introduction to this section.

The 'Kaba' is the building in Mecca which is the focus of Islamic Pilgrimage.

Gabriel, Michael and others in this story are angels, several of whom are seen as having specific functions: Gabriel is often God's messenger, Israfil will blow the trumpet on Judgement Day, Azrail is the angel of death. When mentioning the names of angels, prophets, and revered figures in the tradition of Islam, usually some phrase such as 'Peace be upon him' is added.

Iblis is also called Shaitan (Satan), and the two names are used interchangeably.]

Word went forth from God: 'Angels, I shall create a Khalifa upon the earth.' The angels said, 'Will You place on earth one who will fill it with tumult and bloodshed?—when we are ever speaking of You and declaring Your goodness and remembering Your holiness?' God replied, 'I know that which you do not know.' Then the Lord of the Worlds commanded Gabriel (on whom be peace) to bring a handful of soil from the earth. At God's command Gabriel (on whom be peace) at once descended from the height of heaven upon the earth and reached that place where the Kaba now stands. He went to take up a handful of soil, but the earth said, 'I adjure you by God not to take soil from me; for God will create his vicegerent from it, and his progeny will be sinful and wicked and will cause great distress...' Gabriel (on whom be peace) heard, and gave up his intention, and returned as he had come. And Michael and Israfil too (on whom be peace) could not perform this task.

Then God sent Azrail. And the earth would have forbidden him too, but Azrail rejected its plea and said, 'He by Whom you adjure me is He by whose command I have come. I will not disobey Him and will surely take your soil back to Him.' And he stretched out his hand and took a handful of soil and returned to the world above and said, 'Lord, you are all-knowing and all-seeing, and I have brought this to You.' Then Almighty God said to him, 'Azrail, from this soil I shall make one who shall be my vicegerent on earth, and [when the time comes for Me] to take his soul it is you whom I shall appoint to do this task.' Then at God's command the angels placed that handful of soil between Talf and Mecca. The rain of God's mercy rained upon it and in two years it became clay, and in the fourth year it hardened and in the sixth year it became potters' clay and in the eighth year it assumed the form of Adam.

One day Iblis with a train of seventy thousand angels came to see the form of Adam lying on the ground, and looked down upon it with contempt.

Iblis tries to interfere in Adam's creation, but his efforts are brought to nothing. The elaborate stage-by-stage process of putting life into Adam is then described:

Adam sneezed and at once, by God's inspiration, cried out *'al hamd ul illah'** the response of which, prescribed by God was *'yar hamuk ullah'*.† And that is why when someone sneezes and says 'al hamd ul illah' those who hear must respond 'yar hamuk ullah'.

When Adam rose up from the ground, then by God's command he put on a crown of gold and a robe and went and sat on a throne,

---

* Praise be to God.
† 'God have mercy on you'. Like most religious exclamations, these are phrases in the language of the Quran.

a throne that extended for forty miles in Paradise, and was studded with gold and jewels. Then God commanded all the angels to bow down before Adam—this was to honour him, not to worship him—and all did so except Iblis. He was proud, and would not bow down, and refused God's command. When they raised their heads again they saw that Iblis was standing there and had not bowed down. Thereupon they again bowed down. The first bowing down was a bow of obedience, and the second a bow of thanksgiving.

Then the Lord of the Worlds said to Iblis, 'How is it that you refused to bow down to that which my two hands have created?' Iblis said, 'I am better than him, because You made me of fire and him of clay. Besides, I bow down to You. How can I bow to any other?' Then Almighty God said, 'Leave this! I reject you and My curse is upon you until Judgement Day.' (Divines differ over the interpretation of 'Leave this!'. Some say it means 'Abandon the true faith' while others think it means 'Leave your angelic form and assume the form of Iblis.') Whereupon by God's wrath his form changed and his eyes descended to his chest. Then accursed Satan opened his mouth and said, 'O Cherisher of all, You have forsaken and rejected me. And it is because of Adam that this has befallen me.... Give me leave until the dead come to life that I may enter into the flesh and bones and veins of men and be hidden from their sight.' And God gave him leave. Satan said, 'I swear by Your honour that I will lead all men astray except your chosen ones.' And God said, 'This is the truth, and I speak nothing but the truth; I shall fill hell with you and with all those who follow your path.'

Then by God's command the angels took Adam's throne and set it down in Paradise, and God bestowed upon him all manner of good things. But in spite of this Adam was not happy and not at peace, because for his peace and comfort every creature needs the fellowship of one of his kind. So God sent him to sleep, a sleep in which he was neither fully asleep nor fully awake, and had Gabriel take a bone from his left side. He felt neither pain nor distress. (If he had, men would never have loved women as they do.) And from this bone he made Eve [in Islam: Hava]... When Adam (on whom be peace) awoke and saw her he wanted to lay hands upon her at once, but the voice of God spoke: 'Adam, mind you do not touch her! Until you are married to her she is forbidden to you.'

At Adam's request God then married them and arranged for all the other observances which characterize a Muslim marriage. God then allowed them all pleasures, but forbade them to go near a particular tree.

Of this tree it is related that its roots were of silver and its branches of gold and its leaves of green emerald. God said to Adam, 'I have presented this tree to you, but do not eat its fruit.' Adam said, 'Oh God, when you have given it to me why do you forbid me to eat from it?' God replied, 'You are a guest in my house. This is *your* tree. It is out of the question that while you are my guest you should eat anything of your own.'

Adam then heard voices, one addressing him and one addressing wheat (which, it appears, is the fruit of the beautiful tree). The voice that spoke to Adam urged him to be resolute in observing God's command, and the one that spoke to the wheat urged it not to flag in its efforts to tempt Adam, and suggested that it call Satan to its aid. Fate asked God why He was permitting all this, and God replied that it was in accordance with a secret purpose.

They say that there are four things which are not there in Paradise—hunger, thirst, nakedness and the excessive heat of the sun.

When Adam saw that all the gates of Paradise were closed he felt freed from all fear. 'Satan is out there in the world and I am here in Paradise. I need not worry about his wiles.' One day accursed Iblis decided that he would get to Adam in Paradise. He knew three of the great names of God. Reciting these, he traversed the seven skies and arrived at the gates of Paradise. Finding them closed he began to think up tricks that would get him in. It so happened that there was a peacock sitting on the battlement of Paradise. He saw that here was this person reciting the great name. The peacock said, 'Who are you?' He replied, I am one of the angels of Almighty

God.' The peacock said, 'Why are you sitting there?' Satan said, 'I can see Paradise, and I want to go in.' The peacock said, 'I have been commanded by God that as long as Adam is in Paradise I am not to let anyone in.' Satan said, 'If you'll take me in I'll teach you a prayer—a prayer which if anyone says and acts according to, he will get three boons: he will not grow old; he will not die; and he will live in Paradise for ever.' Iblis recited this prayer, and both left the battlements and went to the gate of Paradise, where the peacock told the snake all that had happened. The moment the snake heard it he was afraid. He closed the gates, poked his head out, and asked Iblis, 'Who are you? And where have you come from to sit here and recite the great name?' He said, 'I am one of the angels of Almighty God.' The snake said, 'Teach me that prayer.' Satan said, 'I will on condition that you take me into Paradise.' The snake said, I have been commanded by God that as long as Adam is in Paradise I am not to let anyone in.' Iblis said, I will not set foot in Paradise. I'll stay in your mouth and not put a foot outside it.' Then the snake opened its mouth wide and accursed Iblis stepped into it, and the snake took him into Paradise and closed the gates of Paradise behind them.

Then Satan said, 'Take me to the tree that God has forbidden Adam to eat of.' When he reached the tree he began to weep hypocritically, there inside the snake's mouth. He was the first person who ever wept hypocritically. All the *houris* and *ghilmans*,* hearing the sound of weeping, gathered around. They said, 'None of us has ever heard the sound of weeping coming from a snake's mouth before,' and Eve asked the snake, 'Why are you weeping?' Satan replied, 'I am weeping because Almighty God will expel you from Paradise because He has forbidden you to eat the fruit of this tree; yet whoever eats the fruit of this tree will stay in Paradise and not be expelled.' Satan said to Adam, 'Adam, shall I show you the tree which will give you eternal life and your kingdom will not

---

* *Houri* is a beautiful woman, and *ghilman* a beautiful boy. Both serve the faithful in paradise.

fail?' And he said, 'I swear by God that I tell you truly. I do not seek to harm you and am advising you for your own good.' So Adam fell, a prey to this deception. The first person who ever swore a false oath was this accursed Satan. Eve was convinced by this oath that he was speaking the truth. She fell into his snare and reaching out her hand plucked three grains of wheat from the tree. One she ate herself and two she brought to Adam. Muaz Razi Ullah, in his commentary, has said that when she plucked these ears of wheat, the place from which she had plucked them turned red, and a drop of blood dripped from it. Then Almighty God swore by Himself and said, 'Until the Last Day I shall befoul your daughters with blood once a month and you and they shall make reparation to this my tree in this way.'

Then Adam went and sat on his throne; and the wheat grains approached him of their own accord. Adam smelt their sweet smell and said to his throne, 'Take and set me down far away from here, for Almighty God has forbidden me to eat this food.' The throne took him away to a distance of a twelve thousand years' journey. When he stepped down from the throne the grains were there too. In short no matter where Adam went, the grains went too. Then one of the grains said, 'Adam, what God has fated to happen will come to pass. Go to a distance of a journey of a million years, but you cannot escape.' Then Eve took the two grains of wheat to Adam. Adam said, 'What is it?' Eve said, 'It is the fruit of the tree that God forbade us to eat. I have eaten one grain, and I have brought two for you.' Adam said, 'What does it taste like?' She said, 'Sweet and delicious.' He said, 'I will not eat it. I have made covenant with God not to eat the fruit of that tree.'

Eve was very disappointed that she could not persuade Adam to eat. So she went and fetched a bowl of wine and gave it him to drink. Adam lost his senses and took and ate the two grains and broke his convenant. Before the two grains had gone down his throat the crown flew from his head and he fell off his throne, and their private parts were uncovered. They tried to pluck leaves to cover them. All the trees they went to refused them, until they went to the fig tree, and it lowered its head and said, 'Take leaves from me and cover your genitals.' And they did so. And they took leaves to cover their genitals from the *ud** tree too. And the voice of God came and said, 'Fig tree, you have been kind to them; I have banished evil and decay from you and made you so that any who eats your fruit seventy times will feel fresh delight each time.' And He addressed the ud and said, 'I have endeared you more than any other to all so that when they put you on the fire they may smell your fragrance.'

Then the dwellers in paradise began to cry out, 'Adam and Eve have both sinned in the sight of God and are roaming like madmen around Paradise.' God summoned them three times, but they did not respond. Then Gabriel came to them and said, 'Adam, your Lord is calling you.' And Adam said, 'I stand before You. O Lord, we feel shame before you.'

God reminded them of His warning. And they responded weeping.

And God said, 'You are to live on earth, and you will work there, and live and die there, and be taken away from there.' Then God commanded Gabriel to expel Adam and Eve and the snake and Satan and the peacock from Paradise and place them in the world. And Gabriel went to Adam and told him. Adam as soon as he heard it became agitated and began to weep copiously at his banishment from Paradise. Eventually he took a piece of wood from there to use as a toothstick, and this stick was handed down in his family from generation to generation until it became the staff of Moses. Then Adam and Eve and the peacock and the shake and Satan were all five expelled from Paradise. First Adam was set down on Sarandip [Sri Lanka], which is an island belonging to India; and Eve was set down in Khurasan and the peacock in Sistan and the snake in Isfahan and Satan (curses be upon him) on the mountain of Damawand [all in Central Asia]. At that time the snake had four legs, like a camel. Because of what had happened Almighty God

---

* *Ud*: Generally translated as aloes-wood. It makes a pleasant smell when it burns.

took them from it so that it should crawl on its belly in the dust and eat there. And when Adam was set down in Sarandip he wept over his sin for forty years or, according to another tradition, three hundred years, so that rivers of his tears began to flow, and on their banks grew dates and cloves and nutmeg. And from Eve's tears henna and indigo and collyrium were created, and from the teardrops that fell into the sea pearls were made, so that these might be made into jewellery for her girls.

One day Gabriel came to Adam and said, 'Adam, before you die perform the Pilgrimage to Mecca.' At the mention of his death he felt afraid. He at once rose up and determined to perform the Pilgrimage. At every place where his footsteps fell a village or a settlement came into being. And wherever he rested after a day's journey, the blessing of his footsteps caused a town to come into being. And some learned divines say that thirty paces brought Adam to Mecca... When Adam sat down to rest he saw Eve coming from the direction of Jeddah. And he rose up and took her in his arms.

Sikandar, Khizar and
the Water of Life

Sikandar determined to march towards the East. He enquired of wise and learned men, 'Have you read in any books what thing confers long life?' One of them replied, 'Refuge of the World, I have read in Adam's testament that Exalted God has created in the darkness of the mountains of Qaf a spring of the Water of Life, whose water is whiter than milk and colder than ice and sweeter than honey and more bland than butter and more fragrant than musk. Whosoever shall drink it shall not die, and shall live on till Judgement Day. And the name of this water is the Water of Life.'

Then Sikandar desired to drink the Water of Life. He said to his wise men, 'Tell me, which steed is the swiftest and most alert among animals?' They said, 'An Arab mare that has not born a foal.' Then he took a thousand horsemen, mounted on picked Arab mares, and appointed Khizar as the guide of the whole force. Then he said, 'When we go into the darkness surely no man will be able to find his neighbour. What will happen then?' The wise men said, 'If in Your Majesty's court there be a regal ruby or pearl, take it along; when this stage comes we shall make our way by its light.' Then he took from his royal treasury a gem, the Lamp of Night, and entrusted it to Khizar, and gave his throne and crown and kingdom into the charge of a wise and prudent man in his service, and, promising to return in twelve years, departed, and taking provision of food and drink, set out for the darkness of Qaf in search of the Water of Life.

When they came to the mountains of Qaf they lost their way, and wandered there for a year; and Khizar lost contact with the armies and found himself in another region of darkness. He took the gem, the Lamp of Night, from his pocket and set it on the ground, and its light dispelled the darkness. By the grace and favour of Allah he came upon the spring of the Water of Life. He washed his face and hands in it, and drank it and rendered thanks to God. Thus did Khizar gain eternal life. Then, returning from there, he came to another place of darkness. Again he took out the gem, the Lamp of Night, and set it on the ground. Its radiance shone forth, and all the armies that had been lost in the darkness came and gathered around him.

Sikandar had told his armies, 'Stay here. I will go forward to see a strange and wonderful sight, and will return.' So saying he went forward; and there came in sight a balcony of such kind that its four Walls were suspended in the air. In it he saw many birds and winged creatures. And the birds said to him, 'Why have you left your habitation and come to this darkness?' He said, 'I have come to drink the Water of Life.' Then the one of them that was king of the birds said, 'Sikandar, the time has now come when all men will put on clothing of silk, and build fine houses, and, setting their hearts on Worldly things, will give themselves up to play and pastime and pleasure and luxury.' So saying, it flapped its wings, and what should Sikandar see but that the whole balcony was now all made of gems. Then it said, 'Sikandar, the time has come for the sounding of the lute and the tabor.' So saying it again flapped his wings, and what should he see but that the whole balcony was now made of rubies and garnets. Seeing this he was astonished. The bird then said to him, 'Do not fear. This is Iblis's [Satan's] handiwork.' Then it said, 'Now confusion will become manifest. Does "There is no god but God" abide, or not?' Sikandar said, 'It abides.' Then it asked, 'Among God's creation is uprightness still the right way, or not?' Sikandar said, 'It is the right way.' Then the bird left that place and went to another place.

It is related that this bird said to Sikandar, 'Go onto the balcony and see what is there.' Then Sikandar went, and what should he see but a man who was standing on one leg and had a horn put to his mouth and was looking up at the sky. They say that it was Asrafil, the angel who will sound the last trump on Judgement Day. He said to Sikandar, 'Sikandar, why have you left your kingdom and the light of your country and strayed into this darkness? Was not that enough for you?' He said, 'I have come to drink the Water of Life, so that the Water of Life may give me increase of days and I may worship God.' Then Asrafil (on whom be peace) put into Sikandar's hand a stone like the head of a cat, and said, 'I have awakened you from heedlessness. Now go! And restrain your greed!'

Then Sikandar, without gaining the Water of Life, came back to his armies. And all joined forces and went their way together. In the darkness of the way they saw beneath the trees growing on heaps of refuse, pieces of rock gleaming like rubies that illumine the night. They asked, 'What is all this?' Luqman, the wise man, replied, 'These are stones. He who picks them up will in the end repent it. And he who does not pick them up will in the end repent it.' In the end some picked them up and some did not. When they came out from the darkness what should they see but that all were gems—rubies, and beryls and garnets and turquoises and emeralds. Then those who had not taken any began to regret it, and those who had taken some regretted that they had not taken more.

Sikandar asked Luqman the Wise, 'What is the meaning of the stone that Asrafil gave me?' Luqman said, 'Put your stone on one side of the balance and the stones of all the others on the other side. See which stone is heavier.' And they saw that Sikandar's stone was the heavier. Then he asked Luqman the Wise, 'What is the mystery of this?' He said, 'Now take all their stones off the balance and put a handful of dust in the scale.' When he did so then both scales of the balance came level. Then he asked Luqman, 'What is this?' Luqman said, 'Exalted God has given you kingship from the East to the West. Even so you were not satisfied. But your belly will be filled with a handful of the dust of the grave.'

When Sikandar heard these words he sent all his armies away from him. And they went away each to his own country, and Sikandar remained there and occupied himself in worship. After some days he died, and was buried there in a coffin of gold. The story is told that at the time of his death Sikandar declared his testament to his mother: 'After my death grant my soul this heavenly reward, and feed those that are fatherless and motherless, and the poor and helpless, and the widows and destitute and needy.' When his mother heard this she began to weep bitterly; and she fulfilled his wish.

Guests are Pests

KHWAJA HASAN NIZAMI

It was December, and very cold. Twelve o'clock at night. Lightning flashing and thunder rumbling, and rain falling. My servants had gone home to sleep, and my wife and children, snug in their quilts, were also fast asleep. I too, wrapped in two quilts, was asleep—two, because one is not enough to keep me warm. Suddenly I was awakened by the noise of people shouting and knocking at the outer gate. Several of them were shouting together. 'Wake Khwaja Sahib up! He has visitors! Open the door! We're getting wet through!' Pyare Shah Peshawari's lodging was near the gate, and he had a servant with him, but neither of them spoke, either because of the cold and rain or because after a full day's hard work they were sleeping so soundly that they did not wake up. I got up, wrapped a blanket around myself and went out. I was shivering and my teeth were chattering and I could not speak. But out of consideration for these visitors I went to the gate and opened it. Meanwhile my servant too had woken up, heard me calling him, and come out. I saw five men standing there, soaked to the skin, and shivering with the cold. None of them had bedding with him.

It was dark. I could not see their faces, and I did not recognize any of their voices. All the same I invited them into the men's part of the house, switched on the light, and asked them to sit down. I then enquired where they had come from at this time of night, and who they were. One of them replied, 'First get us some dry, warm clothes. We'll talk when we've recovered from the cold.' I told the servant to open the box and get out blankets and loincloths and give them to them. My visitor said, 'Loincloths? In this cold? Good sir, get us warm paijamas and shirts.' I said, 'I keep blankets and quilts for any visitors who may come, but I am sorry to say I have not had warm paijamas and shirts made. Please forgive me. For the present, take off your wet clothes, put on these loincloths and wrap yourself up in the blankets. I'll send for a brazier right away and you'll soon be warm.' My visitor got cross at this and said, 'We came here thinking that it was a godly man's house we were coming to and he'd have everything that guests need. But I see there's practically nothing here. All right, give us the loincloths. We don't want to catch pneumonia. We've been wearing wet clothes for the last hour.' Then, in the next breath, 'All right, order some tea for us. We'll eat a little later. For the present tea will do. It'll warm us up. If you tell them to put cloves and cinnamon in the tea we'll enjoy it more, and it will warm us up better. And order eggs for our meal, with quite a lot of chillies.'

Up to that point I had overlooked their rudeness in my concern to take care of their needs, but when I saw that here they were, complete strangers behaving as though they owned the place, and without any regard for the inconvenience they were causing others, I laughed and said, 'No, my good sir, just wrap yourselves in your blankets and go to sleep. It's bad for your health to drink tea in the middle of the night, and as for food, it's virtually poison at this time. Just keep repeating the name of God and you'll very soon be warm.' Meanwhile my servant brought the brazier in and set it down between the beds. My visitors laughed out loud, and one of them said, 'Just look! This saintly man is like a stone. We'll get nothing out of him.' He went on, 'Listen, good sir. We've had nothing to eat all day. There's nothing along the line from Nagda. You can't get anything to eat anywhere. And the train was late. When we got to Nizam-ud-Din it was twelve o'clock. We asked the ticket collector where we could stay and he sent us to you. "He's a godly man," he said, "and an extremely hospitable one. He always has room for hundreds of guests."'

I said, 'Listen to me. When I intend to visit someone I inform my host eight days beforehand. I tell him that I will arrive at such and such a time, and shall have my servant with me, that I don't eat rice and don't drink tea, and that I shall bring my bedding with me and stay only one night. And I expect anyone who wants to stay with me to do likewise. That is what "courtesy" means, or, in English, "behaving like a gentleman." And when people go against these standards—come without warning, at an inconvenient time, without previous acquaintance, I call them not guests but pests.'

At this he got angry and said, 'I see! You've embraced the New Light.* We've made a grave mistake in coming here, and I can promise you we'll never come here again. But at the moment we need tea and food. If we get neither we'll be dead by morning and you'll have to get five graves dug and provide five shrouds.'

I said, 'No matter. To provide graves and shrouds is a meritorious act, and I will gladly do you this service. And if you care to express any last wishes I shall hear what you have to say and fulfil your bequests.'

One of them was a maulvi,† and he now began to expound the merits of hospitality towards guests. 'What evil times we live in!' he said. 'Even people like you have banished, both from your hearts and your conduct, the concept that guests are a blessing. Your predecessor Sultanji even on his deathbed asked whether any guests had come, and said that if so they should be "made welcome."'

I said, 'Have I not made you welcome in getting out of my warm bed in all this cold and rain and inviting you in and giving you shelter? My servant is only human, like yourselves. He's already done a full day's work. How can I ask him to make tea at this time of night? This place is a village. I can't get milk at this time.' He said, 'You must have tinned milk in the house.' I said, 'In the first place, I don't like tinned milk. And secondly, even if I did, I'm not willing to trouble either my wife or my servant at such a time. So

---

* The New Light: Adopting British ways and abandoning traditional customs. See p. 289.
† *Maulvi*: see note on p. 43.

goodnight—sleep well. If we live, we'll meet in the morning.' He said, 'So are we to spend the night repeating *qul ho vallah*.'*

I said, 'Yes. First recite qul ho vallah, then, "in the name of God" and then *auz o billah*,† so that God may bless you and make you human, so that you will never again have the effrontery to arrive anywhere in the middle of the night and announce "Like it or not, we are your guests."'

I did then signal to the servant and he brought tea and biscuits and eggs. I stayed awake until two o'clock, and when they had had tea and food and gone to sleep I too went to bed.

My visitors woke up at ten o'clock and took a bath in hot water. My servant had dried their wet clothes in front of the fire, and they got dressed. After they had had their breakfast I began to converse with the maulana, the expounder of Islam.

I said, 'Maulana, if you found anything I said to you last night offensive, please forgive me.'

He said, 'Your conduct was unforgivable. You ridiculed me, and he who ridicules even the slipper of a Muslim divine is an infidel.'

I replied, 'Perhaps you do not know that on five occasions, fatwas have been issued declaring me to be an infidel, each bearing the signatures of a hundred and fifty maulvis. If by insulting you I have again become an infidel, well, I was a five-fold infidel already. What difference can that make?'

He said, 'Do you know how hospitable to guests Hazrat Ibrahim‡ (peace be upon him) was? Even angels from heaven used to come to him in the form of guests. And our holy prophet Muhammad (peace and security be on him and his progeny) used to entertain even guests who were not Muslims. He would give a guest all the food he had in the house and himself go to bed hungry. He would give up his own bed for his guest to sleep in. On one occasion a

---

* *qul ho vallah*: 'God is one'. But there is a play upon words here. The Arabic words are thought to sound like the rumbling of an empty belly.

† *auz o billah*: 'Refuge in God'—the key words in the sentence, 'I seek refuge in God from accursed Satan.'

‡ Ibrahim: see p. 121. *Hazrat* is a title of great respect.

non-Muslim guest excreted in his bedding and ran off while it was still dark. The prophet washed the excrement off with his own hands. His companions pressed him to let them do it, but he refused and said, "This is my guest's excrement. I will wash it myself." It so happened that this guest came back to collect something he had forgotten, and saw what Muhammad was doing. Whereupon he fell at his feet and became a Muslim. Your leader and Imam of all, Hazrat Ali, acted in the same way. And this was the custom of all the most revered men of God. If you revere Hazrat Ibrahim and the Prophet of God, then you should not behave to your guests as you did to us last night.'

I replied, 'Respected Maulana Sahib, I am familiar with the hospitality of the prophets and saints and the Muslims in general, and I revere them for it. But in the days when there were no roads, no railways, no cars, and no inns and hotels, simple humanity demanded that hospitality to travellers be looked upon as a matter of honour, and pride, and religious merit. Those were days when because of the difficulties that faced travellers, people very rarely travelled. Travel was regarded as a torment. But today there is rail and motor transport, running from morning to night and carrying passengers in hundreds of thousands from place to place. There are inns and hotels everywhere. And now the same degree of hospitality is not required. And since there are many unemployed and idle people who have made it their trade to make themselves uninvited guests and, on the plea that their luggage has been stolen, asking you to pay their fare, I entertain only those guests who give me previous notice of their arrival or whom I know. These professional guests I look upon as pests. And my apologizing to you was a matter of courtesy; because I still think that what I said to you last night was absolutely right. And I tell my followers too to beware of entertaining uninvited guests like you. Moreover, I am opposed to the entertainment customarily offered at weddings and occasions of mourning—to such an extent that I consider even the marriage banquet in present day conditions to be an occasion for display and hypocrisy.'

When I said this the expounder of Islam was beside himself with rage. He told his companions that to lodge with a person like me, and to accept his food and drink was a sin. His four companions said nothing. The maulana told them again and again to get up and get moving. 'I am not going to stay here,' he said. I smiled and said, 'If you wish I will send for salt and water.' He stared at me and said, 'Why?' I said, 'Because you have eaten and drunk forbidden things last night and this morning. You need to bring all that up, and you cannot do that without salt and water. Or I can send for a peacock feather. Put that down your throat and move it about and you will soon vomit everything up.'

At this the maulana stood up and said, 'Curses on any man who ever stays in your house again, and triple pronouncement of divorce of the wife of any man who eats and drinks anything at your table.' I put my hands together and with folded hands said, 'If your honour will give me your spouse's address I will write to her today to inform her that you have divorced her in the presence of five Muslim witnesses.' The maulana's four companions burst out laughing, and the maulana himself laughed. Then he sat down and put on a serious air and said, 'Shahji,* I like your bluntness. And it is marvellous how in the course of what you had to say you spoke of travellers' luggage being stolen. You seem to be a man of great spiritual powers, because that is exactly what happened to us. All five of us had our luggage stolen during the rail journey. And now we haven't a single penny left. You will at least have to give all five of us the fare for our journey home.' I said, 'Most gladly. I have work for you. There are book pages and newspaper pages here that need to be folded. I will give you your two meals a day and two annas a head as your wages. When you have saved enough to get you home you can go. If you accept, you can have the servants' quarters to stay in.' The maulana again got very angry and began to swear at me. And at his insistence his four companions got up and left. And that was the end of the matter.

---

* A common form of address for a saintly man.

I was asked to speak on this theme, and that is why I have told you a story of my own experience. I frequently have experiences of this kind, and Delhi Radio station probably gave me this subject to speak on so that I should present you with some useful lessons to be drawn from it.

But now I should show you the other side of the picture, and tell you that hospitality and entertainment of guests is the most valuable thing in our Asian culture and eastern way of conduct. If we can get rid of those professional, sham guests that I spoke of and still maintain our standards of hospitality, we shall be preserving an excellent trait in our Asian, Eastern way of life.

The late Hakim Ajmal Khan once told me of two incidents that occurred during his travels in Europe. On one occasion, he was the guest of an Englishman, and there was enough food on the table to feed several others besides. At this point a poor man, an Englishman, came to his host and said that he had had no food for the last three mealtimes, and was hungry. The host told him he could go to such and such a place that provided food as a charity, and when the man had gone said to the Hakim Sahib, 'I don't know whether this man was really hungry or not. There are plenty of bad characters who make up stories like this.'

Some time later the Hakim Sahib went to Constantinople, the Turkish capital, where he stayed in a hotel. In the evening he went out for a walk and came upon a big garden at the roadside. He thought it was a public garden, and went inside. But in fact, it belonged to the wife of a high-ranking Turkish officer, who observed purdah. (This was in 1911, when Turkish women used to observe purdah.) A maidservant saw the Hakim Sahib and called out, 'Who are you? And why are you in this purdah garden?' He replied, 'I am a visitor.' As soon as she heard the word 'visitor' the woman said, 'A visitor? You are most welcome. Please take a seat in that room in front of you. The pasha is out, and his lady is in purdah. I will bring you some refreshment at once.' The Hakim Sahib said, 'I am staying in a hotel. I do not need any refreshment.' The woman said, 'Can a visitor come to a Turkish Muslim's house and go away without having had anything to eat or drink? Impossible! That would be the worst insult, the worst humiliation that a Turk could be offered.' The Hakim Sahib took a seat in the room. The woman first brought him the latest newspaper and a little later, a tray of fruit and sweets and tea, and with it a message from her lady that she was grateful to him for visiting her house and only sorry that the pasha was out and so would not have the pleasure of meeting him. 'When he comes I will congratulate him on his good fortune in having had an Indian Muslim visit his house.'

These two incidents illustrate very clearly the difference between the West and the East and between European and Asian standards of hospitality.

In that same year, 1911, I too travelled in Islamic countries. In Damascus I went into a restaurant to eat. There were a number of Turks and Arabs already sitting eating at one of the tables. I greeted them and sat down at a table and the owner of the restaurant served me food. The Turks and Arabs said farewell to me and left. When I asked the owner for my bill he said, 'The Turks have paid for your food.' I said, 'Why? Why have they paid? We're not acquainted. I don't know them and they don't know me.' He said, 'They were Muslims, and so are you. They were already here when you came, and that makes you their guest. It's not necessary to know one's guests. They weren't doing you a favour when they paid for your food—merely showing that they were good Muslims.'

These examples show that hospitality is an excellent quality in Eastern peoples, and no instances of guests being pests should make us abandon it. We can learn from the west how to avoid the evils of hospitality, but to lose the quality of hospitality would be to turn our backs on our culture and our standards of good conduct.

LOVE POETRY
GHAZALS OF MIR AND GHALIB

Classical Love Poetry

From the time that Urdu speakers first began to use their mother tongue as a vehicle for literature, poetry dominated the scene; and poetry remains to the present day that part of their literature which Urdu speakers most value. Urdu speakers most emphatically do not suffer from that 'successfully cultivated distaste for poetry' which the English have, with much justification, been accused of by one of their fellow countrymen.

Their classical poetry includes verse in a number of different genres, but by far the most popular of these was, and still is, a form called the ghazal. It is the ghazal therefore, which forms the subject matter of this section, and other genres are not represented in this book.

Love in Muslim Society

The ghazal's central theme is love; and to fully appreciate ghazal poetry, one needs to understand how the society and time which produced this form of poetry viewed passionate love.

The ghazal celebrates a love which, in that social context, could *only* be illicit. Romantic love was regarded as a menace to ordered social life—and indeed, it still often is. Marriages were (and often still are) alliances between two families, not unions of two lovers.*
The purdah system evolved as a way of making falling in love impossible, and when it could not be prevented it was drastically

---

* See the earlier extract by Shaukat Thanavi, *Love and Prudence*.

punished. From puberty onwards boys and girls were kept strictly apart. Houses were divided into two separate parts, one for the men and one for the women, but a boy and a girl from the same neighbourhood might perhaps catch an accidental sight of each other, which might be enough for them to believe themselves in love. To persist in the course of love took great courage, especially on the part of the girl, who (as in almost all societies) was penalized even more cruelly than the boy. Even where she returned his love, she would feel the need to put his steadfastness to the test, treating him with what seemed to him great cruelty until she felt sure that no matter what it cost him he would be true to her.

All these situations are frequent themes in ghazal poetry; and it is not surprising that the illicit—often dangerous—nature of the love it depicts gives rise to particularly intense expressions of feeling.

Ghazals and Mushairas

Though a ghazal is primarily a love poem, it has many other possible themes as well. It consists of a series of loosely linked couplets, each independent in meaning—called *sher* in Urdu, as well as in English (by Urdu and Hindi speakers, mostly). In a typical ghazal there may not be common theme between the couplets. So you can think of a ghazal as a collection of independent two-line poems. (Rarely will a poet compose a 'continuous' ghazal on a single theme. I have included a couple of examples; but these are exceptions.)

For Urdu speakers, the ghazal is primarily something they *hear*, not read. Poets air their ghazals in gatherings called *mushairas*; only later will some of their poems get into print and be read. You will get a sense of the atmosphere of a mushaira in a later section of this book, in Farhatullah Beg's *A Memorable Delhi Mushaira*. The form of the ghazal is intimately connected with this way of presenting it. Every couplet is spoken and appreciated separately, and the audience responds immediately. The mushaira is often an all-night affair, and therefore, monotony of theme and mood has to be avoided if the poets are to make their impact. Within one ghazal the mood may vary startlingly from couplet to couplet, so that lines of intense sadness might be followed by others of broad comedy. Poets enable their audience to relax between the highly charged couplets by including verses that say nothing much, but say it competently. Urdu speakers know all this—they take it in their stride, and enjoy it all; but what they remember afterwards are the good verses.

What binds the couplets together and makes them part of the same ghazal is not their theme, but a very strict unity of form—rhyme and metre—and, as this is poetry to be *heard*, ghazals work best when these features are strongly marked. All the couplets of a ghazal must use exactly the same metre, and follow a strict rhyme scheme: the lines of the first couplet rhyme (AA) and in all following couplets the second line must rhyme with that initial couplet (BA, CA, DA and so on.) Once the audience has heard the first couplet they can anticipate the shape and sound of all those that will follow, and this enhances the pleasure they feel. Sadly, this is a pleasure largely lost in translation. The metrical patterns in Urdu are far more complex and varied than those commonly used in English, and while in Urdu rhymes are abundant and rhyming is easy, that is not the case in English. Only very rarely can a translator find a good, consistent rhyme which can be maintained throughout the poem.

Two other conventions of the ghazal need explaining. First, every ghazal poet takes a pen name, a *takhallus*, and they must introduce this in the last couplet of the ghazal, rather like a signature. So in the last couplet it often sounds as if poets are addressing themselves, or as though they were someone else talking about the poet.

Then there is the question of grammatical gender. Mushairas were traditionally part of cultured aristocratic society, and largely male affairs, though courtesans were an accepted part of their social world and many were skilled poets. But the grammatical convention is that it is the male lover who speaks. In medieval literatures conventions of this kind were strict and binding, and though it was true that the poet generally *was* masculine and that this fixed the convention, it was no less true that convention was binding on all poets, so that women ghazal poets also spoke of themselves in the masculine. The beloved, too, is always spoken of in the masculine, and though this could in some cases have reflected a real-life love of man to man, in most cases it is clear that a female beloved is intended: this is a grammatical convention only. A similar but opposite convention is found in much of Bhakti poetry. There the archetype is that of the love of Radha—a woman—for Krishna—a male god—and *all* lovers, male and female alike, speak of themselves in the feminine gender. In both forms of poetry both men and women listening feel no difficulty in identifying with the poet-lover.

Illustrating the Themes of the Ghazal

Because English readers encountering the ghazal for the first time are likely to find it difficult to put aside the expectation that a poem should have a unity of theme and tone, I have taken the *sher*—the couplet—as the essential poetic unit, rather than presenting whole ghazals. I have illustrated the ghazal's recurrent themes primarily through a selection of couplets taken from two of its greatest exponents. Mir (1723–1810) is by universal consent the greatest eighteenth-century ghazal poet, and the greatest love poet of all Urdu literature. Ghalib (1797–1869) is the greatest nineteenth-century poet, and in many people's view the greatest Urdu poet of all. His ghazals are extensively quoted today, and far more Urdu speakers know by heart large stretches of Ghalib's ghazals than educated English speakers know of Shakespeare. At the end of the section, to give you a feel of a typical ghazal where each couplet is on a different theme, I have included several couplets from a number of well known ghazals of Ghalib.

A few ghazals—untypically—do have a continuous theme, and I have included examples of this at the beginning of the section, one ghazal each by Hasrat Mohani (1875–1951) and Momin (1800–1851).

Readers who know Urdu will want to know the originals of the couplets I have included, so I have given these alongside the translations, in roman script. Many different ways are used to transcribe the sounds of Urdu in English letters. I have not used diacritics but rather, employed a simple transcription using the phonetic sounds of the words. For help with pronunciation, see my note on Urdu pronunciation in the appendix.

Lovers' Meetings

I begin with two continuous ghazals which vividly capture the social context of love in traditional society. The first, by Hasrat Mohani, gives a picture of how lovers will manage to find moments to be together, despite the restrictions. In older parts of towns the houses often adjoin one another, and in the hottest weather people take their midday siesta up on the flat roof and sleep there at night. Lovers who are bold enough may stay awake and cross surreptitiously from one roof to another:

> I still recall when first I fell in love
> The silent tears I shed, all night, all day.
>
> The thousand fears, the hundred thousand longings
> I felt when first I gave my heart away.
>
> The days when I would gaze up at your window
> And you would meet the challenge of my eyes.
>
> When first we met, the boldness of my passion,
> Alarming to you, taken by surprise.
>
> I quickly raised the corner of your curtain
> You raised your scarf to hide your face from view.
>
> I made to kiss your feet, thinking you sleeping
> You smiled and pushed my head away from you.
>
> The days when no one else but I yet loved you
> Just tell me, do you nurse those memories too?

At nights, when there was no one there to see you
And stop you, you would steal away to me

In the midday heat, you'd come barefoot to call me
And tell me all you had to say to me.

The secret places where I used to meet you
Long years ago, I still can see them all

And though I pray to God to make me pious
Those lusty days are days I still recall.

> chupke chupke raat din aansu bahaana yaad hai
> hum ko ab tak aashiqi ka vo zamaana yaad hai
>
> baa hazaaraan iztaraab o sad hazaaraan ishtiaaq
> tujh se vo pehle pal dil ka lagaana yaad hai
>
> baar baar uthna usi jaanib nigaah e shauq ka
> aur tira ghurfe se vo aankhen laraana yaad hai
>
> tujh se kuchh milte hi vo bebaak ho jaana mera
> aur tira daanton mein vo ungli dabaana yaad hai
>
> khainch lena vo mera parde ka kona daffatan
> aur dupatte se tera vo munh chhupaana yaad hai
>
> jaan kar sona tujhe vo qasad e paabosi mera
> aur tera thukra ke sar vo muskaraana yaad hai
>
> jab siva mere tumhaara koi deevaana na tha
> sach kaho kuchh tum ko bhi vo kaar-khaana yaad hai
>
> dopehr ki dhoop mein mere bulaane ke liye
> vo tira kothe pe nange paaon aana yaad hai
>
> chori chori hum se tum aakar mile thhe jis jagah
> muddatein guzrin par ab tak vo thikaana yaad hai
>
> bavajuud e iddi'a e ittiqa Hasrat mujhe
> aaj tak ahd e havas ka vo fasaana yaad hai

This poem expresses the exuberance of youth, and a mood in which the lovers give no attention to the price they would have to pay for their love if it were discovered. But the price could have been a formidable one. Lovers who were discovered could be killed by their families, and where the families shrank from so violent a punishment, forcible separation and the strongest condemnation of the lovers was the norm. So the joy that the lovers felt in loving each other could seldom last. The lovers' relationship usually ended because they themselves accepted the prevailing social values and gave in to pressure. This ghazal by Momin conveys the sense of inevitable loss:

> Once we made a pledge we would always love—
>   and I wonder, do you remember it?
> And that come what may we would still be true—
>   and I wonder, do you remember it?
>
> In those days you always were kind to me,
>   days when in every moment you cherished me
> And I recall every smallest thing,
>   and I wonder, do you remember it?
>
> Ever new complaints, ever new resentments,
>   and with it, stories of all our joys
> Times when all I did would provoke a frown—
>   and I wonder, do you remember it?
>
> I would sit in company, facing you,
>   and our gestures served us in place of words
> That proclaimed our passion quite openly—
>   and I wonder, do you remember it?
>
> When fortune favoured us we would meet,
>   and with every breath would speak our love
> And complain of kinsfolk who censured us—
>   and I wonder, do you remember it?

And if something happened to cause you pain,
    and you had a mind to complain of it
You forgot it all before words would come—
    and I wonder, do you remember it?

Those were days when both of us were in love,
    days when both would want to communicate
Days when you and I were each other's love—
    and I wonder, do you remember it?

Yes, some years have passed since you promised me
    you would always, always be true to me.
Have you kept that promise? I ask it now—
    and I wonder, do you remember it?

I am he whom you called your lover once,
    he who you were sure would be true to you
I am still that lover of whom you spoke—
    and I wonder, do you remember it?

> vo jo hum mein tum mein qaraar tha, tumhein yaad ho
>   ki na yaad ho
> vuhi yani vaada nibaah ka, tumhein yaad ho ki na yaad
>   ho
>
> vo jo lutf mujh pe the beshtar vo karam ki tha mere
>   haal par
> mujhe sab hai yaad zara zara, tumhein yaad ho ki na
>   yaad ho
>
> vo nae gile vo shikaayatein vo maze maze ki hikaayatein
> vo har ek baat pe ruthna, tumhein yaad ho ki na yaad ho
>
> kabhi baithe sab mein jo rubaru to ishaaraton hi se
>   guftagu
> vo bayaan shauq ka barmala, tumhein yaad ho ki na
>   yaad ho
>
> hui ittifaaq se gar baham to vafa jataane ko dam ba dam
> gila e malaamat e aqriba, tumhein yaad ho ki na yaad ho

koi baat aisi agar hui ki tumhare ji ko buri lagi
to bayaan se pehle hi bhoolna, tumhein yaad ho ki na
    yaad ho

kabhi hum mein tum mein bhi chaah thi kabhi hum se
    tum se bhi raah thi
kabhi hum bhi tum bhi thhe aashna, tumhein yaad ho
    ki na yaad ho

suno zikr hai kai saal ka ki kiya ik aap ne vaada tha
so nibaahane ka to zikr kya, tumhein yaad ho ki na yaad
    ho

jise aap ginte thhe aashna jise aap kehte thhe baa-vafa
main vuhi hoon Momin e mubtala, tumhein yaad ho ki
    na yaad ho

Mir: The Ideal Ghazal Lover

The eighteenth-century poet Mir is often described as 'the poet of love'. Throughout his ghazals and other semi-autobiographical poetry, he wrote movingly of his own intense and often traumatic experiences in love. He exemplifies the concept of a lover who is steadfast in his love, regardless of the obstacles.

In couplet after couplet he describes the immediate, overwhelming impact of a woman's beauty:

> I caught a glimpse of you with hair dishevelled
> And my distracted heart was yours for life.

> zulfein khole tu to tuk aaya nazar
> umar bhar yahaan kaam e dil barham raha

> She came but once, but do not ask what left me as she went—
> My strength, and faith, and fortitude, and will and heart and soul.

> hosh o sabr o khirad o deen o havas o dil o taab
> uss ke ek aane mein kya kya na gaya—mat poochho

> Where lovely women gather my beloved shines among them
> As when the shining moon appears among the twinkling stars.

> jama e khubaan mein mera mehboob is maanind hai
> jun mah e taabinda aata hai kabhu taaron ki beech

Until you see her walk you will not know
What grace and poise and matchless beauty are.

> sargarm e jalva us ko dekhe koi so jaane
> tarz e khiraam kya hai, husn o jamaal kya hai

Now and then she passes smiling, and for me the roses bloom
All the advent of spring is in the grace of her approach.

> aa nikalta hai kabhu hansta to hai bagh o bahaar
> uss ki aamad mein hai saari fasl e gul aane ki tarah

A body beautiful as hers I never saw or knew of
As flawless is her form as if cast in a perfect mould.

> itni sudaul dehi dekhi na hum suni hai
> tarkeeb us ki goya saanche mein gayi hai dhali

As the pure pearl shines through the limpid water
So does the beauty of her body shine.

> saath us husn ke deta tha dikhai vo badan
> jaise jhamke hai para gauhar e tar paani mein

For you I live—whose tightly clad, firm body
Teaches my soul what joy it is to live.

> tangi e jaama zulm hai e baais e hayaat
> paate hain lutf jaan ka hum tere tan ke beech

Her body yields such joy, I know no longer
Whether it is her body or my soul.

> lutf us ke badan ka kuchh na poochho
> kya jaaniye jaan hai ki tan hai?

Her wakening eyes, half-opened, seem to hold
All the intoxicating power of wine.

> Mir un neem baaz aankhon mein
> saari masti sharaab ki si hai

In that house where the moonlight of your radiance lies
  spread
The moonlight seems as lustreless as does the spider's web.

  jis ghar mein tere jalve se ho chaandni ka farsh
  vahaan chaadar e mahtaab hai makri ka sa jaala

I never saw the stars so bright before:
It was her eyes that taught them how to shine.

  chashmak e anjum mein itni dilkashi aage na thi
  seekh li taaron ne us ki aankh jhamkaane ki tarah

Perhaps when it passed by that way my love was combing
  out her hair:
The scented breeze of morning brings a fragrance into
  every lane.

  ab jo naseem muattar aayi shaayad baal khule uss ke
  sheher ki saari galiyaan ho gayin goya anbar saara aaj.

By following his heart he faces the censure of society:

  I take my stand for her—the world turns and assails me:
  I am her friend—and all creation is my enemy.

    uss ki taraf jo li hum ne hai apni taraf se phira aalam
    yaani dosti se us but ki dushman saari khudaai hui.

  Whom all the world reviles and persecutes, that man am I—
  Struck down by fate, and by her cruelty, and my distress.

    kare hai jis ko malaamat jahaan vo main hi hoon
    ajal raseeda, jafa deeda, iztiraab zada.

*He sometimes feels that he would have done better to do what most of his
fellows did, and take care never to fall in love:*

  Would that mankind had been immune to love,
  For it spares neither lover nor beloved.

muhabbat na ho kaash makhlooq ko
na chode ye aashiq na maashooq ko.

Live in the chains of slavery, and die in jail
But do not fall into the snare of love.

zindaan mein phanse, tauq pade, qaid mein mar jaaye
par daam e muhabbat mein giriftaar na hovay.

*Speaking of himself in the voice of someone else (this is the last couplet of
the ghazal where he is expected to use his pen-name):*

Mir's last behest to me was only this:
'Do what you will, my son, but do not love!'

vasiyat Mir ne mujh ko yehi ki
ki sab kuchh hona tu, aashiq na hona.

*But for himself, he chose to love, minimizing neither the pain nor the joy
that love brought him. He knew the price he might be called upon to pay,
and was ready to pay it:*

At the first trial your life may be demanded.
If you're afraid, don't come into the field.

ishq mein gaam e avval apne ji se guzarna pesh aaya
iss maidaan mein rakh ke qadam kya marne se dar
        jaavein hum

Just sacrifice your life, and fear is banished.
Go on your way; all danger will have vanished.

guzar jaan se aur dar kuchh nahin
rah e ishq mein phir khatar kuchh nahin

*A man's love for a woman might awaken in her a consciousness of her own
beauty and give her a sense of power over him:*

A man may die, and she will never care.
Oh God! Oh God! Just see how proud she is!

marjaao koi parva nahin hai
kitna hai maghroor! Allaah! Allaah!

The study of her beauty occupies her. What are you?
Though you desire her and petition her day in, day out.

vo mahv e jamaal apne hai, parva nahin us ko
khaahaan raho tum ab, ki talabgaar raho tum

Such pride in your fair symmetry, my love?
God marred you when He made you beautiful.

tanaasub pe aza ke itna tabakhtur!
bigaada tujhe khubsoorat banaakar

I nurse a wounded heart; she laughs and turns away.
Such is my heavy grief: so light she makes of it.

main ji sambhaalta hoon vo hanske taalta hai
yahaan mushkilein hain aisi vahaan ye masaahile hain

My lips returned no answer to all the world's revilings;
But what was that to you, love? You did not even notice.

bin kuchh kahe suna hai aalam se maine kya kya
par tu ne ye na jaana, aye bevafa, ki kya tha

See your own beauty and rejoice: I never said 'Do not do so.'
But sometimes spare a glance for me, and see what it has
    brought me to.

karta hai kaun mana ki saj apni tu na dekh?
lekin kabhi to Mir ke kar haal par nazar

But if she is cruel to him, no matter. He can bear all that she can inflict:

The arrows of your pride fly fast against the target of our
    breasts,
But iron breastplates are the hearts of those that pledge
    their love to you.

tere teer e naaz ke jo ye hadaf hue hain, zaalim
magar aahani tavve hain jigar e niyaaz mandaan

Compared to contemptuous indifference, even her anger is welcome:

I rouse your wrath,—and when I do at least you glance this
way.
If only I could make you angry with me all the time!

hote ho be-damaagh toh dekho ho tuk idhar
ghussa hi hum pe kaash ke aksar raha karo

*At times, he pretends that he does not understand why she behaves as she
does:*

I cannot see why you should act the stranger,
For you and I sprang from a common source.

vajah e begaanagi nahin maaloom
tum jahaan ke ho, vahaan ke hum bhi hain

I sit in silent wonder at your beauty,
And you? What is it that has struck *you* dumb?

hum to tumhaare husn ki hairat se hain khamosh
tum hum se koi karte nahin baat, kya sabab?

*He humorously envisages a situation which would have made a difference
to the way things stand:*

We have no common ground on which to meet.
If only *you* had been a poet too!

kuchh vaseelo nahin jo us se miloon
sher ho yaar ka shaayar aye kaash!

*—or he points out to her how popular he is with others and asks her to
follow their example:*

Beauty you have—now find fair words to match it.
This is what makes men speak so well of Mir.

> husn to hai hi—karo lutf e zabaan bhi paida
> Mir ko dekho ki sab log bhala kehte hain

Men come from south and east and west in hopes to get a
  glimpse of me—
Sad, that it should be you alone care nothing for my company.

> dakkhin poorab pacchim se log aakar mujko dekhein hain
> haif ki tum ko parva nahin hai mutlaq meri suhbat ki

*At all events he does not give up, and dreams of what he hopes may one
day happen:*

The spring has come, the flowers bloom cheek by cheek—
Would you and I might stand thus in the garden!

> bahaar aayi gul phool sar jode nikle
> rahein bagh mein kaash is rang hum tu

'Sleep in my arms!'—no, these are words I cannot find the
  strength to say
You need not speak; you need not stop; just pause as you
  pass by this way.

> sabr kahaan jo tum ko kahiye lag ke gale se so jao
> bolo na bolo, baitho na baitho, khade khade tuk ho jao

My love, I cannot tell the tale of all the things I want from
  you.
A hundred longings fill my soul, a thousand yearnings
  throng my heart.

> kya kahiye kya rakhein hain hum tujh se, yaar, khvaahish
> yak jaan, sad tamanna—yak dil hazaar khvaahish

Joy of my life, her body overflows with all delights.
Ah for the day when she will come and sleep in my embrace!

lutf se labrez hai us kaam e jaan ka sab badan
mukhtalif hojaaye hum se jo kabhu to, haaye, vo

*There are signs that such a day may come—moments when she is content
to let him see her as she is:*

You use no charms, no sidelong glance, no wayward airs to
win me now—
Nothing but your simplicity—and this has won me heart
and soul.

ek faqat hai saadagi, tis pe bala e jaan hai tu
ishva karishma kuchh nahin, aan nahin, ada nahin

There are hesitations, but in the end she comes to him:

Time after time she broke her word, but when she came at
last
I saw her from afar and knew: to see her was to love her.

der bad ahd vo jo yaar aaya
door se dekhte hi pyaar aaya.

And when she does come there is initial shyness:

Her sweet reluctance fires me with a keener love for her
And her resistance gives a joy compliance cannot give.

iqraar mein kahaan hai inkar ki si khoobi
hota hai shauq Ghalib us ki 'nahin! nahin!' par

We pass the long nights naked in each other's arms. How
strange
That in the daytime still she shyly veils her face from me.

raaton paas gale lag sote nange hokar—hai ye ajab
din ko be-parda nahin milte hum se sharmaate hain hanoz

He tells her that all he can offer her is his love:

> Now you have come I've nothing left to offer you but this:
> I'll draw you into my embrace and love you all day long.

> aaj humaare ghar aaya to kya hai yahaan jo nisaar karein?
> ila khainch baghal mein tujh ko der talak hum pyaar
>   karein

In a long poem (called a masnavi*) Mir tells the story of his own separation from his beloved. Here is the relevant passage in prose translation:*

One day she said to me, 'No good can come of our love; how long can we go on pining for each other like this?' I was too consumed by love to see the truth of her words, but today I think of them and weep.

How can I describe what I suffered in separation from her? At nights I imagined her with me, but the days were unbearable. For years we did not see each other again. I was indifferent to the world, and to my wife and my children and my family. I would think with longing of the days when, in spite of all difficulties and dangers, I would sometimes come to her and sit silently by her. For her sake all my relatives and friends had set their faces against me and called me mad, and the meanest and most contemptible people had taunted me to my face. At last the grief of separation became more than either of us could bear. We met, and this time satisfied all the yearning of our hearts. We were together for several days, but there came a day when we again had to part. It was not her fault. Our fate was against us. She said, 'It is best that we should part for some time. In love, there comes a stage when such things have to be faced. Do not think I am forsaking you, and do not grieve too much. As long as I live, you will be in my heart. I too grieve at this parting. But what can I do? My honour must be my first concern.' I could not speak in reply. I sat stunned and silent before her, trying to keep back the tears and speaking only if she spoke. After night fell, we parted, and I went from her lane as one who leaves behind him everything that is precious in the world.

I bear my sorrow alone. There is no one to whom I can tell my secret. Sometimes a message comes from her and I live again, but mostly nobody comes. How can I live parted from her like this? The memory of her is always with me—her loveliness, her tender love for me, her gentle speech, her grief at my distress, her longing to see me happy—and every memory brings the tears to my eyes. I long to be with her again, and without her I shall die.

In his ghazals he deals constantly with this theme:

> The candle gutters in the draught, and my life too must waste away.
> Like it I weep, and burn, and melt, and pine away parted from you.
>
> > gayi umar meri saari jaise sham e baad ke beech
> > yehi rona, jalna, galna, yehi iztiraab tujh bin
>
> How happily the days would pass when she was with me day and night.
> It is a different picture now: the nights and days are not the same.
>
> > vasl mein us ke roz o shab kya khoob guzarti thi apni!
> > hijraan ka kuchh aur hai saamaan ab vo lail o nahaar nahin
>
> We whispered to each other then; now you don't speak to me.
> Well, those were other times, and now another age has dawned.
>
> > har aan thi sargoshi ya baat nahin gaahe
> > auqaat hai ik ye bhi, ik vo bhi, zamaana tha

When I was sad she used to run and throw her arms about
   me—
She whom the whole world worshipped—but, alas, those
   days are gone.

   ab vo samaan nahin hai ki vo kaam jaan e khalq
   maghmoom hum ko dekh ke daura lipat gaya

I loved to see her wake from sleep, and rub her eyes, and
   stretch and yawn.
The beauty of this scene lives on unfading in my memory.

   ye bhi samaan khush tarkibon ka Mir na apne dil se gaya
   sote se uthkar aankhein mali hain, le angraai jamaahen
      hain

My eyes still see you; *you* live in my heart
Though years have passed since you would come and go.

   rehte ho tum aankhon mein phirte ho tumhin dil mein
   muddat se agarche yan aate ho na jaate ho

*Yet—in these linked couplets in a single ghazal—he affirms that he has
no regrets:*

Much have I suffered in my love for you—
Cruelty, persecution, and much more
And life-long deprivation of the joys
I spent the years in endless yearning for.
Yet from my heart I pity any man
Who never stood a suppliant at your door.

   zulm o jaur o jafa sitam bedaad
   ishq mein tere hum pe kya na hua
   hum to naa-kaam hi jahaan mein rahe
   yahaan kabhu apna mudda'a na hua

   Mir afsos vo ki jo koi
   uss ke darvaaze ka gada na hua

In the symbolism of the ghazal, the sufferings of love crush the heart to blood. But it is love, with all its suffering, that gives joy to life:

> I passed my life in love's intoxication
> Drunk with the rose-red wine of my heart's blood.

> umar bhar hum rahe sharaabi se
> dil e pur khoon ki ik gulaabi se

Ultimately, the fact that he can no longer see her does not matter:

> The bond of love does not depend on seeing you each day
> Come only once; you will be with me still my whole life
>   through.

> roz aane pe nahin nisbat e ishqi mauquf
> umr bhar ek mulaaqaat chali jaati hai

> This is a realm where near and far are one;
> With her or parted from her, you must love.

> ishq mein vasl o judaai se nahin kuchh guftagu
> qurb o bod is ja baraabar hai—muhabbat chaahiye

He knew from the start the risk that he was running:

> When once our hearts catch fire no power avails to save us
>   from our fate
> Like lamps that burn throughout the night we too are
>   steadily consumed.

> dil jalte kuchh ban nahin aati haal bigadte jaate hain
> jaise chiraagh e aakhri shab hum log nibarte jaate hain

> I knew that love would take my life as forfeit.
> When I began I knew how I would end.

> ishq jaana tha maar rakhega
> ibtida mein thi intiha maaloom

I asked the breeze, 'Where shall I find the vagabonds of love?'
It gathered up a little dust and raised it in the air.

> aavaaragaan e ishq ka poochha jo main nishaan
> musht e ghubaar le ke saba ne uda diya

We are fated to love, just as in the Urdu and Persian poetic tradition the nightingale is fated to love the rose*, and the rose to be indifferent to its love, and the lightning to strike somewhere—though no one knows beforehand where:

Burn in the red fire of the rose in silence—
Lightning must strike, and it has struck your nest.

> aatish e rang e gul se kya kahiye?
> barq thi, aashiyaan par aayi

---

* See note on p. 83.

Ghalib's More Nuanced View of Love

Not all poets loved as Mir loved, with the complete commitment that his verses teach. The ghazals of Mir's greatest successor, Ghalib, reveal a more complex view, both of himelf and of his relationship to the beloved.

~

Like Mir he has verses which express the delights of love, and a capacity to enjoy them to the full:

> He who sits in the shade of his beloved's wall
> Is lord and king of all the realm of Hindustan.
>
> > baitha hai jo ki saaya e deevaar e yaar mein
> > farmaan-rava e kishvar e hindostaan hai
>
> Sleep is for him, pride is for him, the nights for him
> Upon whose arm your tresses all dishevelled lay.
>
> > neend us ki hai damaagh us ka hai raatein us ki hain
> > teri zulfein jis ke baazu par pareshaan hogain
>
> All that she is puts Ghalib's soul in turmoil
> All that she says, and hints, and looks, and does.
>
> > bala e jaan hai, Ghalib, us ki har baat
> > ibaarat kya, ishaarat kya, ada kya

I shall write to you even without cause
Simply to write your name fills me with love.

> khat likhenge garche matlab kuchh na ho
> hum to aashiq hain tumhaare naam ke

He also knows the dangers of love:

No one can govern love, Ghalib. This is a kind of fire
No one can kindle; and, once kindled, no one can put out.

> ishq par zor nahin, hai ye vo aatish, Ghalib,
> ki lagaaye na lage aur bujhaaye na bane

O foolish heart, what has befallen you?
Do you know know this sickness has no cure?

> dil e naadaan tujhe hua kya hai?
> aakhir is dard ki dava kya hai?

You ask what balm will soothe the wounded heart—
Its main ingredient is diamond dust.

> na poochh nuskha e marham jaraahat e dil ka
> ki us mein reza e almaas juzv e aazam hai

The rose's scent, the heart's complaint, smoke rising from
   the lamp—
None comes from your assembly but distraught, in disarray.

> bu e gul, naala e dil, dood e chiraagh e mehfil
> jo teri bazm se nikla so pareshaan nikla

Sometimes her sudden anger entrances him:

Thousands of signs of love cannot match one averted gaze.
Thousands of self-adornings cannot match one flare of wrath.

> laakhon lagaao ek churaana nigaah ka
> laakhon banaao ek bigadna etaab mein

He is disappointed at her lack of sustained interest in him:

> The thought that beauty would be kind possessed me.
>   What simplicity!
> Your coming was no more than just the prelude to your
>   going.

> humaari saadagi thi iltifaat e naaz par marna
> tera aana na tha, zaalim, magar tamheed jaane ki

But he loves her, and any kind of feeling she has for him is better than none:

> All wrath? All cruelty? Be what you may
> I wish that all you are had been for me.

> qahr ho ya bala ho, jo kuchh ho
> kaash ke tum mere liye hote

> Do not break off the bond uniting us—
> If nothing else, grant me your enmity.

> qata keeje na ta'alluq hum se
> kuchh nahin hai to adaavat hi sahi

But unlike Mir, he is not prepared to commit himself unreservedly, and many of his verses written to or about his beloved are far from adoring. In reply to her taunt that what he suffers from is not love, but madness:

> 'It is not love, but madness'? Be it so.
> My madness is your reputation though.
> *(That is, it is my mad love for you that makes you famous.)*

> ishq mujh ko nahin, vahshat hi sahi
> meri vahshat teri shuhrat hi sahi

> To every word that I utter you answer, 'What are you?'
> *You* tell me, is *this* the way, then, I should be spoken to?

> har ek baat pe kahte ho tum ki 'tu kya hai'?
> tumhi kaho ki ye andaaz e guftagu kya hai

If this is testing, can you tell me, what would persecution be?
It was to *him* you gave your heart; what do you want with
    testing *me*?

    yehi hai aazmaana to sataana kis ko kehte hain?
    adu ke ho liye jab tum to mera imtihaan kyon ho?

Is this affliction not enough to work one's ruin utterly?
With you as friend, what need is there for fate to be an
    enemy?

    ye fitna aadmi ki khaana veeraani ko kya kam hai?
    huey tum dost jis ke dushman us ka aasmaan kyon ho?

Jealousy says, Alas! Alas! Her love is for my rival!
Reason says, One cold as she cannot love any man.

    rashk kehta hai ki, 'us ka ghair se ikhlaas, haif!'
    aqal kehti hai ki, 'vo be-mehr kis ka aashna?'

To think desire is adoration is to be a fool
How should I *worship* her who treats me with such tyranny?

    khvaahish ko ahmaqon ne parastish diya qaraar
    kya poojta hoon uss but e be-daadgar ko main?

All that the nightingale can do provokes the rose's laughter
What men call love is really a derangement of the mind.

    bulbul ke kaarobaar pe hain khandaha e gul
    kehte hain jis ko ishq khalal hai dimaagh ka

Mystic Love

For most ghazal poets it is Mir's view of love rather than Ghalib's that has prevailed. Love is absolute, unconditional and never failing, and what the lover learns through devotion to his beloved forms the foundation of an outlook which informs his whole life and conduct. To appreciate what this implies, we need to understand another dimension of what ghazal poets understand by 'love'.

In the ghazal, as in the poetry of medieval Europe, 'love' was of two kinds: love of two human beings for one another, and love of the truly religious person for God. Inspired by Sufi traditions, the early ghazal poets understood the love of God to be all-embracing—the primary experience of love (called *haqiqqi*)—and saw the experience of longing for a human beloved (*majazi*) as a reflection of the fundamental impulse to seek union with God.

The themes of these two kinds of love not only dominate the ghazal; they are very closely intertwined, and there are innumerable verses which can be taken in either sense. Indeed many couplets can imply both senses at the same time.

A ghazal of Dard (1721–1785), Mir's contemporary, includes these (thematically linked) couplets:

> As long as I can seek it will be you I seek
> As long as I can speak it is of you I speak.

> mera ji hai jab tak tera justuju hai
> zabaan jab talak hai yahi guftagu hai

The longing that I feel is longing for you
And when I yearn, it is for you I yearn.

> tamanna teri hai agar hai tamanna
> teri aarzu hai agar aarzu hai.

This garden of the world—I roamed all through it
No flower can match the scent and hue of love's flower.

> kiya sair sab hum ne gulzaar e duniya
> gul e dosti mein ajab rang o bu hai

What is it draws my inner eye towards you?
No matter where I turn you are before me.

> nazar mere dil ki pari Dard kis par
> jidhar dekhta hoon vahin ru ba ru hai

Urdu has no capital letters, and no one can tell whether the English translator should write 'you' or 'You'. Nor does it matter. The lines are equally valid in both senses, and every Urdu reader takes this for granted. Urdu readers also accept without difficulty the most sensuous expressions of love for another human being as valid allegorical statements of love for God. So did medieval Europeans. (Perhaps an example of this parallelism best known to English readers is in the Song of Songs in the Old Testament, where, for example, the human lover's very sensual, detailed description of his beloved's body is titled, 'Christ sets forth the graces of the Church'.)

In the South Asian Muslim context the parallelism between the two kinds of love is closer than is immediately evident. Mystics incurred a fierce hostility from the orthodox religious establishment, for their search for God was entirely personal and gave no credence to official interpreters of Islam. So the poet's love for his God is just as illicit as that of the lover of a human beloved. It impels him to assail the pillars of conventional society, and to face the consequences. In the ghazal the poet is always depicted as facing up to this hostility gladly and defiantly.

Further, this situation makes it natural for him to accept and exalt all love. To the ghazal poet, as Hasrat Mohani puts it, 'All love is unconditionally good'. In terms of human beloveds, this could be both heterosexual and homosexual, so the ghazal has a surprisingly modern ring. All this sits easily in poetry which moves simultaneously on two levels, and there is almost no couplet which cannot be taken in this sense. Hasrat Mohani's full couplet is:

> All love is unconditionally good
> Be it for God, be it for human beauty.

> muhabbat khair e mutlaq hai baharhaal
> vo haq se ho ki ho husn e bashar se

For the modern reader it is necessary to make another point. In medieval societies ideals of life and conduct were necessarily conceived of as religious ideals. Whatever your principles in life, you regarded them as God's commands to you, and there was no other intellectual framework available within which you could conceive them. In the twentieth century there are, of course, still many for whom this remains true, but there are also many others who formulate their ideals in entirely secular terms, and Urdu poetry will speak to them more powerfully if they think of the poets' assertion of their love of God as an assertion of their love of, and commitment to, their highest ideals of life and conduct.

Neither Mir nor Ghalib were mystics in the literal sense, but they were steeped in the traditions and values of ghazal poetry, and like all ghazal poets drew closely on the concepts of early poets, who were themselves genuine mystics. They both seek God in the sense that they strive to be ever closer to Him.

Mir writes:

> I seek you like the morning breeze that with each dawn
>   goes forth again
> From house to house, from door to door, from town to
>   town, from lane to lane.

jaise naseem har sahr teri karun hoon justaju
khaana ba khaana, dar ba dar, sheher ba sheher, ku ba ku

For Ghalib this search—for God, or the ultimate meaning of life—
is deeper and more comprehensive. He is convinced that He can be
found, even if a lifetime is too short a span in which to complete
the search. To those who give up he says:

> You are the ones who do not know the music of His secrets,
> Hidden no more than melody lies hidden in the lute.

> mahram nahin hai tu hi navaaha e raaz ka
> yan varna jo hijaab hai parda hai saaz ka

You can look at almost all the couplets already quoted and read
them in this additional sense, as allegorical statements of mystic
love, or a commitment to deeply held values. When Ghalib writes
about having suffered because of his love, he may mean any one of
this infinite range of loves—as in this couplet (where 'in pledge to'
means 'a victim of'):

> Though I have passed my life in pledge to all the age's
>   cruelties
> Yet never was the thought of you once absent from my
>   mind.

> go main raha raheen e sitamha e rozgaar
> lekin tere khayaal se ghaafil nahin raha

To summarize, the ghazal exalts that person who is steadfast in love
in the face of affliction, knows that this commitment is certain to
entail suffering, and may demand the sacrifice of his life. His love
may be for a fellow human being, for God, for his country, for his
people, for his community, or for any moral, social or political ideal
in which he passionately believes; and the ghazal poets conceive of
all these loves as being simply aspects of a single love that embraces
them all, or at any rate that which can embrace them all.

The Challenge to Orthodoxy

From these mystical concepts ghazal poets draw far-reaching conclusions which lead them into violent collision with the religiously orthodox, and towards a strong commitment to the values of humanism.

In these days when resurgent Islamic fundamentalism makes the headlines it cannot be stressed too strongly that a very different kind of Islam, which challenges the fundamentalists, has existed for centuries and has exercised an enormous influence. It pervades the Urdu ghazal, and had been equally prominent in Persian poetry centuries earlier.

The passionate love of God is its starting point, and it has some parallels in the Christian tradition too. Joinville in his *Life of St Louis* relates how a friar met an old woman in Damascus who was carrying a bowl of burning coals in one hand and a flask of water in the other, and who, when he asked her what they were for, replied that the fire was to burn paradise to ashes and the water to put out the fires of hell, so that people could live their lives no longer motivated by the hope of paradise and the fear of hell but solely by their love for God. This sentiment is common in the ghazal poets.

The true lover of God attaches little or no importance to the traditional religious observances. Strict Muslims pray five times a day, fast during daylight hours in the month of Ramzan and make every effort to make a pilgrimage to Mecca once in their lifetime. Clearly, these can be inspired by true love for God, but it is more likely that they will be motivated by mere convention, or even a pharisaical desire to feel self-righteousness—and in the ghazal they are always regarded as being so motivated.

Mir writes scathingly of the things that are supposed to attract men to paradise—houris, beautiful women, and ghilmans, beautiful boys, who are said to serve the faithful in paradise:

> Houris and boys and palaces and streams of Paradise—
> Cast every one of them to Hell, and I will love my Love.
>
> > hoor o qasoor o ghilmaan, nahr o naeem e jannat
> > ye kulluhum jahannum! mushtaaq e yaar hain hum

He looks with pitying contempt on those who are consumed by the anxiety to 'earn' paradise:

> To save their souls they kill themselves with care.
> A Paradise like that can go to Hell!
>
> > jaaye hai ji najaat ke gham mein
> > aisi jannat gayi jahannam mein

Ghalib writes similarly:

> God's will be done, but not from greed for heaven's wine
>   and honey
> Take hold of paradise, someone, and cast it into hell!
>
> > taa'at mein ta rahe na mai o angabeen ki laag
> > dozakh mein daal do koi lekar bahisht ko

> Abstinence wins no praise from me. What though it be
>   sincere?
> Behind it lies raw greed to win reward for virtuous deeds.
>
> > kya zuhd ko maanun? ki na ho garchi riyaai
> > paadaash e amal ki tama e khaam bahut hai

Ghalib, more than any other Urdu poet, is sceptical about the promised joys of paradise:

> I know the truth regarding Paradise, but all the same
> Since it gives happiness, Ghalib, the thought of it is good.

> hum ko maaloom hai jannat ki haqeeqat, lekin
> dil ko khush rakhne ko, Ghalib, ye khayaal achcha hai

And if it does exist, it cannot compensate for all the troubles one has to undergo in this world:

> They offer paradise to make up for our life below.
> It needs a stronger wine than this to cure our hangover.

> dete hai jannat hayaat e dahr ke badle
> nasha baa-andaaza e khumaar nahin hai

Even its pleasures are no match for the joys of this world. He tells his mistress paradise will please him only if she is there:

> The radiance that lights your lane lights paradise as well.
> The scene is just the same, but where's the joy in living there?

> kam nahin jalvaagari mein tere kooche se bahisht
> yehi naqsha hai, vale is qadar aabaad nahin

> I will not cry for more if I may only look at you
> But there among the houris let me look upon your face.

> taskeen ko hum na royein jo zauq e nazar mile
> hooraan e khuld mein teri soorat magar mile

Mir has many verses attacking the 'shaikh'—the personification in the ghazal of an orthodox, bigoted religious leader:

> Shaikh says his prayers? Don't be deceived by that.
> Prayer is a load he lowers from his head.

shaikh ki tu namaaz par mat ja
bojh sar ka sa daal aata hai

Sometimes he adds the honoroific 'ji'—normally a mark of respect, but here clearly sarcastic:

If pilgrimage could make a man, then all the world might
    make the pilgrimage.
But shaikh ji is just back, and look at him—an ass he went:
    an ass he has returned.

haj se koi aadmi ho to saara aalam haj hi kare
makke se aaye shaikh ji lekin ve to vohi hain khar ke khar

You're going to make the Pilgrimage? Then take the shaikh
    along;
If you're to reach the Kaba you must take an ass with you.

qasd e haj hai to shaikh ko le chal
kaaba jaane ko ye bhi khar hai shart

He went to Mecca, and Medina, and to Karbala
And what he was, he still remains now that he has returned.

makke gaya, madeene gaya, karbala gaya
jaisa gaya tha vaisa hi chal phir ke aa gaya

His attitude towards the shaikh and the preacher is nearly always bitterly contemptuous:

I grant you, sir, the preacher is an angel
To be a man, now—that's more difficult.

hum ne ye maana ke vaaiz hai malak
aadmi hona bahut mushkil hai, miyaan

I worked at it for years, and only then
Could trace his lineage back to Father Adam.

barson taeen jab hum ne taraddud kiye hain tab
pahunchaaya hai aadam taeen vaaiz ke nasab ko

He ridicules the shaikh's claim to understand serious poetry:

Mir's every word has meaning beyond meaning—
More than a worthless shaikh can understand.

Mir sahib ka har sukhan hai ramz
be-haqeeqat hai shaikh—kya samjhe?

Yes, shaikh, you understand Mir perfectly!
Bravo! You worthless dolt. Bravo! Bravo!

shaikh tu ne khoob samjha Mir ko
vah va, ai be-haqeeqat, vah vah!

Ghalib is usually more light-hearted, and dismisses such people with
mockery rather than with loathing. He sees the shaikh as one who simply
repeats traditional beliefs that have no real religious validity—as in this
verse, about the supposed gardens of Paradise, tended by the keeper Rizvan:

The shaikh sings loud the praises of the gardens of Rizvan;
    to us
They lie, a bunch of faded flowers, upon oblivion's shelf.

sitaaish gar hai zaahid is qadar jis baagh e razvaan ka
vo ik guldasta hai hum bekhudon ke taaq e nasiyaan ka

He ridicules the shaikh's love of honey and abhorrence of wine, suggesting
that he would do better to reverse his attitudes:

Abstemious one, why do you push the cup away?
It's wine! It's not the vomit of the bee!

kyon rad e qadah kare hai zaahid?
mai hai ye, magas ki qai nahin hai

And what does he know about wine anyway? Without knowing what wine tastes like, how can he sing the praises of the 'wine of purity' promised to the faithful in paradise?

> Preacher, you cannot drink it, nor can you give *us* to drink
> What then is all this talk about your 'wine of purity'?

> vaaiz na tum peeo na kisi ko pila sako
> kya baat hai tumhaari sharaab e tuhoor ki?

~

For the poet lover of the Divine Beloved, his love, like his earthly loves, is something that liberates him from all the cramping restrictions that orthodox Islam and strong social convention alike impose upon his natural feelings. So also do wine and music—wine which orthodox Islam entirely forbids and music, of which it strongly disapproves. The poet will have none of these prohibitions and restrictions, and if violating them brings drastic consequences, so be it. The consequences are frequently painful.

In a series of thematically linked couplets, Ghalib warns those who are just embarking on this experience:

> Newcomers to the assembly of the heart's desires,
> Beware, if it is wine and music that you seek!

> Look well at me, if only you have eyes to see;
> Listen to me, if you have ears to hear me speak.

> The *saki's** charm will steal away your faith, your wits.
> The minstrel's song will rob you of your sense, your powers.

> At night you see the carpet laden all with bloom—
> A gardener's apron, filled with fresh, sweet-scented flowers.

---

* *Saki*: The cup-bearer, traditionally a beautiful young man, who serves the assembled company with wine.

The saki walks, the flute plays on enchantingly,
Heaven to the eyes, paradise to the ears of all.

Come in the morning: Look at the assembly then,
Life, joy, wine, music—all are gone beyond recall.

Bearing the scar of parting from its erstwhile friends,
One candle stands, burnt out. Know: this is how it ends.

> e taaza vaaridaan e bisaat e hava e dil
> zinhaar! agar tumhein havas e nai o nosh hai
>
> dekho mujhe jo deeda e ibrat nigaah ho
> meri suno jo gosh e naseehat niyosh hai
>
> saaqi ba jalva, dushman e eemaan o aagahi
> ba naghma rahzan e tamkeen o hosh hai
>
> ya shab ko dekhte thhe ki har gosha e bisaat
> daaman e baaghbaan o kaf e gul farosh hai
>
> lutf e khiram e saaqi o zauq e sada e chang
> ye jannat e nigaah, vo firdaus e gosh hai
>
> ya subh dam jo dekhiye aakar to bazm mein
> ne vo saroor o soor na josh o kharosh hai
>
> daagh e firaaq e suhbat e shab ki jali hui
> ik shama rah gai hai, so vo bhi khamosh hai

The mystic lover of his Divine Beloved is guided by his strong instinctive sense of what is right. Ghalib says, since God knows all the secrets of His servants' hearts, genuine regret for sin is enough:

> What wonder if His mercy should accept in expiation
> The shame that will not let me ask forgiveness for my sins.
>
> rahmat agar qabool kare, kya baeed hai
> sharmindagi se uzr na karna gunaah ka

Mir believes:

> Your heart will guide you on the path of love
> This is your guide, your Prophet and your God.

> tareeq e ishq mein hai rahnuma dil
> payambar dil hai, qibla dil, khuda dil

He reminds his listeners of the words with which Muslims begin any serious undertaking— 'In the name of God, the Compassionate, the Merciful':

> It is God's mercy that we sinners speak of;
> Fasting and prayer are never mentioned here.

> hum muznibon mein sirf karam se hai guftagu
> mazkoor o zikr yahaan nahin saum o salvaat ka

He is so confident that 'sinning' is right that he calls upon the orthodox to 'sin' too—for instance inviting them to drink wine—and suggests that the rainy season, a time of great delight after the intense heat of the preceding months, is an especially appropriate time:

> Come on out, recluse! Leave your cell and see the green
>   plants growing
> And black clouds sent from Mecca swaying high above the
>   taverns.

> tu bhi ribaat e kuhn se soofi, sair ko chal tuk sabze ki
> abr e siya qibla se aakar jhoom pada maikhaanon par

> Come to the tavern, recluse, now, for joy has left the mosque.
> The rain falls, and the breeze blows soft, and all your body
>   glows.

> kah soofi chal maikhaane mein, lutf nahin ab masjid mein
> abr hai baaraan, baad narmak, rang badan mein jhamka hai

> Do people lead the holy life when clouds sway overhead?
> In days like these, ascetic, you should see if you can sin.

taa'at koi kare hai jab abr zor jhoome?
gar ho sake to zaahid is vaqt mein gunah kar

And he recalls the joys that sin has brought him:

What days those were!—when I would drink and climb up
  to the tavern roof
And fall asleep, the white sheet of the moonlight over me.

kya lutf tha ki maikade ki pusht e baam par
sote thhe mast chaadar e mahtaab taan kar

*Ghalib, as he often does, goes further than Mir. He not only values his
sins, but feels a deep regret that life has not afforded him the possibility of
sinning much more than he has:*

The urge to sin should match the scale of yearning in my
  heart.
The seven seas would do no more than wet my garment's
  hem.

baqadr e hasrat e dil chaahiye zauq e ma'aasi bhi
bharoon yak gosha i daaman gar aab e haft darya ho

There is an echo here of a verse of Dard, which has become proverbial:

Shaikh, if my cloak is wet that does not mean I should be
  censured;
Angels could make ablution with the water wrung from it.

tar-daamani pe shaikh hamaari na jaaiyo
daaman nichod dein to farishte vuzu karein

*—but Ghalib has taken the image further. He pictures sin as a vast ocean
and wishes that it could have been even bigger:*

Sin's ocean was not vast enough; it dried right up
And still my garment's hem was barely damp with it.

darya e muaasi tunak-aabi se hua khushk
mera sar e daaman bhi abhi tar na hua tha

It calls to mind the number of scars of thwarted yearnings
So do not ask me, God, to count the number of my sins.

aata hai daagh e hasrat e dil ka shumaar yaad
mujh se mire gunaah ka hisaab e khuda na maang

Note too how I regret the sins that I could not commit
O Lord, if you would punish me for these committed sins.

naa-karda gunaahon ki bhi hasrat ki mile daad
ya rab, agar in karda gunaahon ki saza hai

The Humanist Values
of the Ghazal

As might be expected, this generous spirit also finds expression in a passionate humanism, and a belief in the equal value of all humankind—and this too brought them into conflict with orthodox views. The poets derive their view from the Islamic belief that when God created Adam He exalted him (and through him all humankind) above the angels and commanded the angels to prostrate themselves before him. Satan refused to do so and was cursed and banished forever from God's presence.* All human beings are, in the common Muslim phrase, *ashraf ul makhluqat*—the best of created things. But orthodox Islam tended to equate 'humankind' with 'Muslim humankind'; not so the poets. For them God had granted to *all* the descendants of Adam the same exalted status.

This assumed a special significance in India, where Muslims were a minority and the overwhelming majority of their fellow Indians were Hindus—and thus, in the language of the orthodox, 'infidels' and 'idolators'. Urdu poets consistently challenge this narrow Islamic orthodoxy, and often used Hindu imagery in a positive way, to make their point more powerfully.

Mir asserts that all true lovers of God, no matter under what name they

---

* For the commonly accepted Muslim telling of the story of the creation, see pp. 124.

worship Him, and in what kind of building, are equally favoured in
God's eyes:

> What does it mean to me? Call me 'believer', call me 'infidel'.
> I seek His threshold, be it in the temple or the mosque.

> > kis ko kahte hain nahin main jaanta islaam o kufr
> > dair ho ya kaaba matlab mujh ko tere dar se hai

*He links the Kaba (the building in Mecca which is the focus of the Muslim
pilgrimage) and Somnath (the site of one of the most famous of Hindu
temples) as equally capable of inspiring religious devotion:*

> It is the power of *His* beauty fills the world with light,
> Be it the Kaba's candle or the lamp that lights Somnath.

> > uss ke farogh e husn se jhamke hai sab mein noor
> > shama e haram ho ya ki daya Somnath ka

*To orthodox Muslims, the worship of idols is anathema; but Mir—in
common with the mystics—uses idolatry as a symbol of a truer devotion to
God than that of orthodox ritual. For an idol is a symbol of beauty, and
beauty is the manifestation of God. So Mir says:*

> True Musalman am I, for to these idols
> I pledge my love. 'There is no god but God.'

> > hain musalmaan—un buton se humein
> > ishq hai—la illaah ilaillaah

*'There is no god but God' are the first words of the Muslim profession of
faith. There could not be a more forceful way of asserting that God and
'these idols'—that is, God and beauty—are one and indivisible.*

> The very men who thought it blasphemy to worship idols
> Sit now before the mosque and put the caste mark on their
> brow.

jo kufr jaante thhe ishq e butaan ko, vo hi
masjid ke aage aakhir qashqah lagaa ke baithe

The bond of love is all—Islam and unbelief are nothing:
Take rosary *and* sacred cord and wear them on your neck.

maqsood dard e dil hai—na islaam hai na kufr
phir har gale mein subha o zunnar kyon na ho?

The rosary here is the symbol of Islam, while the zunnar, *translated here as 'sacred cord', is a very comprehensive symbol. In an Indian context it first suggests the sacred thread worn by the high-caste Hindu, but it is also used for the cord worn by Eastern Christians and Zoroastrians. Ghalib too uses these images:*

Put on the sacred thread, and break the hundred-beaded
    rosary.
The traveller takes the path he sees to be the even one.

zunnar baandh subha e sad daana tod daal
rah-rau chale hai raah ko hamvaar dekh kar

(The beads of the rosary are like hills over which the fingers have to pass, whereas they pass smoothly and evenly over the thread.)

The sense of solidarity with all humankind is often expressed in verses which raise no questions about their religious beliefs or lack of them. The Urdu poets follow the creed of the great fourteenth-century Persian poet Hafiz who declared:

Do not distress your fellow men, and do what else you will
For in my Holy Law there is no other sin but this.

In a similar vein, another unidentified Persian poet wrote:

Drink wine and burn the Holy Book, and set fire to the Kaba
Dwell in the idol temple—but don't harm your fellow men.

Here Mir virtually incorporates Hafiz's words:

> Go to the mosque; stand knocking at the door—
> Live all your days with drunkards in their den—
>
> Do anything you want to do, my friend,
> But do not seek to harm your fellow men.

> dar e masjid pe halq e zan ho tum
> ki raho baith khaana e khummaar
>
> ji mein aave so keejiyo pyaare
> ek hona na darpai e aazaar

He stresses his oneness with all his fellows:

> I heard the lamentation of the prisoner in his cage—
> It was *my* heart that ached, and I that was held captive there.

> ji khainch gaya aseer e qafas ke fughaan ke or
> thhi chot apne dil ko giriftaar hum hue

> What do you need to render what is due?
> Nor wealth nor learning enters into it.

> haq ko dene ko chaahiye hai kya?
> yahan na asbaab ne hunar hai shart

He dismisses with contempt those who think they can be near to God without feeling anything for humankind:

> They cannot feel the grief that wounds His servant's heart,
> Yet every worthless fellow here 'communes with God'.

> bande ke dard e dil ko koi nahin pahunchta
> har ek be-haqeeqat yahaan hai khuda raseeda

God and Humankind

The conviction of human greatness is so strong that it raises questions about the behaviour of God himself. If God so honoured Adam at his creation, why does He now humiliate Adam's descendants?

Mir writes:

> What have the angels got to do with man?
> The highest rank belongs to him alone.
>
> > aadmi se malak ko kya nisbat?
> > shaan arfa hai Mir, insaan ki

Ghalib is particularly insistent. He writes:

> Today we are abased. Why so? For yesterday You would not
> brook
> The insolence the angel showed towards our majesty.
>
> > hain aaj kyon zaleel? ki kal tak na thi pasand
> > gustaakhi e farishta hamaari janaab mein

And why is man judged merely on the record presented by the recording angels and given no right to have anyone speak in his defence?

> The angels write, and we are seized. Where is the justice
> there?
> Did *we* have no one present when they wrote their record
> down?

pakde jaate hain farishton ke likhe par naa-haq
aadmi koi hamaara dam e tahreer bhi tha?

*Why does God, when it is His will that determines everything, falsely
allege that man is free to act as he chooses? Mir writes:*

You call us free? You slander us unjustly.
Your will is done—and *we* must take the blame.

naa-haq hum majbooron par ye tuhmat hai mukhtaari ki
chaahte hain so aap karein hain hum ko abas badnaam
kiya

All that we 'free' men do is under duress
Mind that you do not force us to speak out!

munh na hum jabrion ka khulvao
kehne ko ikhtiyaar sa hai kuchh

*Ghalib, speaking in some sense as the spokesman of humankind, demands
of God that He treat him with proper respect:*

We serve You; yet our independent self-respect is such
We shall at once turn back if we should find the Kaba closed.

bandagi mein bhi vo aazaada o khud-been hain ki hum
ulte phir aae dar e kaaba agar vaa na hua

*There are verses which hint pretty clearly that though man was God's
creation, he has potentialities greater than any which God himself has been
able to comprehend.*
    Mir writes:

Such as we are, God fashioned us close to His heart's desire:
If we had been what we had wished, what might we not
have been!

ab aise hain ki saane ki mizaaj oopar baham pahunche
jo khaatir khvaah apne hum hue hota to kya hota!

Oh God, what sort of men are they who love to be Thy
    servants?
I would have been beset with shame even had I been God.

illahi kaise hote hain jinhein hai bandagi khvaahish?
humein to sharm daamangeer hoti hai khuda hote

And Ghalib, in the same vein,

He gave me both the worlds and told Himself, 'He is content.'
And I, tongue-tied with shame, had not the heart to ask for
    more.

donon jahaan de ke vo samjhe ye khush raha
yan aa pari ye sharm ki takraar kya karein

Would that I could have looked out from an even greater
    height
Would that I had my dwelling place above the throne of God.

manzar ik bulandi par aur hum bana sakte
arsh se udhar hota kaash ke makaan apna

*He uses a story of Musa (Moses) asking God to show Himself to him. God
said that Musa could not look upon him, but might look at the mountain,
Tur. 'If it abide in its place then shall thou see Me.' But God's radiance
reduced the great mountain to dust and Musa fell down in a swoon. But I,
says Ghalib, could have sustained Your revelation:*

You should have let Your radiance fall on me, not on the
    Mount of Tur
One pours wine in the measure that the drinker can contain.

girni thhi hum pe barq e tajalli na toor par
dete hain baada zarf e qadah khvaar dekh kar

*Even the very purpose of creation is challenged. If man was destined to the
misery he has had to suffer, why did God need to create him? Mir asks
Him:*

My eyelids opened, and I saw what none should have to see;
I slept in non-existence: why did You awaken me?

aankhein khulin to dekha jo kuchh na dekhna tha
khvaab e adam se hum ko kaahe ke taeen jagaaya

Or why, as Ghalib asks Him with impudent humour, did He not equip him better to withstand it all?

When, Lord, you fated me to bear such grief
You should have given me more hearts than one.

meri qismat mein gham gar itna tha
dil bhi, ya rab, kayi diye hote

Why did God create things which charm man's senses, distracting his attention and making him forget that they are only manifestations of God?

When all is You, and nought exists but You
Tell me, O Lord, why all this turmoil too?

These fair-faced women, with their coquetries,
Their glances, airs and graces, what are these?

Why the sweet perfume of their coiling tresses?
Why the collyrium that adorns their eyes?

jab ki tujh bin nahin koi maujood
phir ye hangaama, e khuda, kya hai?

ye pari-chehra log kaise hain?
ghamza o ishva o ada kya hai?

shikan e zulf e anbareen kyon hai?
nigah e chashm e surma sa kya hai?

And why, he asks himself, did God create me?

When nothing was, then God was there; had nothing been,
God would have been.

My being has defeated me. Had I not been, what would
have been?

na tha kuchh to khuda tha, kuchh na hota to khuda hota
duboya mujh ko hone ne, na hota main to kya hota?

*(almost suggesting that but for the act of creation, he and God
would have been indistinguishable.)*

*Whatever the answers to these far-reaching questions may be, it seems best to
leave God to his own devices and expect nothing from Him—and certainly
to ask nothing more from Him than He has already granted. Ghalib jokes:*

If you would solve your problems, prayer's enchantment
does not work
O Lord, accept my supplication: Long may Khizar live!

hareef e matlab e mushkil nahin fasoon e nayaaz
dua qabool ho ya rab ki umr e khizar daraaz!

*(God had already granted Khizar eternal life!)**

But it is certain that one has to search further than traditional forms suggest:

The object of my worship lies beyond perception's reach.
For men who see, the Kaba is a compass, nothing more.

hai pare sarhad e idraak se apna masjood
qible ko ahl e nazar qibla-numa kehte hain

*People who follow the path of love, in all its senses, are told by people
of 'good sense' that they are mad. Mir here represents himself as having
heeded their advice, but now regretting it:*

Good sense has come to fetter me. Before that
I knew the joy of life, for I was mad.

khiradmandi hui zanjeer varna
guzarti khoob thi deevaanepan mein

---

* For the story of the Water of Life see p. 132.

The Poet in Society

Themes of love in this wide-ranging sense predominate in the ghazal, but they are far from being its only subject. Any thought that can be encapsulated in a single couplet can find its place in the ghazal, so its range is practically unlimited.

Both Mir and Ghalib were self-conscious about their role as poets in society. A century apart, they both lived in Delhi for the greater part of their lives, experienced traumatic changes in the city they loved, and were deeply distressed by the conditions of the age.

In 1701, when Aurangzeb, the last great Mughal Emperor, died, the empire had been at its greatest extent, covering all but the extreme south of the subcontinent. As its capital, Delhi was then, in Percival Spear's words, 'the largest and most renowned city...of all the East, from Constantinople to Canton'. But after 1707 its decline was catastrophic. In 1739, when Mir was in his teens, the Iranian king Nadir Shah invaded from the north-west, crushingly defeated the Mughal armies, occupied Delhi, massacred something like 20,000 of its inhabitants and stripped it of all its great accumulated wealth—so great that on his return to Iran he remitted for three years the revenue of his whole kingdom. The Empire, and Delhi, never recovered; and until the British established their control over Delhi in 1803, increasing anarchy and lawlessness prevailed.

Mir's poetry shows how deep was the impact upon him of this catastrophic decline of the Mughal Empire and of Delhi, to which he felt the deepest attachment even when conditions forced him to leave it and live elsewhere. All standards of honourable conduct were abandoned. There were repeated invasions and lootings. Rivals for power stopped at nothing to achieve their ambitions. A chief minister, before being invested by the Emperor with the robe of office, swore on the Holy Quran never to betray him. That same morning he deposed him, imprisoned him and blinded him. Mir lamented the abandonment of honourable standards of conduct, contrasting the age he lived in with a (partly imaginary) past; in the Mughals' greatest period, the innovative and tolerant reign of Akbar (1556–1605), standards were indeed higher, though not as high as Mir imagined.

By the time Ghalib was born (1797), Mir was already an old man, and conditions had changed markedly. In his early teens Ghalib came from his native Agra to live in Delhi, and by then the British conquest had at any rate brought some stability. But though there was now order in the city, Ghalib equally looked back to an earlier age as one with higher standards of conduct.

They saw their poetry as a high calling, a means of asserting the values that really mattered. They felt that all around them were people who considered themselves poets, but only a few had anything significant to say. Ghalib defined poetry as 'the creation of meaning, not the matching of rhymes'. Mir felt the same. Muhammad Husain Azad,* who wrote lively accounts of the lives of the great poets, tells us how Mir responded to a young nobleman who requested him to initiate him into the art of poetry. Mir said, 'Young sir, you are a noble and the son of a noble. Practice horsemanship and archery and the handling of the lance. Poetry is a task for men whose hearts have been seared by the fire of love and pierced by the wounds of grief.'

~

Mir speaks often of physical desolation and spiritual decline:

> This age is not like that which went before it
> The times have changed, the earth and sky have changed.

* See p. 241.

is ahd ko na jaaniye agla sa ahd Mir
vo daur ab nahin, vo zameen aasmaan nahin

Here where the thorns grow, spreading over mounds of
   dust and ruins
These eyes of mine once saw the gardens blooming in the
   spring.

jis ja ki khas o khaar ke ab dher lage hain
yahaan hum ne inhi aankhon se dekhi hain bahaaren

Here in this city where the dust drifts in deserted lanes
A man might come and fill his lap with gold in days gone by.

udti hai khak sheher ki galiyon mein ab jahaan
sona liya hai god mein bhar kar vahin se hum

These eyes saw only yesterday house after house
Where here and there a ruined wall or doorway stands.

kal dekhte humaare baste thhe ghar baraabar
ab ye kahin kahin jo deevaar o dar rahe hain

Metaphors drawn from this desolation recur in his verse:

Tears flow like rivers from my weeping eyes
My heart, like Delhi, lies in ruins now.

deeda e giryaan hamaara neher hai
dil kharaaba jaise Dilli sheher hai

You ask me of the ruin of my heart by pain and grief
It is a city looted by an army on the march.

kharaabi dil ki kya anboh e dard o gham se poochho ho?
vuhi haalat hai jaise sheher lashkar loot jaata hai

The city of my heart—alas!—was once a wondrous sight
Her going razed it to the ground; none will live there again.

kharaabi dil ki kya anboh e dard o gham se poochho ho?
vuhi haalat hai jaise sheher lashkar loot jaata hai

Burnt in the flames till every building was reduced to ashes—
How fair a city was the heart that love put to the fire!

jal jal ke sab imaarat e dil khaak ho gayi
kaise nagar ko, ah, muhabbat ne di hai aag!

He bemoans the conditions of the time:

Ours is a dark age; men have lost all trace of love and loyalty
In former days it was not so; these things were second
　　nature then.

ahd humaara tera hai ye jis mein gum hai mihr o vafa
agle zamaane mein to yehi logon ki rasm o aadat thi

Roaming from land to land I sought for loyalty
Grief tears my heart; it is not to be found.

sau mulk phira lekin paai na vafa ik ja
ji kha gayi hai mera is jins ki naayaabi

The cult of human decency has vanished from the world.
What men are there upon the earth! What times we live in
　　now!

rasm uth gayi duniya se ik baar muravvat ki
kya log zameen par hain! kaisa ye samaan aaya!

Such friends I had—and one by one they died and turned
　　to dust.
I am a fool—nobody grieves for anybody now.

kya kya azeez dost mile Mir khaak mein
naadaan yahaan kisu ka kisu ko bhi gham hua

What man would want to live in times like these?
When doing good means wishing yourself ill.

ye zamaana nahin aisa ki koi zeest kare
chaahte hain jo bura apna bhala karte hain

Ghalib echoes these feelings:

How can I tell the virtues of the men to whom this age
    gave birth?
He does me harm to whom I have done good repeatedly.

kahun kya khoobi e ausaaf e abna e zamaan Ghalib?
badi ki us ne jis se hum ne ki thi baarha neki

Extremely difficult an easy task can prove to be
Not every man will manage to achieve humanity.

bas ki dushvaar hai har kaam ka aasaan hona
aadmi ko bhi muyassar nahin insaan hona

Mir regards the nobility, as those who set the tone for society, with special disfavour:

Although the fortunes of the age have not shown favour to
    me
So that the ways of wealth and grandeur could not be my
    ways,

Praise be to God that I am poor and mean—for none can
    class me
With the great ones whom men delight to honour in these
    days.

go tavajjuh se zamaane ki jahaan mein mujh ko
jah o sarvat ka muyassar sar o saamaan na hua

shukr sad shukr ki main zillat o khvaari ke sabab
kysi unvaan mein hum chashm e azeezaan na hua

I will write verses showing that I hold the great
In that same honour as the great have held my verses.

jaisi izzat mere deevaan ki ameeron mein hui
vaise hi un ki bhi hogi mere deevaan ke beech

My verses are all liked by high society
But it is to the people that I speak.

sher mere hain sab khivaas pasand
par mujhe guftagu avaam se hai

Since evening fell, the flame within my heart
Burns dimly, as it were a poor man's lamp.

shaam se kuchh bujha sa rehta hai
dil hua hai chiraagh muflis ka

Both feel that their poetry is not valued as it should be. Mir writes:

My verse is not like any other poet's
The way I speak to you is all my own.

nahin milta sukhan apna kisu se
hamaari guftagu ka dhab juda hai

In every region, every city, far and wide my fame is known
The beauty of my poetry is spoken of in every home.

door tak rusva hua hoon shehron shehron mulk mulk
meri sher o shayri ka tazkara ghar ghar hai ab

Ghalib, ironically feigning ignorance of Mir's status, classes himself with him:

Ghalib, you aren't the only one supreme in Urdu verse
They tell me that in former times there lived a certain Mir.

rekhte ke tumhin ustaad nahin ho, Ghalib
kehte hain, agle zamaane mein koi Mir bhi tha.

And yet he asserts his own distinctive contribution:

The world holds others too who write good poetry
But Ghalib's style, they say, is something else.

hain aur bhi duniya mein sukhanvar bahut achche
kehte hain ki Ghalib ka hai andaaz e bayaan aur

He gives himself freely to those who really value his poetry:

I give my poetry away, and give myself along with it
But first I look for people who can value what I give.

bik jaate hain hum aap mata e sukhan ke saath
lekin ayaar e taba e khareedaar dekh kar

I am collyrium freely given for the eyes of men
My price the recognition of what I confer on them.

surma e muft e nazar hoon; meri qimat ye hai
ki rahe chashm e khareedaar pe ihsaan mera

*(Collyrium—kohl—surma—is a dark eyeliner used to make the
eyes seem brighter, but was also believed to sharpen the sight.)*

*They speak to an audience that cannot appreciate what they are saying, and
they feel a keen regret that this should be so. Mir writes:*

How could I tell my tale in this strange land?
I speak a tongue they do not understand.

rahi nagufta mere dil mein daastaan meri
na is dayyaar mein samjha koi zabaan meri

I wrote in every metre, wasting all my years
Bringing up pearls for men who did not know their price.

har bahr mein ashaar kahe umr ko khoya
is gohar e naayaab ki kuchh baat na paai

Why bother, Mir, to speak to this assembly of the deaf?
One speaks to those who listen: what's the good of
    speaking here?

phira mat Mir sar apna giraan goshon ki majlis mein
sune koi to kuchh kahiye bhi is kehne ka kya haasil?

Ghalib, having tried his fortune without success beyond the bounds of his own homeland, asks himself:

> Ghalib, who honoured you at home, that other lands
>   should value you?
> Be frank: you are the straw that does not feed the bonfire's
>   flame.

> thi vatan mein shaan kya, Ghalib, ki ho ghurbat mein qadr?
> be-takalluf hoon vo musht e khas ki gulkhan mein nahin

> I may be good, I may be bad—I live in ill-matched
>   company—
> A flower thrown on the bonfire, or a weed among the
>   flowers.

> na janun nek hoon ya bad hoon, par suhbat mukhaalif hai
> jo gul hoon to hoon gulkhan mein, jo khas hoon to
>   hoon gulshan mein

At times they feel that they would do best to withdraw from human company altogether. Mir says:

> Live out your life away from man's society,
> for men no longer feel that you are one of them;

> Thousands and thousands here were laid low in the dust
> and no one even asked what had become of them.*

> tu jahaan se dil utha yahaan nahin rasm e dardmandi
> kisi ne bhi yun na poochha hue khaak yahaan hazaaraan

And Ghalib (in three linked couplets):

> Now let me go away and live somewhere where no one
>   else will be

---

* Ed: This is a rare example where Ralph Russell used four lines rather than two in translating a couplet, to enable him to convey more fully what is implied.

Where there is none that knows my tongue, where there is
none to speak with me.

There I will build myself a house with, so to say, no doors,
no walls
And live there without neighbours, and with no one to
keep watch for me.

If I fall ill, then there should be no one to come and visit me
And if I die let none be there to weep and wail and mourn
for me.

rahiye ab aisi jagah chalkar jahaan koi na ho
hum sukhan koi na ho, aur hum zabaan koi na ho

be-dar o deevaar sa ik ghar banaaya chaahiye
koi hum-saaya na ho aur paasbaan koi na ho

padiye agar beemaar to koi na ho teemaardaar
aur agar mar jaiye to nauhaakhan koi na ho

Sometimes he is ready to burst with the bitterness he feels:

My heart is vibrant with complaint as is the harp with
music
Give it the slightest touch, and you will see what happens
then.

pur hoon main shikve se yun raag se jaise baaja
ik zara chhediye, phir dekhiye kya hota hai

At other times he contemplates his position with wry humour:

O Lord, they do not understand, nor *will* they understand
my words.
Give them another heart, or else give me another tongue.

ya rab, vo na samjhe hain na samjhenge meri baat
de aur dil unko jo na de mujh ko zabaan aur

I do not long to hear men's praise; I seek no man's reward
And if they say my verses have no meaning, be it so.

> na sitaaish ki tamanna na sile ki parva
> agar nahin hain mere ashaar mein maani na sahi

Mir says of his own poetry:

Don't think me a mere poet—no, my verse
Is made of pain and grief more than you know.

> mujh ko shayqr na kaho, Mir, ke sahib maine
> dard o gham kitne kiye jama to deevaan kiya

Under this guise of poetry Mir speaks the sorrows of his
    heart.
What poetry it is, my friends!—this lover's way of life.

> is parde mein gham e dil kehta hai Mir apna
> kya sher o shayari hai, yaaro, sha'aar e aashiq

*As 'lovers' in the full ghazal sense, they are aware of the transience of life,
and its inevitable sorrow. Ghalib says:*

Spring is the henna on the feet of autumn—nothing more.
In this world lasting sorrow follows transient delight.

> hina e paa e khizaan hai bahaar agar hai bhi
> davaam e kulfat e khaatir hai aish duniya ka

The rose has opened wide her arms for the farewell
    embrace
Come nightingale, it's time to go! The days of spring are
    gone.

> aaghosh e gul kushooda bara e vida hai
> ay andaleeb, chal! ki chale din bahaar ke

And Mir writes:

> The rose's scent, the nightingale's sweet song
> And life—alas! how soon they pass away!

> bu e gul ya nava e bulbul thhi
> umr, afsos! kya shitaab gayi!

> The sun of life sinks fast behind the roof.
> Do what you have to do, Mir; night comes on.

> hai lab e baam aaftaab e umr
> kar le so kiya hai Mir din thoda

Ghalib's Personal Philosophy

Ghalib's ghazals are particularly rich in philosophical reflections. The ghazal's highly condensed form means that his thoughts are expressed elliptically, but by piecing them together, one gradually builds up a picture of his personal philosophy.

~

He often feels that the universe exerts its powers to annihilate everything delicate and beautiful:

> It makes my heart quail when I see the effort of the blazing sun
> I, a mere drop of dew that hangs upon the desert thorn.

> larazta hai mera dil zahmat e mihr e darakhshaan par
> main hoon vo qatra e shabnam ki ho khaar e be-aabaan par

> Not one created atom here but what is destined to decay
> The sun on high a lamp that gutters in the windy street.

> hain zavaal aamaada ajza aafreenish ke tamaam
> mihr e gardoon hai chiraagh e rahguzaar e baad yan

He is sure he has something of value to contribute. He may be a lone figure, but he has his own resources to keep him company:

> Each of us is a world in which all kinds of fancies throng
> I sit in an assembly even though I am alone.

> hai aadmi baja e khud ik mahshar e khayaal
> hum anjuman samajhte hain khalvat hi kyon na ho

Yet his sense of his own unique importance is also something he must subdue, if he is to fulfil the tasks he has set himself:

> For all the expertise I have acquired in breaking idols
> As long as *I* exist a heavy stone still blocks my path.

> harchand subuk-dast huey but-shikani mein
> hum hain, to abhi raah mein hai sang e giraan aur

> In my construction lies concealed the stuff that is to ruin
>   me—
> The hot blood of the peasant holds the lightning for his
>   crops.

> meri tameer mein muzmar hai ik soorat kharaabi ki
> hayoola barq e khirman ka hai khoon e garm dehqaan ka

He needs to know what it is he is living for, and he repeatedly makes clear that the guidance which orthodox Islam provides is not enough. In several verses he refers to the legendary figure of Khizar, who accompanied Sikandar (Alexander the Great) in search of the water of immortality.* Khizar found it and drank, but Sikandar did not, and there is some suggestion that Khizar contrived it so. Khizar now wanders immortal and tradition says that he comes to the aid of travellers who are lost, and guides them onto the right way.

Ghalib says he will find his own way:

> I am not bound to take the path that Khizar indicates.
> I'll think an old man comes to bear me company on my way.

> laazim nahin ki Khizar ki hum pairvi karein
> jaana ki ik buzurg humein hamsafar mile

---

* See p. 132.

You know how Khizar treated Alexander—
How then can one make anyone one's guide?

    kya kiya Khizar ne Sikandar se
    ab kise rahnuma kare koi?

He is prepared to value whatever others can teach him, but will not surrender his own judgement:

I go some way with every man I see advancing swiftly
So far I see no man whom I can take to be my guide.

    chalta hoon thodi door har ik tezrau ke saath
    pehchaanta nahin hoon abhi raahbar ko main

He suggests that God Himself may now be prepared to reveal secrets that He had hitherto kept to Himself:

Why should we think that all who go will get the same reply?
Come on, let us too make the trip to see the Mount of Tur.*

    kya farz hai ki sab ko mile ek sa javaab?
    aao na hum bhi ser karen koh e toor ki

In this verse the saki—the handsome young cup-bearer—is a metaphor for one who conveys God's message, which inspires him as wine inspires the drinker; and he suggests that he may acquire the wine of insight in unorthodox ways:

If you dislike me, saki, pour the wine in my cupped hand
I may not have the cup? So be it. Let me have the wine.

    pila de ok se saaqi jo hum se nafrat hai
    piyaala gar nahin deta na de sharaab to de

The search for meaning is never-ending. He wants to observe everything steadily, good and bad alike:

* For the story of the Mount of Tur, see p. 194.

Ghalib, it is the rose's beauty teaches us to gaze.
No matter what the scene, no one should ever close his eyes.

bakhshe hai jalva e gul zauq e tamaasha, Ghalib,
chashm ko chaahiye har rang mein vaa hojaana

—and learn to see in the smallest phenomena the implication of larger things:

Unless the sea within the drop, the whole within the part
Appear, you play like children; you still lack the seeing eye.

qatre mein dajla dikhaai na de aur juzv mein kul
khel ladkon ka hua, deeda e beena na hua

Though no one can control the course of events, all that happens is to be welcomed, for it adds to his experience and understanding:

The steed of life runs on. None knows where it will stay its
   course
The reins were never in our hands or the stirrups on our
   feet.

rau mein hai rakhsh e umar, kahaan dekhiye thame
ne haath baag par hai na paa hai rikaab mein

He wants to play an active part in life, not simply waiting for experience to come, but creating our own:

The staring mirror's brightness is discoloured in the end
The standing water grows its own green surface in the end.

safa e hairat e aaina hai saamaan e zang aakhir
taghair aab e barja maanda ka, paata hai rang aakhir

He believes in extracting from life every enjoyment it can bring:

What if I cannot move my hands? My eyesight is still sound
So let the goblet and the flask stand there before my eyes.

go haath ko junbish nahin aankhon mein to dam hai
rehne do abhi saaghar o meena mere aage

If beauty is transient you should dwell not on the transience but the beauty;
and if something is a source of joy, feel that joy, even where it is not you but
others who experience it:

Spring is soon fled? What of it? It is spring.
Sing of its breezes, of its greenery.

The fair are cruel? What of it? They are fair.
Sing of their grace, their swaying symmetry.

nahin bahaar ko fursat, na ho, bahaar toh hai
taraavat e chaman o khoobi e hava kahiye

nahin nigaar ko ulfat, na ho, nigaar to hai
ravaani e ravish o masti e ada kahiye

If he incurs misfortune in doing so, that is because the irresistible urging of
his heart drives him on regardless of the consequences:

I grapple with that fragment of ill fate that is my untamed
    heart,
The enemy of ease, the friend of reckless wandering.

main aur ik aafat ka tukda vo dil e vahshi ki hai
aafiyat ka dushman aur aavaaragi ka aashna

We pass our lives in journeying in constant restlessness
And tell our years not by the sun's course but the
    lightning's flash.

raftaar e umr qat e rah e iztiraab hai
is saal ke hisaab ko barq aaftaab hai

All too often it is grief and sorrow that falls to his lot, but he must welcome
this too:

Though you play only strains of grief, my heart, yet I must
  treasure them
The music of this lute of life will all be stilled one day.

  naghmaha e gham ko bhi, e dil, ghaneemat jaaniye
  be-sada ho jaaega ye saaz e hasti ek din

My heart, this pain and sorrow too is precious, for the time
  will come
You will not heave the midnight sigh, nor shed your tears
  as morning dawns.

  dila, ye dard o alam bhi to mughtanim hai, ki aakhir
  na girya e sahri hai na aah e neemshabi hai

Home is not home unless it holds the turmoil of strong
  feeling
If there are cries of grief, not songs of joy, then be it so.

  ek hangaame pe mauquf hai ghar ki raunaq
  nauha e gham hi sahi, naghma e shaadi na sahi.

He longs for things he cannot have:

  Desires in thousands—and at each I die and then revive anew
  And many longings were fulfilled—many, but even so too few.

    hazaaron khvaahishein aisi ki har khvaahish pe dam nikle
    bahut nikle mere armaan, lekin phir bhi kam nikle

*But he mocks those, including himself at times, who think that they have
a right to good fortune:*

  We cry to fate, 'Restore to us the life of ease that once was
    ours!'
  We think our looted wealth a debt the robber owes to us.

    falak se hum ko aish e rafta ka kya kya taqaaza hai!
    mata e burda ko samjhe huey hain qarz e rahzan par

Sometimes it is better not to voice one's grief:

> Would that I had not voiced my grief but how was I to
>   know, my friend
> That this would only make more keen the pain within my
>   heart?
>
> na karta kaash naala! mujh ko kya maaloom tha, humdum
> ki hoga baa'is e afzaa'ish e dard e daroon vo bhi?

There are times when he feels despair:

> What is the autumn? What the season men call spring?
>   Throughout the year
> We live on, caged, lamenting still that once we had the
>   power to fly.
>
> khizaan kya? fasl e gul kehte hain kisko? koi mausam ho
> vuhi hum hain, qafas hai, aur maatam baal o par ka hai

*And he sometimes feels that it is his own nature that will inevitably bring
him loss:*

> I feel no joy though clouds should mass a hundred times
>   above my fields
> To me it means that lightning seeks thus early to find out
>   my crop.
>
> khushi kya khet par mere agar sau baar abr aave?
> samajhta hoon ki dhoondhe hai abhi se barq khirman ko
>
> Ghalib, no matter how I toil my labour bears no fruit.
> Lightning will strike my granaries if locusts spare my fields.
>
> Ghalib, kuchh apni sa'i se lahna nahin mujhe
> khirman jale agar na malakh khaae kisht ko

But he will not give up:

> I have not ceased to struggle; I am like the captive bird
> Who in the cage still gathers straws with which to build his
>   nest.

> misaal ye meri koshish ki hai ki murgh e aseer
> kare qafas mein faraaham khas aashiyaan ke liye

To long for something is enough in itself:

> I too gaze on the wonders that my longing can perform
> It matters nothing to me whether I attain my wish.

> hoon main bhi tamaashaai e nairang e tamanna
> matlab nahin kuchh isse ki matlab hi bar aave

The great thing is to struggle, even when you know you will not win:

> Back! Thronging hosts of black despair, lest you reduce to
>   dust as well
> The one joy left to me—the joy that unavailing struggle
>   brings.

> bas hujoom e naa-umeedi! khaak mein mil jaayegi
> ye jo ik lazzat hamaari sa'i e be-haasil mein hai

> Grief nourishes us lovers in the bosom of adversity
> Our lamp shines through the tempest like the coral
>   through the stormy sea.

> gham aaghosh e bala mein parvarish deta hai aashiq ko
> charaagh e raushan apna qulzum e sarsar ka marjaan hai

*He holds on to the knowledge that it is love which gives meaning to life,
even though to love is to court one's own destruction:*

> I pledge myself entire to love—and love of life possesses me.
> I worship lightning—and lament the lightning's handiwork.

saraapa rahn e ishq o naaguzir e ulfat e hasti
ibaadat barq ki karta hoon aur afsos haasil ka

We who are free grieve only for a moment
And use the lightning's flash to light our homes.

gham nahin hota hai aazaadon ko besh az yak nafas
barq se karte hain raushan sham e maatam-khaana hum

Images and Allusions

I hope that these translations have conveyed something of the poetic quality of the original. They cannot of course convey it all, for the vocabulary of the ghazal is full of words that have multiple connotations. A few examples will illustrate this.

Mir writes:

> Your long black tresses come to mind and glistening
>   teardrops dim my sight.
> And all is dark; the rains have come; the fireflies glimmer in
>   the night.

> teri zulf e siyah ki yaad mein aansu jhamakte hain
> andheri raat hai, barsaat hai, jugnu chamakte hain

In India, the season of the rains, when the clouds cover the sky and the nights are really dark, has the same romantic connotations as spring does in Europe. But the second line not only evokes the atmosphere with a few vivid strokes, it also suggests the elements which make up the first line, for the 'long black tresses' of the beloved are regularly compared with the long black night, and tears with rain, while the 'glistening' tears and the 'glimmering' fireflies (the two Urdu words used are equally close) also suggest each other. Every one of these connotations is relevant and contributes to the vivid intensity of the picture.

The conventional ghazal images can say a great deal more than is at once evident. In this verse of Mir's:

I asked how long the rose would bloom.
The rosebud heard my words and smiled.

> kaha maine kitna hai gul ka sabaat?
> kali ne ye sunkar tabassum kiya

The word 'smiled' conveys several meanings. The rosebud smiles at
the foolish hopes that lie behind so naive a question. But 'to smile'
is also a regular metaphor for the blooming of a flower—and the
moment the bud blooms, it loses its existence as a bud. The rose
itself will fade and pass out of existence as quickly and irrevocably.

Another apparently simple couplet is:

You'll find Mir lying in the shade of someone's wall:
What have such idle fellows got to do with love?

> kaha maine kitna hai gul ka sabaat?
> kali ne ye sunkar tabassum kiya

The first line is an effective example of the idiom of the ghazal. At
first reading it conveys plainly enough the immediate impression
that his worldly-wise critics receive when they see him—that here
is an idle fellow who does not care where he lies so long as it is
in the shade. But Urdu speakers familiar with the ghazal would
know at once that the 'someone' is his mistress, and that far from
being an idler, the devoted lover is watching and waiting constantly
in her lane or outside her house. The word 'shade', too has many
implications in addition to the obvious meaning. The cool shade is
a pleasant concept in English, but it is even more so in a country
where the intensity of the heat becomes almost unbearable in some
seasons of the year, and in Urdu a wide range of metaphorical use
reflects this fact. For example, when a child's father dies, leaving
him helpless and unprotected, it is said that he has been deprived
of the 'shadow' of his father, in which he could rest, protected from
the heat and dust of life. In this verse it suggests two things: first, an

ironic situation in which what appears to others to be a life of ease and comfort passed in the cool shade is in fact the life of the lover, with all its inevitable and never-ending suffering; but secondly, it also suggests a proud acceptance of all the pleasant connotations of shade as indeed applying to the life of the true lover, for with all its suffering, it is his unbreakable constancy in love which provides the whole meaning and content of his life and brings him a profound spiritual happiness.

Ghalib has a couplet:

> You, and the coiling tresses of your hair—
> I, and my endless, dark imaginings.

> tu aur aaraa'ish e kham e kaakul
> main aur andeshaaha e door o daraaz

At the level of the poet's love for his mistress, the couplet shows him admiring her beauty and at the same time anxious in case this self-adornment is intended to please not him, but some unknown rival for her love. The comparison between her long black hair and his 'endless, dark imaginings' is clear. And 'coiling' suggests perplexity and anguish. But this image of the beautiful woman whom he loves may stand for anything else to which he dedicates himself with equal whole-heartedness—to his Divine Beloved, whose ways are inscrutable and who may have unimagined tribulations in store for him, or his high ideals in life, commitment to which may bring heavy penalties. All these things would suggest themselves to an Urdu reader to whom the ghazal tradition has been familiar since childhood.

Sometimes the poet will use one of the standard symbols in an unusual way. The 'saki' (cup-bearer) is a beautiful youth who pours the wine for you, wine which in an allegorical sense, is the intoxicating message of divine love; so he is generally a figure from whom something good is expected. But in one verse of Ghalib this is not his role. He is the symbol of fate, from which Ghalib expects nothing but evil. Fate is determined by the revolution of the seven

skies, and Ghalib pictures these as seven upturned cups. It is the saki
who has turned them, and so emptied them of every drop of wine
they had once contained. So Ghalib says:

> How should the saki of the skies pour you the wine of
>   happiness?
> He sits there with his—one, two, four—his seven cups
>   upturned.

>> mai e ishrat ki khvaahish saaqi e gardoon se kya keejiye?
>> liye baitha hai ik do chaar jaam e vaazhgoon vo bhi

Legendary figures serve the same purpose, but allusions familiar to
Urdu speakers would need explanation to make them intelligible
to an English reader. One such allusion is to the story of Jamshed,
a legendary king of Iran, who was said to have a marvellous
cup. When he looked in it, he could see all that was happening
throughout the world. Mir refers to this to reflect on the transience
of life—not even the powerful or the miraculous will last:

> The great Jamshed who made the wine cup, where is he
>   today?
> Where are the revellers whom wine and music used to thrill?

> His cup is gone—save that the tulip still preserves its shape.
> Only the poppy's shoulder now supports its wine bowl still.

> A fragment of the tavern keeper's skull closes the vat
> The willows sway where slender youths once came to
>   drink their fill.

>> jamshed jis ne vaz kiya jaam, kya hua?
>> ve suhbaten kahaan gayin? kidhar ve naavnosh?

>> juz laala us ke jaam se paate nahin nishaan
>> hai koknaar us ki jagah ab subu badosh

>> jhoome hai bed jaaye javaanaan e mai-gusaar
>> baala e kham hai khisht e sar e peer e naifarosh

Ghalib says, anyway, why bother with such things? Keep to simple values:

> I will go and get another from the shop if it should break
> No goblet of Jamshed for me! This cup of clay is good!

> aur baazaar se le aayenge agar toot gaya
> saaghar e jam se mera jaam e sifaal achcha hai

However close a translation gets to the original, there may be layers of meaning it cannot convey. One of Mir's most powerful couplets is this:

> You must have heard what happened to Mansur—
> Here, if you speak the truth, they crucify you.

> mansoor ki haqeeqat tum ne suni hi hogi
> haq jo kahe hai, us ko yahaan daar khainchte hain

Even if you know nothing else about Mansur, the verse itself tells you that he was someone who spoke the truth to a hostile world and paid the penalty for it. In Mir's original, *haqq* is the word which I have translated as 'the truth', but this is only one of several meanings the word can have. The Urdu reader would know this, and know who Mansur was. In the ghazal he is *the* examplar of a devoted lover of God, whose ecstatic cry *anal haqq*—'I am God'—expressed a sense of complete oneness with his Divine Beloved; but to the orthodox it was horrendous blasphemy, punishable by death.

A whole stock of other symbols, not represented in the selections in this book, serves a similar purpose, and makes possible a conciseness and richness of expression which is one of the hallmarks of a good ghazal.

Eleven Ghazals of Ghalib

I invite you now to read a few ghazals. They are not complete: from each I have selected couplets that Urdu speakers are most likely to be familiar with, and which don't need much explanation. The essential thing to remember is that each couplet stands on its own in terms of meaning, and needs to be appreciated on its own. In the first three ghazals I have attempted to give some of the unifying effects of the rhyme scheme, while in others, the beat of the metre is intended to convey something of the same effect. Sometimes, as in the Urdu, the rhyming phrase is several words long, (as 'Like this' in ghazal II, or 'before my eyes' in ghazal III) and the repetition of this phrase has the effect of creating a sense of association with the otherwise quite separate couplets.

I

The fair are cruel? What of it? They are fair
Sing of their grace, their swaying symmetry.

 nahin nigaar ko ulfat na ho, nigaar to hai
 ravaani e ravish o masti e ada kahiye

Spring is soon fled? What of it? It is spring.
Sing of its breezes, of its greenery.

 nahin bahaar ko fursat, na ho, bahaar to hai
 taraavat e chaman o khoobi e hava kahiye

Your ship has reached the shore. Why cry to God
Against your captain's cruel tyranny?

> safeena jab ki kinaare pe aa laga, Ghalib
> khuda se kya sitam o jaur e naa-khuda kahiye

II

You stand away, and purse your lips, and show their rosebud
  form
I said 'How do you kiss?' Come, kiss my lips and say, 'Like
  this!'

> ghuncha e naa-shagufta ko door se mat dikha ki yun
> bose ko poochhta hoon main, munh se mujhe bata ki yun

How does she steal your heart? Why ask? She does not
  speak a word—
But every gesture, every grace, is telling you 'Like this!'

> pursish e tarz e dilbari keejiye kya, ki bin kahe
> us ke har ik ishaare se nikle hai ye ada ki yun

At night, and flushed with wine, and in my rival's
  company—
God grant that she may come to me, but not, O god, like this.

> raat ke vaqt mein piye, saath raqeeb ko liye
> aae vo yahaan khuda kare par na kare khuda ki yun

How should I not sit silent facing her in her assembly?
Her silence is itself enough to tell me, 'Sit like this!'

> bazm mein us ke ru-ba-ru kyon na khamosh baithiye?
> us ki to khaamoshi mein bhi hai yehi mudda'a ki yun

I said, 'From love's assembly every rival should be banished.'
What irony! She heard me, sent me out, and said, 'Like this!'

> main ne kaha ki 'bazm e naaz chaahiye ghair se tihi'
> sunke sitam zareef ne mujh ko utha diya ki 'yun!'

If people say, 'Can Urdu, then, put Persian verse to shame?'
Recite a line of Ghalib's verse and tell them, 'Yes! Like this!'

> jo ye kahe ki 'rekhta kyonke ho rashk e faarsi?'
> gufta e Ghalib ek baar padhke use suna ki yun

III

The world is but a game that children play before my eyes,
A spectacle that passes night and day before my eyes.

> baazeecha e atfaal hai duniya mere aage
> hota hai shab o roz tamaasha mere aage

The throne of Sulaiman is but a toy in my esteem,
The miracles that Isa worked, a trifle in my eyes.*

> ik khel hai aurang e Sulaimaan mere nazdeek
> ik baat hai ejaaz e maseeha mere aage

You need not ask how I feel when I am away from you;
See for yourself how you feel when you are before my eyes.†

> mat poochh ki kya haal hai mera tere peechhe
> tu dekh ki kya rang hai tera mere aage

My faith restrains me while the lure of unbelief attracts me
That way, the Kaba: and this way, the Church before my eyes.

> imaan mujhe roke hai jo khainche hai mujhe kufr
> kaaba mere peechhe hai, kaleesa mere aage

A raging sea of blood lies in my path. Would that were all!
For perils more than these may yet arise before my eyes.

> hai maujzan ik qulzum e khoon kaash yehi ho
> aata hai abhi dekhiye kya kya mere aage

---

* Sulaiman and Isa are, respectively, the Biblical Solomon and Jesus.
† I feel in your absence all the agitation you feel in my presence.

What if I cannot move my hands? My eyesight is still sound
So let the goblet and the flask stand there before my eyes.

> go haath ko junbish nahin aankhon mein to dam hai
> rehne do abhi saaghar o meena mere aage

He shares my calling, shares my ways, he shares my inmost
    thoughts;
Do not speak ill of Ghalib; he finds favour in my eyes.

> hum-pesha o hum-mashrab o hum-raaz hai mera
> Ghalib ko bura kyon kaho, achcha mere aage

IV

This was not to be my fate that all should end in lovers
    meeting;
Even had I gone on living, I should still be waiting, waiting.

> ye na thhi hamaari qismat ki visaal e yaar hota
> agar aur jeete rehte yehi intizaar hota

Did your promise save my life? Yes!—for I knew you would
    not keep it.
Would I not have died of joy if I had thought you would
    fulfill it?

> tere vaade par jiye hum to ye jaan jhoot jaana
> ki khushi se marna jaate agar aitibaar hota

Am I still to call it friendship when my friends start
    preaching at me?
Someone should have brought me comfort, someone
    should have shared my sorrows.

> ye kahaan ki dosti hai ki bane hai dost naasih
> koi chaara-saaz hota, koi gham-gusaar hota

Grief wastes our life away—and yet how shall we flee the
     heart within us?
Had we not known the grief of love, we would have
     known the grief of living.

> gham agarchi jaan-gusil hai, pe kahaan bachein? ki dil hai
> gham e ishq gar na hota gham e rozgaar hota

With what style you handle, Ghalib, all these themes of
     mystic teaching!
What a saint we would have thought you if you had not
     been a drinker!

> ye misaa'il e tasavvuf, ye tera bayaan Ghalib
> tujhe hum vali samajhte jo na baada-khvaar hota!

V

Since I have made my home, without your leave, right by
     your door,
Do you think, even now, you'll need directing to my house?*

> gar jab bana liya tere dar par kahe baghair
> jaanega ab bhi tu na mera ghar kahe baghair?

She says, when I no longer even have the power of speech,
'How should I know a man's heart if he does not speak to
     me?'

> kehte hain jab rahi na mujhe taaqat e sukhan
> jaanun kisi ke dil ki main kyonkar kahe baghair?

I have to do with her of whom no man in all the world
Has ever spoken yet without calling her 'cruel one'.

> kaam usse aa pada hai ki jis ka jahaan mein
> leve na koi naam sitamgar kahe baghair

---

* I've constantly asked you to visit me and your excuse has always been 'I
don't know the way.' But now...

I have nothing to say to you; else I am not the man
To hold my tongue; I would speak out though it cost me
   my head.

> ji mein hi kuchh nahin hai humaare vagarna hum
> sar jaaye ya rahe na rahen par kahe baghair

I will not cease to worship her, that infidel, my idol
Though all creation never cease to call me infidel.

> chhodunga main na us but e kaafir ka poojna
> chhode na khalq go mujhe kaafir kahe baghair

I mean her airs and graces, but I cannot talk of them
Unless I speak in terms of knives and daggers that she wields.

> maqsad hai naaz o ghamza vale guftagu mein kaam
> chalta nahin hai dashna o khanjar kahe baghair

I talk of contemplating God, but cannot make my point
Unless I speak of wine-cup and intoxicating wine.*

> har chand ho mushaahida e haq ki guftagu
> banti nahin hai baada o saaghar kahe baghair

Since I am deaf I make a claim to double kindness from you;
I cannot hear what you have said unless you say it twice.†

> behra hoon main toh chaahiye doona ho iltifaat
> sunta nahin hoon baat mukarrar kahe baghair

Ghalib, you must not lay your plea repeatedly before her;
All that you feel, she knows; you need not speak a single
   word.

> Ghalib na kar huzoor mein tu baar baar arz
> zaahir hai tera haal sab un par kahe baghair

---

* An acceptance of the conventional metaphors of the ghazal.
† Humorous. He wants her to repeat her words of kindness, and makes the
excuse that he is deaf. Ghalib did in fact become deaf as he got older!

VI

She has foresworn her cruelty—but can she?
She says, 'How can I show my face to you?'*

    jaur se baaz aaye par baaz aaen kya,
    kehte hain hum tujh ko munh dikhlaayein kya?

All night, all day, the seven heavens are turning—
Something will happen; set your mind at ease.

    raat din gardish mein hain saat aasmaan
    ho rahega kuchh na kuchh ghabraayein kya?

She fights me, and I tell myself she loves me:
When she feels nothing, what can I dream then?

    laag ho toh usko hum samjhen lagaao
    jab na ho kuchh bhi to dhoka khaayein kya?

See, I keep pace with him who bears my letter.
Am I then to deliver it myself?†

    ho liye kyon naama-bar ke saath-saath,
    Ya rab apne khat ko hum pahunchaaen kya?

What though a wave of blood should overwhelm me?‡
How can I leave the threshold of my love?

    mauj e khoon sar se guzar hi kyon na jaaye
    aastaan e yaar se uth jaayein kya?

I passed my life waiting for death to take me,
And dead, I still must see what I must see.§

    umar bhar dekha kiya marne ki raah
    mar gaye par dekhiye dikhlaayen kya?

---

* Shame at the thought of her past cruelties makes her hide her face—and that is cruel!

† I keep pace—so impatient am I to have her reply.

‡ What though every conceivable misfortune should befall me?

§ What I must see—what God has in store for me.

She is perplexed. She asks me, 'Who is Ghalib?'
Tell me, someone, what answer can I give?

poochhte hain vo ki 'Ghalib kaun hai?'
koi batlaao ki hum batlaayein kya?

VII

I am no melody, I am no lute—
I am the sound that my own breaking makes.

na gul e naghma hoon na parda e saaz
main hoon apni shikast ki aavaaz

You, and the coiling tresses of your hair—
I, and my endless, dark imaginings.*

tu aur aaraa'ish e kham e kaakul
main aur andeshaha e door o daraaz

Love of my captor holds me in her snare;
It is not that I lack the power of flight.

hoon giriftaar e ulfat e sayyaad
varna baaqi hai taaqat e parvaaz

VIII

None of my hopes can ever be fulfilled;
Seek as I may, I see no way ahead.

koi ummeed bar nahin aati
koi soorat nazar nahin aati

Death surely comes on its appointed day;
Why then does sleep not come the whole night through?

maut ka ek din muayyan hai
neend kyon raat bhar nahin aati?

* See p. 219.

Once I would contemplate my wounded heart
And laugh. Now laughter never comes to me.

> aage aati thi haal e dil pe hansi
> ab kisi baat par nahin aati

The meek ascetic wins reward in heaven.
I know; but I cannot incline that way.

> janta hoon savaab e taa'at o zuhd
> par tabiyat idhar nahin aati

If I keep silent, it is for a reason.
You surely know I have the power to speak?

> hai kuchh aisi hi baat jo chup hoon
> varna kya baat kar nahin aati?

I am so far away that even I
Have not the least awareness where I am.

> hum vahaan hain jahaan se hum ko bhi
> kuchh humaari khabar nahin aati

Ghalib, you have the face to go to Mecca?
But then you never feel a sense of shame.

> kaabe kis munh se jaaoge, Ghalib?
> sharm tumko magar nahin aati

IX

Beneath the shade of every mosque should be a tavern—
Just as the eye, your reverence, is near the brow.*

> masjid ke zer e saaya kharaabat chaahiye
> bhaon paas aankh qibla e haajaat chaahiye

It was for fair-faced women that I learnt to paint;
One needs some pretext, after all, for meeting them.

---

*The mosque, with its arch, is compared to the eyebrow, and the tavern to the eye—and it is obvious which is to be valued more!

seekhe hain mah-rukhon ke liye hum musavvari
taqreeb kuchh to bahr e mulaaqaat chaahiye

What idiot takes to wine in hope of finding joy?
Each day, each night, I seek a refuge from myself.

mai se gharaz nashaat hai kis ru-siyaah ko?
ik guna be-khudi mujhe din raat chaahiye

Tulip and rose and eglantine wear different hues;
With every hue let us affirm the joy of spring.

hai rang e laala o gul o nasreen juda juda
har rang mein bahaar ka isbaat chaahiye

X

Life passes by unused, although it be as long as Khizar's.
He too will ask himself tomorrow, 'What have I achieved?'

be-sarfa hi guzarti hai ho garche umr e Khizar
hazrat bhi kal kahenge ki hum kya kiya kiye?

Had I the power, I would demand an answer from the earth,
'What have you done, vile miser, with all the rare treasures
    you hold?'*

maqdoor ho to khaak se poochhun ki ai la'eem
tu ne vo gunjha e giraan maaya kya kiye?

I hope it was not in *his* company she learnt these ways;
She gives me kisses even when I do not ask for them.

sohbat mein ghair ki na padi ho kahin ye khoo
dene laga hai bosa baghair iltija kiye

When she is obstinate, that's it! But this at least is good:
When she forgets, she can keep scores of promises she made.

---

* The 'rare treasures' mean the great ones who have died and been lost to
the world.

zid ki hai aur baat magar khoo buri nahin
bhoole se usne saikdon vaade vafa kiye

Ghalib, you know yourself what sort of answer you will get;
No matter how you talk, and how she goes on listening.

Ghalib tumhin kaho ki milega javaab kya
maana ki tum kaha kiye aur vo suna kiye

XI

A strong snare lay in wait for me, concealed close to my
    nest;
I had not even taken wing when it imprisoned me.

pinhan thha daam e sakht qareeb aashiyaan ke
udne na paaye thhe ki giriftaar hum hue

You love me now, but that does not atone, for in this world
Much, besides you, has visited its cruelty on me.

teri vafa se kya ho talaafi ki dahr mein
tere siva bhi hum pe bahut se sitam hue

I filled the blood-stained pages with the story of my love
And went on writing even when they had cut off my hands.*

likhte rahe junoon ki hikaayaat e khoon chakaan
har chand usme haath hamaare qalam hue

Asad, I took to begging, but I kept my sense of humour,
And am the suppliant lover now of the munificent.†

chhodi asad na hum ne gadaai mein dil lagi
saa'il hue to aashiq e ahl e karam hue

---

* The original has a characteristic, but untranslatable play on words. *Hath qalam hue* means, 'My hands were cut off'—but the words could also mean, 'My hands became pens.'

† 'Munificent' here is used ironically.

A Living Tradition

I have chosen to present the ghazal with examples taken almost entirely from the work of two of its greatest exponents, Mir and Ghalib. But it cannot be stressed too strongly that the ghazal has always been, and still is, the most popular genre of Urdu verse, and Mir and Ghalib were only two, albeit the greatest two, of the great ghazal poets of their day.

The ghazal is a living tradition. The separate couplets, each complete in itself, lend themselves to being easily memorized and are often used as apt quotations to comment on daily situations. Many Urdu speakers know by heart hundreds of ghazal couplets, and have heard many ghazals sung, Ghalib's being particularly popular.

Some ghazals incorporate already well-known proverbs, like these of Mir, in which the proverb corresponds to the words I have enclosed in quotes:

> Already you bewail your blistered feet?
> 'It's a long way to Delhi yet,' my son.

>> shikva e aabla abhi se Mir?
>> hai pyaare hanoz Dilli door

> What can I do? My heart is in her power.
> 'The earth is hard, the sky is far away.'

>> kare kya? ki dil bhi to majboor hai
>> zameen sakht hai aasmaan door hai

I roam about disgraced, but nothing can be done about it.
What is a man to do, Mir Sahib? 'Service is servitude.'

> laa-elaaji hai jo rehti hai mujhe aavaaragi
> keejiye kya Mir sahib? bandagi be-chaaragi

No one goes to his death with open eyes:
'If you have life, then you have everything.'

> Mir amdan bhi koi marta hai?
> jaan hai to jahaan hai pyaare

Other verses by Mir have themselves become proverbial, like that which makes the same point as 'It's a long way to Delhi':

> Why do you weep? Love's trials have just begun.
> Restrain your tears. See what is yet to come.

> ibtida e ishq hai rona hai kya?
> aage aage dekhiye hota hai kya

Another is often quoted when you part from friends, especially when you do not know when you will see them again:

> Now I must leave the temple of my idols
> I'll come again—if God brings me this way.

> ab to jaate hain but-kade se Mir
> phir milenge agar khuda laaya

(There is an irony in the couplet; the God who abhors idolatry is hardly likely to help you return to the temple.)

One whose meaning is plain:

> Defeat and victory are things that fate alone decides,
> But, Mir, this feeble heart of mine has fought with all its
>   strength.

shikast o fatah naseebon se hai, ai Mir
muqaabala toh dil e naatavaan ne khoob kiya

Urdu speakers (including those who have had little or no formal education) will regularly quote couplets in conversation often without knowing or caring whose couplets they are quoting. For instance they will say of anyone (including themselves!) whom they suspect of embroidering the truth:

> The stories of my love are true—except that here and there I add a touch or two in order to adorn the tale.

> fasaane yun to muhabbat ke sach hain par kuchh kuchh
> badha bhi dete hain hum zeb e daastaan ke liye

Or, urging someone to go boldly for what they want:

> Here wine flows freely, but the timid cannot hope to taste it. Come forward and reach out to take the cup: the wine is yours.

> ye bazm e mai hai yan kotaah-dasti mein hai mahroomi
> jo badh kar khud utha le haath mein meena usi ka hai

Or of someone whose project fails just when success seems certain:

> Just see my luck! The noose I threw has broken When I had almost reached the parapet.

> qismat ki khoobi dekhiye tooti kahaan kamand
> do char haath jab ke lab e baam reh gaya

(The image being that of a lover coming secretly to climb up to the flat roof where his beloved awaits him.)

Of these three couplets the first is by Shefta, a contemporary of Ghalib, the second by Shad, a twentieth-century poet, and the third by Qaim, a contemporary of Mir. Other pieces in this book give examples of how naturally Urdu speakers use ghazal couplets to comment on their everyday lives.

Throughout the history of Urdu literature there have been major figures who owe their fame solely to the fact that they were ghazal poets. Even those modern poets who write mainly in other forms all write ghazals too; and some of the best-known songs in the immensely popular Indian films are ghazals.

The ghazal's lasting popularity is not difficult to understand. It celebrates those who have the courage in the face of all difficulties to stand by their love, be it a human lover, or devotion to God, or to the ideals to which they dedicate themselves. As long as people who do that are honoured, as one hopes they always will be, the ghazal is not likely to lose its appeal.

THE LIVES OF POETS

The Lives of Poets

By the last quarter of the nineteenth century, Urdu was beginning to be more commonly used for prose writing. A major role in producing this change was a modernizing movement called the 'New Light', which I will introduce you to in the following section. But it so happens that some of the best prose writing of this period is about the lives of poets and poetic culture of the preceding age—the period in which Ghalib lived—so it seems appropriate to read these first.

The outstanding example of writing about the classical poets is by Muhammad Husain Azad (1830–1910), in a book called *Ab i Hayat*. (This means 'The Water of Life',* but Urdu titles rarely give any indication of what the book is about. Urdu readers might know the story and understand that Azad is claiming immortality for his work.) It gives a historical account of Urdu poetry in which the liveliest parts are descriptions of the individual poets. *Ab-i-Hayat* is his best and most famous work but he also wrote educational books for schools and a voluminous study of the life and times of the Mughal Emperor Akbar (1556–1605).

The first piece in this section is an extract about Nasikh (1771–1838), a contemporary and friend of Ghalib. In it Azad not only traces his development as a poet, but is also at pains to give a picture of him as a man. We also get a sense of what it was like to be a poet at this time. The ability to compose poetry was regarded as one of the normal accomplishments of an educated

---

* For the story of the Water of Life see p. 132.

man, but anyone who aimed to make his mark as a poet was expected to serve an apprenticeship under an *ustad*—a master-poet—submitting his verses to him for correction until such time as his ustad considered that he no longer needed instruction. Only a minority made poetry a full-time occupation, and unless they were wealthy they would need to find a patron. To support poets and scholars was considered the proper function of those who were in a position to do so. Once a poet had achieved eminence the position of poet and patron was reversed: it was not the aspiring poet who sought the patron but the aspiring patron who sought the poet. Often the patron of a great poet would hope to achieve poetic fame himself, and would appoint the poet as his ustad. Bahadur Shah Zafar, the last Mughal Emperor before the British put an end to the Mughal Empire after the great revolt of 1857, was both the patron and the *shagird* (apprentice in poetry) of Ghalib.

The next piece is by Abdul Halim Sharar (1860–1926). He is mainly known as a historical novelist, but his best work, from which this extract is taken, is a vivid and comprehensive treatment of life in old Lucknow, the capital of the princely state of Oudh[*] (or Awadh) and a centre of cultural life that rivalled Delhi. It is the story of a famous singer, which illustrates that it was not only poets who enjoyed the patronage of the great, and the independence which their great reputation ensured them. Men of learning and accomplished artistes held the same position.

The extract from the writing of Farhatullah Beg (1883–1947) gives a brilliantly imagined account of the last mushaira held in Delhi under the patronage of the Mughal Emperor before the uprising of 1857. The mushaira—described in the section on *Love Poetry*[†]—was a gathering at which a number of poets would recite their verse. All the poets who feature in this one were historical figures, and part of the appeal of his account lies in the knowledge

[*] The eastern half of what is now Uttar Pradesh.
[†] See p. 148.

which the reader has—and which the participating poets did not have—that their world was about to end abruptly in disaster.*

Of all the nineteenth-century poets, Ghalib was the one whom later generations found most memorable. It was his personality as well as his poetry which made so strong an impact—a personality vividly revealed in a book by his younger colleague, Altaf Husain Hali (1837–1914). *Yadgar i Ghalib* (*A Memoir of Ghalib*) was published in 1897. Most of it consists of selections from, and commentary on, Ghalib's Urdu and Persian prose and verse, but the first part portrays his life and character.

Finally, there are a few extracts from Ghalib's own letters. The publication of his Urdu letters was itself a landmark in the history of Urdu prose. There is some irony in this, for he prided himself (justifiably) on his command of classical Persian, and for most of his life he had strongly maintained the opinion that, not only for prose, but for poetry too, Persian was still the only proper medium. When in 1858, an admirer of his suggested publishing a collection of his Urdu letters he emphatically forbade him to do so:

> As for your wish to publish the Urdu letters, that…is unnecessary. Only a few of them were written with proper thought and care, and apart from these few the rest are just what came on the spur of the moment. Their publication would diminish my stature as a writer.

But ten to eleven years later he had changed his view of the matter, and not only approved of publication but himself helped in collecting letters from the friends to whom he had written. The bulk of them date from after 1857, and it was the circumstances of that terrible time that made them what they are—an intimate, vivid and frank picture of himself. A first volume was published in 1869, the year of his death. The seal of approval thus conferred on natural prose by a great poet must have done a lot to bring about general acceptance of Urdu as a literary medium.

---

* On the impact of 1857, see p. 290.

Nasikh: Portrait of a Poet

MUHAMMAD HUSAIN AZAD

Nasikh told one of his friends, 'In those days Mir was still living. My love of poetry was such that I could not restrain my ardour, and one day I went secretly to him and showed him several ghazals. He would not look at them.' (One would like to know what Mir said to him; it is not likely that Nasikh will have told anybody!) 'I went away disappointed. But I said to myself, "Well, Mir Sahib is only a man, not an angel. I'll correct my verses myself." So I would compose verses and put them aside. After some days I would look at them again, make any improvements I felt necessary and again put them aside. After a while I would again look at them at my leisure and revise them. In short, I went on writing. But I never recited anything [at a mushaira] until I was fully satisfied with it.'

> He goes on to say that he would attend mushairas, but so long as the established poets of the day were alive he would only listen, and never recite. 'When the field was clear I began to recite.'
>   Like anyone with a classical education he knew the numerical value assigned to each letter of the alphabet, and used this in daily life. For instance when he said 'Ya Ghafur!' (Ghafur being one of the names of Allah—the forgiving one) the numerical value of the letters added up to 1297. So:

...From his earliest years he loved physical exercise. He would do 1297 press-ups daily, that being the numerical value of *Ya Ghafur*. He did this exercise regularly, and without fail, and on occasion would increase the number of press-ups. His physique was well-suited to all this. He was tall, and broad in the chest. He kept his head shaved, and would sit there wearing nothing but a loincloth, like a lion about to spring. Even in the winter he wore only a shirt of fine cloth, or at the most one made of chintz.

He took only one meal every twenty-four hours, but he would then make up for all the meal times he had missed, and eat five kilos of the finest food. When a particular fruit was in season, on any day when he felt like eating it, he would not take a regular meal. For example, when mangoes were in season he would one day have several basketsful brought to him, have some troughs filled with water, put the mangoes in them, and not stop eating until he had emptied all of them. When he ate corn on the cob, as he often did, he would finish up with the cobs piled in heaps around him. He dined in this way on fruit, each in its season, only two or three times in the season, and two or three friends would join him in this.

He usually dined alone. Everyone knew when his mealtime was. When the time for the zuhr prayer drew near everyone would leave him. [A friend of his told me:] 'Once or twice I had occasion to eat with him. That day he had had food sent for from the bazaar. There were four or five bowls of *qurma* and kababs. In one bowl was the meat of some bird. There were turnips, beetroot and two kinds of lentils—and all this for him alone. But he finished it all. It was a rule with him to finish off one bowl at a time. The servant would take away the empty bowl and set another down in front of him. It was out of the question for him to put two kinds of food in his mouth at once. He used to say that if you mixed things you spoilt their taste. Then he would eat pulao (or some other rice dish). Then lentils, and after every four or five mouthfuls, chutney, or pickle or whatever... He used to say, "I'm an old man, but I eat better than you youngsters..." But he was a huge man, and strong with it, and when you looked at him you would feel that four or five kilos of food were nothing to him.'

...The late Agha Kalb e Husain Khan often used to invite him to his house, where he would detain him as his guest for months together. One day he had his cook prepare some special dishes for him. This took a little longer than usual. Nasikh saw some servants bringing their food and called them across. 'Who is this food for?' he asked. They said, 'It's for us.' He said, 'Bring it here,' had four or five of them set down their food before him, ate it all, wiped the bowls, gave them back to them and told them, 'When my food comes you can eat that.'

His routine was to begin his exercises three hours before dawn and go on with them until the morning... Then he would bathe and have cane chairs set out in the spotlessly clean courtyard; or, when he sat inside, the room would be furnished with carpets and adorned with other things. During the morning his friends and pupils in poetry would come to visit him. At midday they would all leave, and he would close the doors and sit down to eat. This was heavy work, and he would then take up this heavy load and take a rest. Visitors would begin arriving again at *asar*.* At *maghrib* they would all leave. He would close the doors, send the servants away, and lock the door from the inside. On the flat roof he had a room to which he could retire. He would go there, sleep a while, and then begin to compose poetry. The world would be sleeping, and dead silence prevailed. And he, instead of sleeping, would write the poetry into which he poured his heart's blood. When his pupils brought him their verses to correct his servants would put them in a coarse cloth bag and put it down beside him. [During the night] he would correct them. Then, when the last watch of the night began, he would put the papers away and begin his exercises again.

He was a stickler for etiquette. He would sit with his back against a bolster. His pupils, most of whom were the sons of well-to-do and noble families, would come and sit respectfully at the edge of the carpet, not daring to breathe a word. He would be thinking, and writing something. Then he would put down the

---

* *Asar* and *maghrib*: The two prayers said respectively in mid-afternoon and just after sunset.

paper he had been writing on and give a grunt. One of them would begin to recite his ghazal. Wherever all that was needed was a change of words, or of the word-order, he would make the necessary correction. Or he would say, 'That's nothing. Cut it out,' or 'The first (or the second) line of the couplet isn't good. Change it.' Or, 'That's a good rhyme, but it isn't appropriate here. Try harder.' When the first one had finished, the second would read out his verse. Nobody dared to speak.

He was a very courteous man, but was often so lost in his own thoughts that people who did not know him thought him indifferent or arrogant. [One visitor, an accomplished poet of Urdu, tells how he once visited him.] 'He was sitting on a stool with a few of his friends around him seated on cane chairs. I went and stood before him and paid my respects to him. He said in a voice even deeper than his huge body would have led one to expect, "Well, sir? What brings you here?" I said, "There is a couplet of a classical Persian poet which I do not understand." He said, "I am not a Persian poet," and at once turned to talk to someone else. I was sorry I had come, and reproached myself for having done so.'

One day someone came to call on him. He was sitting with some of his friends in the small courtyard. His visitor was carrying a stick, and it so happened that there was a little mound of earth just in front of where he was standing. As people commonly do, he began to demolish this with the end of his stick. Nasikh called a servant, and when the man came said to him, 'Fill a basket with earth and put it down in front of this gentleman. Then he can amuse himself to his heart's content.'

On one occasion a friend had given Nasikh a present of three glass spoons. Spoons like this were a novelty in those days and were really very beautiful. Nasikh had placed them on a niche at his side. A young nobleman who had come to visit him noticed them and asked him, 'Where did you buy these spoons, sir, and how much did they cost?' Nasikh told him how he had come by them. His visitor picked up a spoon and said how much he admired it. Then as he went on talking he kept tapping the floor with it until he tapped too hard and it broke in two. Nasikh took another spoon, handed it to him and said, 'Now play with this one.'

One day he was being pestered by a visitor who sat there showing no sign of leaving. Nasikh called a servant and told him to bring him the box in which he kept his documents. When he did so Nasikh took out the deeds of his house, laid them before his visitor, and said to the servant, 'Now bring some men to move the furniture out.' His visitor looked at him aghast, and the servant too was dumbfounded. Nasikh said, 'What are you staring at? He's taken possession of the house. I don't want him to miss out on the furniture.'

Nasikh never entered anyone's service. He had resources of his own, and the generosity of his admirers enabled him to live in affluence. On the first occasion of his coming to Allahabad, Raja Chandu Lal [a would-be patron] sent him twelve thousand rupees and invited him to come to him. Nasikh wrote to him, 'I have a patron who is a Sayyid,* and I cannot leave him. When I leave here I shall go to Lucknow.' The Raja wrote again, and sent him fifteen thousand rupees, urging him to come. 'If you come,' he wrote, 'I shall have you made Poet Laureate. You will not be required to attend regularly at court; you may come to see me whenever you please.' He declined the offer, and deposited the money with Agha Kalb e Husain Khan and drew on it when he needed it. And this was not his only resource. Nawab Motamid ud Daula, [an important noble at the court of the king of Oudh] and his son were always visiting him, and gifts and tributes would reach him from all sides. He ate well on the proceeds and enabled others to do so too, entertaining Sayyids and funding pilgrims to Mecca and visitors to shrines. He lived an independent life, visiting and staying as a guest wherever he pleased, and his hosts considered it an honour to have him.

Ghazi ud Din Haider, the King of Oudh, formally acknowledged that he ruled as the vassal of the Mughal Emperor. Though the British

---

* Sayyids claim to be descended from the Prophet's daughter Fatima and are revered accordingly.

*acknowledged the Emperor, they encouraged Ghazi ud Din Haidar to
assume the title of King, thus virtually declaring independence. It seems
that Nasikh disapproved of their doing so:*

On one occasion when Nasikh was at the height of his fame Ghazi
ud Din Haidar said to his minister, 'If Shaikh Nasikh will attend
my court and recite an ode in my praise I will confer on him
the title of Poet Laureate.' When the minister, who was Nasikh's
respectful pupil, conveyed this message to him he was much put
out, and said, 'Mirza Sulaiman Shikoh [the representative of the
Mughal Emperor in Lucknow] can bestow that title when he is
king. Or the British Government can. What do I want with *his*
title?' Whereupon the king banished him from Lucknow... But
when Ghazi ud Din Haidar died he came back.

Nasikh died in his own home and was buried there. People
say that he was sixty-four or sixty-five when he died, but [my
informant says that] he must have been nearly 100.

The King and the Singer

ABDUL HALIM SHARAR

In the days when Ghazi ud Din Haidar was King of Oudh [1814–1827] there lived in Lucknow, in Gola Ganj, a superb singer named Haidari Khan. Because of his awkward, independent nature people called him Crazy Haidari Khan. Ghazi ud Din Haidar very much wanted to hear him sing, but so far had not been able to.

One afternoon he went out, carried in his palanquin, to take the air by the riverside. As they passed under the Rumi Gate someone saw Haidari Khan passing by. They told the king, 'Light of the World, that is Haidari Khan.' Ghazi ud Din Haidar was very pleased and ordered him to be brought to him. The King said, 'Well, Haidari Khan, won't you ever let me hear you sing?' He replied, 'Certainly I will but I don't know where you live.' The King burst out laughing and said, 'All right, come with me. I'll take you there myself.' 'Very well,' he said, and went along with him. They had almost reached Chattar Manzil [the King's palace] when Haidari Khan flew off the handle and said, 'I'm coming with you, but I won't sing unless you give me puris and cream to eat.' The King promised he would. They reached the palace and the King sat down and began to listen to his singing. In no time at all he was so overwhelmed by it that he was lost in ecstasy. At this Haidari Khan stopped singing. The King asked him to continue, but instead he said, 'This tobacco you have in your hookah seems very, very good. What shop do you get it from?' The King too was a man of unpredictable temperament and his eccentric behaviour was well known. He was put out by this question, but his companions told him, 'Light of the World, you know that he's crazy. He still doesn't know who he's talking to.'

At the King's direction they now took Haidari Khan into another room, where they gave him puris and cream and a hookah to smoke. He took puris weighing half a pound and cream weighing a quarter of a pound, asked for a small quantity of sugar and despatched all this to his wife. (He used to do this wherever he was.) While all this was happening the King was drinking, and when he was drunk he again remembered Haidari Khan. He at once sent for him and commanded him to sing; but he had no sooner begun than the King stopped him and said, 'Haidari Khan, listen to me. If you simply make me happy and don't also make me weep then mark my words, I'll immediately have you drowned in the Gomati [the river that runs through Lucknow].' Haidari Khan was stunned. Realizing that the King might carry out his threat he replied, 'Your Majesty, as God wills,' and proceeded to put all that he had into his singing. By God's power, or rather because the appointed term of Haidari Khan's life was not yet up, the King quickly felt the impact of the singing and began to weep in spite of himself. He felt pleased with Haidari Khan and said to him, 'Haidari Khan, ask me a boon. What do you ask?' He replied, 'Will you give me what I ask?' The King promised that he would. Haidari Khan made him repeat his promise three times, and then said, 'Your Majesty, what I ask is that you never send for me and never have me sing to you again.' The King was astonished. 'Why?' he asked. Haidari Khan replied, 'What is it to you? If you have me put to death there will never again be another Haidari Khan. Whereas if *you* die there'll at once be another King.' The King was much displeased, and turned away, and Haidari Khan seized the opportunity to make his escape.

A Memorable Delhi Mushaira

FARHATULLAH BEG

A mushaira in aristocratic circles was conducted in accordance with a strict etiquette, as Beg's description conveys. The setting is the court of the last Mughal emperor. The mushaira begins late in the evening and will continue throughout the night. The poets take their seats on the carpet. When proceedings begin, a lighted candle is passed around, and when it is set down before a poet this means that it is his turn to recite. Every poet who participates, from the youngest to the oldest and most eminent, faces the critical assessment of his audience. Couplet by couplet they courteously but uninhibitedly let him know their estimate of its worth. Often the mushaira is hosted by a prominent noble who prescibes a misra-i-tarah—*that is, a half-line of verse which every participating poet has to incorporate in the poem he is to present there. Much importance is attached to a poet's technical skills—his command of metre, rhyme and figures of speech. For even the greatest poets, a mushaira is a contest in which they need the skills not only of a poet, but those of an orator, a public performer and a debater.*

~

The candle was set down before Ghulam Rasul Shauq. He's old now, poor fellow. He leads the prayers in the Azizabadi mosque. In his early days Zauq [now the ustad of the Mughal Emperor] used to submit his verses to him for correction, and on the strength of that he still calls himself Zauq's ustad and thinks that Zauq should still bring his verses to him to correct. He seems to one to have grown somewhat senile. The opening couplet of the ghazal he recited was quite a forceful one, but of the rest, the less said the better.

Ghalib, Momin, Azurda, Sahbai—in short all the masters of the art [of poetry], began to tease Zauq, exclaiming loudly in praise of our friend Shauq's verse. Shauq thought that they were genuinely praising him and could not see that they were making a fool of him. The moment anyone cried out in praise he turned his gaze upon Zauq and said, 'You see? *This* is the way to write poetry.' Zauq, poor man, would laugh and make no reply. One or two of his shagirds would want to reply, but he restrained them.

The next to recite was Alexander Heatherley, whose takhallus [pen name] was Azad. He is French, but he was born and brought up in Delhi, where he lived until he went to Alwar as captain of artillery. He is about twenty or twenty-one years old, and is qualified in medicine too. He loves poetry, and is Arif's* shagird. Whenever he hears that a mushaira is going to be held he comes straight to Delhi. He dresses in his military uniform, but converses in Urdu, and his Urdu is as pure as any Delhi man's. His verse is not bad, and for a Frenchman to compose Urdu verse as he does is something truly remarkable...

Earlier in the mushaira one of the palace officials who recited well had been called upon to recite a ghazal sent by the heir-apparent of the King, who had not himself come to the mushaira. Farhatullah Beg gives four couplets of it and comments:

The ghazal was totally undistinguished, but it was the heir-apparent's, and it needed courage to refrain from praise. But Ghalib and Momin sat absolutely silent. This did not please some of those present who had come from the Fort [i.e. the Red Fort, the seat of the Mughal royal family.] But they knew very well that even if the King himself presented a ghazal which was not up to standard, those two would not so much as nod their heads.

---

* Ghalib's wife's nephew, whom Ghalib looked upon as his son.

...The candle came to Nawab Mustafa Khan Shefta. He is an acknowledged master of the art of poetry. He is a shagird of Momin, but is himself an ustad. When he praises a couplet this establishes its worth, and if he is silent, this devalues it in the eyes of others too. He recited a ghazal [of seven couplets] which was greeted with praise, but praise very soberly expressed. In big mushairas I have seen that those present will encourage newcomers with their praise, but when the time comes for the masters to recite, the atmosphere is more restrained and more solemn, and only those couplets will be praised that deserve to be praised. And this is as the masters wish it to be. If any couplet is praised beyond its worth, this distresses them. They seek praise only for those couplets that they themselves think deserving of praise. And when they recite they look only to their equals, and it is they alone who express their appreciation.

The numerous members of the royal family, sons of numerous wives and concubines, regarded themselves as the arbiters of taste both in dress and in language, and were especially ready to criticize any of their number who had left Delhi to live in other cities, such as Lucknow and Benares. The poet Haya was made to feel this when it came to his turn to recite.

Haya is a man of happy temperament, a good man—intelligent, humorous, and a spontaneous poet. He is about thirty-five or thirty-six and normally lives in Benares, visiting Delhi only occasionally. He looks just like the other princes except that he is clean shaven and dresses in Lucknow style. In poetry, he was at first his father's shagird, then Shah Nasir's, and now Zauq's. He is an excellent chess-player. He learnt chess from Hakim Ashraf Ali Khan, but these days it is Momin that he plays with. He plays the sitar beautifully. He is a good poet too, but he does not work hard at it, and sacrifices meaning to colourful language. He presented a ghazal [of six couplets].

His father rebuked him for a fault in the fifth couplet:

'Since you went to Lucknow you've changed your style of dress. And now you've changed your language too. You've made *saans* [the Urdu word for 'breath'] feminine.' [Haya replied that he had followed Zauq's usage, and quoted a line of Zauq in support, and his father retorted] 'I ask you, can the ustad's usage be any authority when it conflicts with ours? He may write as he pleases. Just tell me this: in the Fort is saans masculine or feminine?' Haya, poor fellow, smiled and said nothing.

> *Other poets defended themselves more vigorously—not to say brazenly, no matter how eminent the critic. Such a one was 'Mir Sahib', (not the great Mir of the eighteenth century.) It was late at night when the candle was set before him, and as soon as people saw that it was his turn to recite all of them roused themselves.*

Some rubbed their eyes. Some got up and splashed water on their faces. No one wanted to doze or sleep any more. The mention of his name had alerted them all. The great poets were smiling and the young ones whispering to one another... There's no one in Delhi who doesn't know Mir Sahib, no mushaira which is not enlivened by his presence, no gathering where his entry does not brighten things up. There may be a handful of people who know his name, but I have never known him as anything but 'Mir Sahib'. He is seventy years old, a tall man withered and dried up, with drooping eyelids, a nose like a parrot's beak, a wide mouth, a long beard, grizzled hair and fair complexion. Describe him, and any child in Delhi will direct you to him. He dresses entirely in spotless white, and wears an impressively grave and solemn expression, but when he gets angry there's no controlling him... At mushairas everyone used to tease him, from the King downwards... He always composed his ghazals off the cuff, and never took the trouble of writing them down beforehand. He saw no need to match the two lines of a couplet. All he was concerned with was the rhyme. Whatever he had to say he would recite with complete aplomb in prose, breaking off in between times to rebut people's objections,

and when he got tired of that he would finish off his 'verse' with
the rhyme. As soon as he started reciting he would be showered
with criticisms from all sides.

> *That night he and his critics ran true to form. He rebuffed a criticism*
> *of Ghalib, telling him that he knew nothing about certain metres. This*
> *lively atmosphere continued practically a full hour...*

> *It was the convention that the most eminent poets' turn to recite would*
> *come last. In this mushaira Momin and Ghalib were two of the last*
> *to recite.*

[Momin was a man of striking appearance.] When the candle
was set before him the assembly quietened, for all were eager to
hear the verse of the master. He picked up the candle and moved
it forward a little, sat up straight, passed his fingers through his
long hair... and in a voice full of emotion began to recite a ghazal
[of eight couplets]. It was as though he had cast a spell on the
assembly. All sat there enthralled, and he too felt the impact of his
own poetry; at those verses which held the strongest appeal his
fingers moved more quickly through his hair... He acknowledged
praise with a slight motion of his head. His style of recitation is
all his own. He gestures very little with his hands. (How could
he when they are so busy with his hair?) It is the modulation of
his voice and the expression of his eyes that casts a spell. When
he had finished his ghazal all the guests present expressed their
praise. He smiled and said, 'Your kindness is the reward of all my
labours. I have already said:

> I seek appreciation; I am not concerned with wealth
> Just critics' praises give me all the recompense I need.'

Ghalib's style is quite different. When the candle was set before
him it was nearly dawn. He said, 'Now gentlemen, I too shall sing
my mournful song.' And he began to recite, raising his voice in a
tone so majestic and so compelling that the whole assembly was
lost in contemplation—a tone that seemed to say that there was no
one who could truly appreciate his worth.

This was the ghazal he recited:[*]

> O foolish heart, what has befallen you?
> Do you not know this sickness[†] has no cure?

>> dil e naadaan tujhe hua kya hai?
>> aakhir is dard ki dava kya hai?

> I long for her, and she is weary of me
> O Lord above, tell me, what does this mean?

>> hum hain mushtaaq aur vo be-zaar
>> ya ilaahi ye maajra kya hai?

> I too possess a tongue like other men
> If only you would ask me what I seek!

>> main bhi munh mein zabaan rakhta hoon
>> kaash poochho ki mudda'a kya hai

> When all is You, and nought exists but You
> Tell me, O Lord, why all this turmoil too?

>> jab ki tujh bin nahin koi maujood
>> phir ye hangaama, e khuda, kya hai?

> These fair-faced women, with their coquetries,
> Their glances, airs and graces, what are these?

>> ye pari-chahra log kaise hain?
>> ghamza o ishva o ada kya hai?

> Why the sweet perfume of their coiling tresses?
> Why the collyrium that adorns their eyes?

---

[*] This ghazal is one of Ghalib's most famous, and illustrates the variety in content of the ghazal's successive couplets very well. The four couplets addressed to God (couplets 4, 5, 6 and 7) form a continuous whole (discussed on p. 195), and are sandwiched between others, in some of which the poet is addressing his mistress (3, 10, 11), and in others someone other than her (1, 2, and 8)—perhaps himself.

[†] Love.

    shikan e zulf e anbareen kyon hai?
    nigah e chashm e surma sa kya hai?

Where does the grass, where do the flowers come from?
What is the cloud made of? What is the breeze?

    sabza o gul kahaan se aae hain?
    abr kya cheez hai? hava kya hai?

See how I look to her for loyalty
Who does not even know what loyalty is.

    hum ko un se vafa ki hai ummeed
    jo nahin jaante vafa kya hai

I would lay down my very life for you
I do not know what *praying* for you means.

    jaan tum par nisaar karta hoon
    main nahin jaanta dua kya hai

I grant that you are right: Ghalib is nothing.
But if you get him free, then what's the harm?

    main ne maana ki kuchh nahin Ghalib
    muft haath aae to bura kya hai?

When Ghalib had finished he smiled and said, 'If even now there is anyone who doesn't understand I must leave him in God's hands.'

Those present knew he was referring to an incident in his early days as a poet, when Hakim Agha Jan Aish had written a poem mocking him for his obscure style, and had recited it at a mushaira at which Ghalib was present:

    What is the point of writing verse which only you can
        understand?
    A poet feels the thrill of joy when others too can
        understand.

We understand the verse of Mir, we understand what
    Sauda wrote;
But Ghalib's verse!—Save he and God, we know not who
    can understand!

Hakim Agha Jan Aish took the point and said, 'Mirza Sahib,* we
must be thankful that at last you've shown some understanding of
the proper style.' In short, praise and humour together.

---

* Mirza: The standard form of address for one who, like Ghalib, was one
of Turkish descent.

A Memoir of Ghalib

ALTAF HUSAIN HALI

Many of the anecdotes in Hali's memoir are examples of Ghalib's cheerful, and openly avowed, refusal to conform to the more inconvenient commands of his Muslim. He drank wine, never said the five prescribed daily prayers, never kept the month-long Ramzan fast (Ramadan), and never performed the pilgrimage to Mecca:

A man, in Ghalib's presence, strongly condemned wine-drinking, and said that the prayers of the wine-bibber are never granted. 'My friend,' said Ghalib, 'if a man has wine, what else does he *need* to pray for?'

He used to take a little wine at bedtime, but he never drank more than the amount that he had prescribed for himself. The key of the box in which he kept his bottles of wine was entrusted to his steward, who had strict instructions that if ever he contemplated drinking more than the fixed amount, he was on no account to agree or to hand over the key.

He often used to compose his verses at night, under the influence of wine. When he had worked out a complete verse he would tie a knot in his sash, and there would be as many as eight to ten knots by the time he retired to bed. In the morning he would recall them, with no other aid to his memory, and would write them down...

When the British forces re-occupied Delhi after the uprising of 1857, Ghalib was summoned for questioning by a British officer, Colonel Burn. Hali writes:

I have heard that when Ghalib came before Colonel Brown [Burn] he was wearing a tall Turkish-style head-dress. The Colonel looked at this strange fashion and asked in broken Urdu, 'Well? You Muslim?' 'Half,' said Ghalib. 'What does that mean?' asked the Colonel. Ghalib said, 'I drink wine, but I don't eat pork.' The Colonel laughed...

Ghalib himself had commented on this incident:

To tell the truth—for to hide the truth is not the way of a man free in spirit—I am no more than half a Muslim, for I am free from the bonds of convention and religion and have liberated my soul from the fear of men's tongues.

Once during Ramzan he was visited by Maulana Azurda, a famous scholar of Islamic law and a poet of Persian, with whom he was friendly. The Muslim calendar is lunar, and over the years Ramzan therefore moves through the whole range of the solar year; that year it was in the hottest season:

The room in which Ghalib spent his day was over the main gateway of the house, and leading off it to one side was another little room, small and dark, and with a doorway so low that one had to stoop right down to go through it. In this room there was a carpet laid on the floor, and in the hot season, when the hot wind was blowing, Ghalib usually spent the day there from ten in the morning until four in the afternoon. One day during the hot season in the month of Ramzan Maulana Azurda came to visit him when the sun was at its hottest. Ghalib was sitting in this little room with a companion playing backgammon... Azurda went in, and when he saw him playing backgammon during Ramzan said, 'I have read in the Traditions* that during Ramzan Satan is held prisoner; but what I see today makes me doubt the authenticity of this tradition.' 'Respected sir,' Ghalib replied, 'the Tradition is completely authentic. But I should perhaps inform you that the place where he is held prisoner is this very room!'

* Traditions: see note p. 85.

His attitude to God was anything but humble.

He was lying on his bed at night looking up at the sky. He was struck by the apparent chaos in the distribution of the stars and said, 'There is no rhyme or reason in anything the self-willed do. Just look at the stars—scattered in complete disorder. No proportion, no system, no sense, no pattern. But their King has absolute power, and no one can breathe a word against Him!'

From all the duties of worship and the enjoined practices of Islam he took only two—a belief that God is one and is immanent in all things, and a love for the Prophet and his family. And this alone he considered sufficient for salvation.

~

Hali gives a moving account of an incident that occurred towards the end of Ghalib's life. He had brought a legal action against a man, and the storm that this raised both surprised and distressed him.

When Ghalib brought his action some little time elapsed, and then people began to send him anonymous letters... cursing him for being a wine-drinker and an irreligious man, and so on, and expressing the fiercest hatred and contempt and condemnation. They had a powerful effect on Ghalib. In those days he was extremely depressed all the time and dispirited, and whenever the postman came with the mail his whole expression would change, from apprehension that there would be some such letter in it. It so happened that in those days I had occasion to go to Delhi with the late Mustafa Khan [Shefta]. I did not know about these contemptible anonymous letters, and in my ignorance one day I committed a blunder the very thought of which always fills me with shame. Those were the days when I was drunk with religious self-satisfaction. I thought that in all God's creation only the Muslims, and of the seventy-three Muslim sects only the Sunnis, and of the Sunnis only the Hanafis, and of the Hanafis only those who performed absolutely meticulously the fasts and prayers and other outward observances, would be found worthy of salvation and forgiveness—as though the scope of God's mercy were more confined and restricted than Queen Victoria's empire, where men of every religion and creed live peacefully together. The greater the love and affection I felt for a man, the more strongly I desired that he should meet his end in the state in which alone, as I thought, he could attain salvation and forgiveness; and since the love and affection I felt for Ghalib were intense, I always lamented his fallen state, thinking, so to say, that in the garden of Rizwan [in Paradise] we should no more be together and that after death we should never see each other again. One day, throwing to the winds all regard for Ghalib's eminence and talent and advanced years, I began to read him a dry-as-dust lecture like an arid preacher. His deafness was by now complete, and one could only converse with him by writing what one had to say. So I wrote a long-winded lecture all about how the five prayers were obligatory and how he must perform them, and laid it before him. It requested him to start saying the five prayers regularly—standing, sitting, by token gestures, in any way at all he found possible; if he could not perform ablution with water before them, then he should use dust to cleanse himself, but he should in no case fail to perform the prayers. Ghalib deeply resented this initiative on my part, and indeed, with every justification—and the more so because in those days anonymous letter-writers were attacking him in the most unseemly terms for his way of life, expressing their hatred and contempt for him in the sort of downright abuse one hears in the market-place. What Ghalib said in reply to my stupid note is worthy of attention. He said, 'I have spent my life in sin and wrong-doing. I have never said a prayer or kept a fast or done any other good deed. Soon I shall breathe no more. Now if in my few remaining days I say my prayers—sitting, or by token gestures—how will that make up for a lifetime of sin? I deserve that when I die my friends and kinsmen should blacken my face and tie a rope round my feet and exhibit me in all the streets and by-lanes and markets of Delhi, and then take me outside the city and leave me there for the dogs and kites and crows to eat—if they can bring themselves to eat such a thing. Though my sins are such that I deserve even worse than that, yet without doubt I believe in the oneness of God, and in the moments of quiet and solitude the words "There is no god but God" and "Nothing exists but God" and "God alone works manifest in all things" are ever on my lips.'

It was perhaps on that same day when this exchange was over and Ghalib was taking his food, that the postman came with a letter... Ghalib concluded that it was another anonymous letter... and handed it to me, telling me to open it and read it. When I looked at it I found that it contained nothing but obscene abuse. He asked me, 'Who is it from? And what does he say?' I hesitated to tell him, and he snatched it out of my hand saying, 'Perhaps it is from one of your spiritual disciples.' Then he read it from start to finish. At one point the writer had even abused Ghalib's mother. Ghalib smiled and said, 'This idiot doesn't even know how to abuse a man. If your man is elderly or middle-aged you abuse his daughter... If he's young, you abuse his wife... and if he's only a boy you abuse his mother. This pimp abuses the mother of a man of seventy-two. Who could be a bigger fool than that?'

~

When Ghalib was not noticeably humble towards God, it was not to be expected that he would fawn upon any of his fellow men. Even with his royal patron Bahadur Shah, while remaining within the conventional formalities he behaves as though he were dealing with an equal.

One day Bahadur Shah, accompanied by Ghalib and a number of other courtiers, was walking in the Hayat Bakhsh or the Mahtab Garden. The mango trees of every variety were laden with fruit, but the fruit of these gardens was reserved exclusively for the King and his queens and members of the royal family. Ghalib looked at the mangoes repeatedly, and with great concentration. The King asked him, 'Mirza, what are you looking at so attentively?' Ghalib replied with joined hands, 'My Lord and Guide, some ancient poet has written:

Upon the top of every fruit is written clear and legibly:
This is the property of A, the son of B, the son of C.

And I am looking to see whether any of these bear my name
and those of my father and grandfather.' The King smiled and the
same day had a big basket of the finest mangoes sent to him.

*The King's real name was Siraj-ud-Din—he took the name Bahadur
Shah when he came to the throne. Once Ghalib composed for his
entertainment a verse which neatly combines a compliment to the King
with a compliment to himself, suggesting that the King matches a
revered medieval saint Nizam-ud-Din in holiness and spiritual power,
while Ghalib matches Amir Khusrau, who was universally honoured
as one of the greatest of the old Persian poets:*

Ghalib frequently recited verses for the King's amusement. On one
occasion when the court was assembled the conversation turned
on the close relations that had existed between Nizam-ud-Din and
Amir Khusrau. Ghalib at once composed and recited the following
verse:

> Two holy guides; two suppliants. In this God's power we see.
> Nizam-ud-Din had Khusrau: Siraj-ud-Din has me.
>
> mile do mursheedon ko qudrat e haq se do taalib
> nizaam ud deen ko khusrau siraaj ud deen ko Ghalib

I have been told that when Ghalib recited the ghazal that ends,

> With what style you handle, Ghalib, all these themes of
>   mystic teaching!
> What a saint we would have thought you if you had not
>   been a drinker!
>
> ye misaa'il e tasavvuf, ye tira bayaan Ghalib
> tujhe hum vali samajhte jo na baada-khvaar hota!

the King commented, 'No, my friend; even so we should never
have counted you a saint.' Ghalib replied, 'Your Majesty counts me

one even now, and only speaks like this lest my sainthood should go to my head.'

~

As a poet he would not express approval of any verse he did not like; but he was generous in his praise of those he did like, even where they were by poets of whom he held a poor opinion. Hali writes:

In our society it is the general rule that when a man recites his verse, every line—good or bad—is greeted with cries of approval, and no one distinguishes between a good line and a bad one. Ghalib's way was quite the opposite of this. No matter how revered and respected a poet might be, until he heard a line that he really liked he never on any account expressed appreciation. Towards the end of his life he became completely deaf, but this was not the case in earlier years. One had to raise one's voice in speaking or reciting to him, but if this was done he could hear perfectly well. Yet until he heard a verse that really appealed to him he would remain quite unmoved. Some of his contemporaries were offended by this attitude, and that is why they found fault with Ghalib's poetry; but although Ghalib was by temperament one who did not like to quarrel with anybody, he never deviated from his practice in this respect.

Yet to any verse that did move him, he gave praise that was almost extravagant—not because he wanted to please anyone, but because his own love of poetry compelled him to praise it. His rivalry with Zauq is well-known. Yet one day when Ghalib was absorbed in a game of chess, the late Munshi Ghulam Ali Khan recited this verse of Zauq to someone else who was present:

Tired of all this, we look to death for our release
But what if even after death we find no peace?

ab to ghabra ke ye kahte hain ke mar jaaenge
mar ke bhi chain na paaya to kidhar jaaenge?

He used to say, 'The moment Ghalib caught some snatch of this he at once left his game and asked me, "What was that verse you recited?" I recited it again. "Whose verse is it?" he said. I told him it was Zauq's. He was astonished, and made me recite it again and again, savouring it every time I did so.'

You may see in his Urdu letters that he speaks of this verse repeatedly, and wherever he quotes examples of good verses, this one is always included. In the same way, when he heard this verse of Momin's:

> I seem to feel that you are by my side
> When all are gone and I am quite alone

> tum mere paas hote ho goya
> jab koi doosra nahin hota

He praised it highly and said, 'I wish Momin Khan would take my whole *diwan* [collection of ghazals] and give me this one verse in exchange.' This verse too he has quoted in many of his letters.

Ghalib's Letters

Ghalib publicly expressed the view that Persian was the real medium of poetry and literary prose, and Urdu much inferior to it, but this was to some extent a pose. This is clear from the pride and joy in his own Urdu verse that he expresses in his private letters. In one written in 1851 he writes:

Today at midday I wrote a ghazal which I shall take and recite to [the King] tomorrow or the day after. I'm writing it out, and will send it to you too. Judge it truly: if Urdu verse can rise to the height where it can cast a spell or work a miracle, will this, or will this not, be its form?

And in 1852:

My friend, in God's name, give my ghazal its due of praise. If this is Urdu poetry, what was it that Mir and Mirza wrote? And if that was Urdu poetry, then what is this?

In other words, my verse is in another class from that of Mir and Mirza (the colloquial names for Mir and Sauda, the two greatest Urdu poets of the eighteenth century)—so much so that you cannot call their work and mine by the same name.

His letters give important insights into his attitude to poetry—both poetry in general, and his own:

The rhythmic speech which men call poetry finds a different place in each man's heart and presents a different aspect to each man's eyes. Men who make poetry all pluck the strings with a different touch and from each instrument bring forth a different melody. Pay no heed to what others see and feel, and bend all your efforts to increase your own perception. Poetry is the creation of meaning, not the matching of rhymes.

> *He was sometimes asked by his friends to compose odes to prospective patrons or to mark a death or birth by composing a chronogram—i.e. a phrase which both refer to an event and at the same time give its date when the numerical value of the individual letters is added up. On occasion he did so, but these were tasks which he undertook very reluctantly:*

My friend, I swear to you by your life and by my faith that I am a complete stranger to the art of the chronogram. You won't have heard of any chronogram by me in Urdu. I have composed a few in Persian, but the position there is that while the verses are mine, the words giving the date were supplied by others. Do you understand me? Calculation is a headache to me, and I can't even add up. Whenever I work out a chronogram I always find that I've calculated it wrongly. There were one or two of my friends who, if the need arose, could work out for me the words which gave the required date, and I would fit them into a verse.

> *On at least one occasion he refused a request for one:*

The lion feeds its cubs on the prey it has hunted, and teaches them to hunt their prey. When they grow up they hunt for themselves. You have become a competent poet, and you have a natural talent. Why should *you* not compose a chronogram on the birth of your child? Why trouble me, an old man grieved at heart? Ala-ud-Din Khan, I swear by your life: I worked out a chronogram-name for your first son and put it into a verse; and the child did not live. The fancy haunts me that this was the effect of my inauspicious stars. No one whom I praise survives it. One ode apiece was enough to dispatch Nasir-ud-Din Haidar and Amjad Ali Shah [Kings of Oudh]. Wajid Ali Shah [the last king] stood up to three, and then collapsed. A man to whom I addressed ten to twenty odes would end up on the far side of oblivion. No, my friend, may God protect me, I will neither write a chronogram on his birth nor work out a chronogram-name. May Exalted God preserve you and your children and confer long life and wealth and prosperity on you all.

He accepted the occasional necessity to write an ode in praise of a patron, but he did not like writing them and certainly did not approve of writing them where there was no need to do so. He writes to his Hindu friend and fellow poet, Hargopal Tufta:

Listen to me, my friend. The man to whom you addressed your ode is as much a stranger to the art of poetry as you and I are to the problems of our respective religions. In fact you and I, in spite of our ignorance of religious matters, at any rate have no aversion to them while this is a fellow whom poetry makes sick... These people aren't fit to be spoken of, much less to be praised.

Much of his correspondence with his friends is occasioned by the fact that, as an eminent poet, many of them made him their ustad—mentor in poetry—and sent their verses to him for correction and improvement. As ustad he was kind, but exacting. He writes to Tufta:

I recall that I had taken your half-line and re-fashioned it into a rhymed couplet... In this form it appealed to me so much that I was tempted not to let you have it back but to use it as the first verse of a ghazal of my own. But then I felt that I must not begrudge it you, and I sent it to you. Your lordship didn't choose to study it. You had been drinking when you wrote to me, and you must have been in the same condition when you went through the corrected verse. Now you are to delete the half-line you have written and let my couplet stand. It's a good one... My friend, when I correct your verses, read the corrections carefully, so that the labour I spend on them is not wasted.

In Urdu and Persian poetics immense importance was attached to precedent. An apprentice-poet whose ustad criticized some expression in his verse would, if he could, justify himself by producing a precedent from the verse of a classical poet. Ghalib was not unduly impressed.

He wrote to Tufta, who had produced a Persian verse, quoting a well-known saying in Persian:

'To find fault with our elders is a fault.' My dear friend, in such instances we should not find fault with the verse of the classical writers; but we should not follow them either. Your humble servant will not tolerate a double plural; nor will he say anything against the great Saib.

And again:

In this couplet Hazin [a classical Persian poet] has written one *hanoz** too many, it is superfluous and absurd, and you cannot regard it as a precedent to be followed. It is a plain blunder, a fault, a flaw. Why should we imitate it? Hazin was only human, but if the couplet were the angel Gabriel's you are not to regard it as an authority, and are not to imitate it.

He replied to a correspondent whose writing he had praised and who had suggested that Ghalib was flattering him:

Your humble servant has many faults, and one of them is that he does not tell lies. Because I am a man of noble family that has had ties with the [British] authorities, I often have occasion to meet persons in authority and to have dealings with them from time to time. I have never flattered any of them. I ask you why should I lie to you, respected sir? Why should I flatter you?

...and similarly, to another correspondent:

Friend, my greetings to you. Your letter came, and I read both your ghazals and rejoiced. Flattery is not your humble servant's way, and if flattery be allowed to enter into matters where the craft of poetry is concerned, then a man's shagird cannot perfect himself. Remember you've never yet sent me a ghazal in which I have not made corrections, especially of Urdu usage. These two ghazals are, in word and content, without blemish.

---

* Hanoz: still, yet (as in 'It's still a long way to go').

Sometimes his replies seem to have got lost in the post:

Lord and Master, it was twelve o'clock, and I was lying on my bed practically naked smoking the hookah when the servant brought your letter to me. As luck would have it, I was wearing neither shirt nor coat, otherwise I'd have rent my clothes in frenzy. (Not that your lordship would have lost anything by that—*I* would have been the one to suffer by it.) Let's begin at the beginning. I corrected your ode and sent it off. I received an acknowledgement. Some of the cancelled verses were sent back to me with a request to be told what was wrong with them. I explained what was wrong with them, wrote in words that were acceptable in place of those to which I had objected, and said that you might now include these verses too in the ode. To this day I have had no reply to this letter. I handed over to Shah Asrar ul Haq the paper addressed to him and wrote to you the verbal message he gave in reply. This letter too your Lordship has not answered.

> My heart is vibrant with complaint as is the harp with music.
> Give it the slightest touch and hear the strains it will pour
>   forth.

> pur hoon main shikve se yun raag se jaise baaja
> ik zara chhediye, phir dekhiye kya hota hai

I think to myself, I sent both letters unstamped. I cannot conceive that they should have been lost. Anyway, it was a long time ago. No point in complaining now. You don't re-heat stale food, and 'service means servitude' [a proverbial saying].

On another occasion he cheerfully admits his own responsibility:

Exalted sir, the ghazal your servant brought has gone where I am going—to oblivion. That is, I have lost it.

His distrust of the British postal services was a long-standing one. Letters that date from as early as 1848 express it, and in 1854 he writes to a friend:

What do you think of the state of the British postal services? I don't know what innovations they've introduced, but all organization is at an end and you simply can't place any reliance on it. An Englishman had one or two of his letters in English go astray. He spoke to the post-office here about it and when nobody paid any attention to him, he addressed a complaint to the head postmaster. He got a reply to say that they accepted no responsibility; he had handed in his letter and they had sent it off; it was not up to them whether or not it reached its destination. Complaints have come from Meerut too, and one hears the same thing in letters from Agra. So far no letter of mine has gone astray, but in a general epidemic who is safe? I've felt obliged to make a new rule. I've sent word to Major John Jacob at Agra and to you at Aligarh and to a cousin of mine—my mother's brother's son—at Banda, and one or two other friends in various districts, telling them that in future we should send our letters to each other unstamped. Neither of us will owe the other anything, and it puts our minds at ease. In future if you send me a letter postage pre-paid I shall be cross with you. Send them unstamped; and get Munshi Hargopal Tufta to do the same; in fact show him what I have written. A lot of pre-paid letters go astray. Unstamped ones can be trusted to get there.

And a few months later:

The post-office department has gone all to pieces. It may have been an idle foreboding, but I had thought it proper, as a precaution, to start sending my letters unstamped. The letter would go to the post-office and I would get a receipt—stamped with a red-ink stamp for a pre-paid letter and a black-ink stamp for an unstamped one. My mind was at rest, because I could look at my mail-book and remind myself on what date I had sent such-and-such a letter and how I had sent it. Now they've put a big box in the post-office. It has an open mouth and anyone who wants to post a letter can go and drop it in the box and come away. No receipt, no stamp, no evidence of posting. God knows whether the letter will be despatched or not. And even if it is, when it gets to the other end there's no prospect of a tip to tempt the postman to deliver it, and no incentive to the authorities to collect what is due on it. They may not even give it to the postman to deliver, and even if they do he may not deliver it. And if it doesn't arrive, the sender has nothing in writing to base a claim on—not, that is, unless he pays four annas extra and sends it registered; and we send off letters all over the place practically every other day. Where are we going to get eight annas and more a week to register them all? Suppose I calculate that a letter weighs three *masha* and stick a half-anna stamp on it. It turns out that it's two *ratti* overweight, and the addressee has to pay double. So you're forced to keep a balance to weigh your letters. The tongue of every balance is different, and shows a slightly different weight. In short, sending off a letter is a headache; it's asking for trouble. I've written this letter on 10th Muharram. Tomorrow I'll send for the necessary stamps, stick them on the envelope and send it off. It's like shooting an arrow in a dark room. If it hits, it hits, and if it misses, it misses.

~

Ghalib had always kept in touch by letter with friends and fellow poets in other parts of India, but after the revolt of 1857 he felt an urgent need to do so. He had been in Delhi when it was in the hands of the rebel soldiers, and witnessed terrible atrocities on both sides. Once the British had taken control they expelled almost all Muslims and Hindus living in Delhi, and Ghalib was only able to stay because he was protected by the Sikh Maharaja of Patiala, who had supported the British throughout. Hindu residents were allowed to return three months later but it was more than two years before Muslims were allowed to. All this time Ghalib was there, and terribly lonely. His friends were scattered far and wide. He comforted himself by writing letter after letter to them. He wrote to Tufta:

In this solitude it is letters that keep me alive. Someone writes to me and I feel he has come to see me. By God's favour not a day passes but three or four letters come from this side and that; in fact there are days when I get letters by both posts—one or two in the morning and one or two in the afternoon. I spend the day reading them and answering them, and it keeps me happy. Why is it that for ten and twelve days together you haven't written—that is haven't been to see me? Write to me, Sahib. Write why you haven't written. Don't grudge the half-anna postage. And if you're *so* hard up send the letter unstamped.

In other letters to Tufta he describes the acute sense of loss which the catastrophe of 1857 caused him. He begins it with a couplet from one of his own ghazals:

If Ghalib sings in bitter strain, forgive him;
Today pain stabs more keenly at his heart.

rakhiyo Ghalib mujhe is talkh navaai mein muaaf
aaj kuchh dard mire dil mein siva hota hai.

My kind friend, first I have to ask you to convey my greetings to my old friend Mir Mukarram Husain Sahib. Tell him that I am still alive and that more than that even I do not know... Listen, my friend, when a man has the means to devote all his days free of care to the pursuit of the things he loves, *that* is what luxury means. The abundant time and energy you give to poetry is proof of your noble qualities and your sound disposition; and brother, the fame of your poetic achievement adds lustre to my name too. As for me, I have forgotten how to write poetry, and forgotten all the verses I ever wrote too—or rather, all except a couplet-and-a-half of my Urdu verse—that is, one final couplet of a ghazal, and one line. This is the couplet. Whenever my heart sinks within me it comes to my lips and I recite it—five times, ten times—over and over again:

Ghalib, when *this* is how my life has passed
How can I call to mind I had a God?

zindagi apni jab is shakl se guzri, Ghalib
hum bhi kya yaad karenge ki khuda rakhte the?

And when I feel at the end of my tether I recite this line to myself: 'O sudden death, why do you still delay?' and relapse into silence. Do not think that it is grief for my own misery or my own ruin that is choking me. I have a deeper sorrow, so deep that I cannot attempt to tell you, and can only hint at it. Among the English whom those infamous black scoundrels slaughtered, some were the focus of my hopes, some my well-wishers, some my friends, some my bosom companions, and some my pupils in poetry. Amongst the Indians some were my kinsmen, some my friends, some my pupils and some men whom I loved. And all of them are laid low in the dust. How grievous it is to mourn *one* loved one. What must his life be like who has to mourn so many? Alas! so many of my friends are dead that now if I should die there will be none to weep for me. 'Verily we are for God, and verily to Him we shall return.' [An Arabic sentence commonly spoken when someone dies.]

He attached great value to personal friendships, and he made them without regard to his friends' religion or race:

I hold all mankind to be my kin, and look upon all men—Muslim, Hindu, Christian—as my brothers, no matter what others may think.

He once wrote to Tufta:

What you have written is unkind and suspicious! Could I be cross with you? May God forbid! I pride myself that I have one friend in India who truly loves me; his name is Hargopal, and his pen-name Tufta. What could you write which would upset me? And as for what someone else may whisper, let me tell you how matters stand there. I had but one brother, who died after thirty years of madness. Suppose he had lived and had been sane and had said anything against you: I would have rebuked him and been angry with him.

He lived on in Delhi for the rest of his life. He describes some of its tribulations in a letter of 1860:

Five invading armies have fallen upon this city one after another: the first was that of the rebel soldiers, which robbed the city of its good name. The second was that of the British, when life and property and honour and dwellings and those who dwelt in them and heaven and earth and all the visible signs of existence were stripped from it. The third was that of famine, when thousands of people died of hunger. The fourth was that of cholera, in which many whose bellies were full lost their lives. The fifth was the fever, which took general plunder of men's strength and powers of resistance. There were not many deaths, but a man who has had fever feels that all the strength has been drained from his limbs. And this invading army has not yet left the city. Two members of my own household are down with fever, the elder boy and my steward. May God restore both of them speedily to health.

~

His own personal life was full of disappointments. He was a very self-conscious aristocrat, inordinately proud of the greatness of his ancestors, and a firm believer in the principle of noblesse oblige; *and he felt correspondingly despondent about his own limited physical and material resources. Four years before his death he wrote:*

Of all the aspirations my Creator placed in me—to roam in happy poverty and independence, or to give freely from my ample bounty—not even a thousandth part of them was realized. I lacked the bodily strength; else I would have taken a staff in my hand, and hung from it a checkered mat and a tin drinking-vessel and a rope, and taken to the road on foot; now to Shiraz, now sojourning in Egypt, now making my way to Najaf I would have roamed. I lacked the means; else I would have played host to a world of men; or if I could not feast a world of men, no matter; at least within the city where I lived none would have gone hungry and unclad...

Within his straitened circumstances he lived as free and independent a life as he could and observed the high standards of conduct which aristocratic values demanded. Here too his aspirations were often thwarted. Patronage

*was meagre, and his own high standards of conduct often led him to clash
with others who proclaimed these same standards but did not observe
them—so much so that he wrote to a friend in 1861:*

You are a prey to grief and sorrow, but... to be the target of the
world's afflictions is proof of an inherent nobility—proof clear, and
argument conclusive.

*Marriage, and the need to incur debts if he were to maintain his
standards, were both an encumbrance to him and a fetter on his freedom.
He writes to a friend who proposed to arrange a second marriage for his
son after his first wife had died, leaving him two sons:*

My friend, you're involving the poor boy in the toils of marriage.
But, God keep them, Abdus Salam and Kulsum are enough to
preserve his name. For my part, my friend, I believe in Ibn-i-
Yamin's words:

> Wise is that man who in this world refrains from just two
>   things:
> He who would pass his days in peace must steel himself to
>   say,
> 'I will not wed, though I might have the daughter of a king;
> I will not borrow, though I get till Doomsday to repay.'

I hope it's not the case that he doesn't want to marry and you are
pushing him into this misfortune.

*He himself was too late to act on the first of these two pieces of advice.
(He had been married at the age of thirteen.) And he felt constrained
by circumstances to saddle himself with debt, a burden which he had to
bear all his adult life.*
*He loved children. In one of his letters he writes to a friend whose baby
son had died:*

My friend, I know exactly what such a loss means. In my seventy-
one years I have had seven children, both boys and girls, and none
lived to be more than fifteen months. You are still young. May
Exalted God give you patience, and another son in his place.

He looked upon his wife's nephew Arif as a son, but Arif and his wife
died within a year of each other in 1851 and 1852 respectively. Ghalib
thereupon took their two sons, then aged five and two, into his own
home, and they brought much comfort to him. When Tufta once wrote to
him apologizing for sending him so many verses to correct, he replied:

Listen, my good sir. You know that the late [Arif] was my 'son' and
that now both his children, my grandsons, have come to live with
me, and that they plague me every minute of the day, and I put
up with it. God is my witness that you are a son to me. Hence the
products of your inspiration are my spiritual grandsons. When I do
not lose patience with these, my physical grandsons, who do not
let me have my dinner in peace, who walk with their bare feet all
over my bed, upset water here, and raise clouds of dust there—how
can my spiritual grandsons, who do none of these things, upset
me? Post them off at once for me to look at. I promise you I'll post
them back to you at once. May God Almighty grant long life to
your children—the children of this external world—and give them
wealth and prosperity, and may He preserve you to look after them.
And on your spiritual children, the products of your inspiration,
may He bestow increase of fame and the gift of men's approval.

To the day of his death he continued to hold himself responsible
for the fortunes of his two 'grandsons', and in his last severe illness
wrote increasingly desperate letters to his then long-time patron, the
Nawab of Rampur, begging him to send money so that he could pay
off his debts—to die in debt was a deep disgrace to a Muslim of noble
family—and to celebrate the wedding of his 'grandson'. The Nawab
did not respond.

From all these disappointments, and from his sense that the good things
in life never seem to last derives much of his philosophy of life. First, he
takes the stand that the pleasures of life are to be enjoyed to the full. He
loved mangoes and his enjoyment of them was uninhibited. They were
one of the many things that he loved in Calcutta, a city in which he had
spent nearly two years in his younger days, and of which he spoke with
great enthusiasm. A Persian couplet which he wrote there says:

> If all the fruits of Paradise lay there outspread before you
> The mangoes of Calcutta still would haunt your memory!

—and in a letter of 1860 to a friend in Marahra he describes how he used to eat them:

You invite me to Marahra and remind me that I had planned to come. In the days when my spirits were high and my strength intact, I once said to the late Shaikh Muhsin-ud-Din how I wished I could go to Marahra during the rains and eat mangoes to my heart's content and my belly's capacity. But where shall I find that spirit today, and from where recover the strength I once had? I neither have the same appetite for mangoes nor the same capacity to hold so many. I never ate them first thing in the morning, nor immediately after the midday meal; and I cannot say that I ate them between lunch and dinner because I never took an evening meal. I would sit down to eat them towards evening, when my food was fully digested, and I tell you bluntly, I would eat them until my belly was bloated and I could hardly breathe. Even now I eat them at the same time of day, but not more than ten to twelve, or if they are of the large kind, only six or seven.

> Alas! how the days of your youth have departed!
> Nay, rather the days of our life have departed!

~

But the transience of human pleasures made him wary of becoming dependent on them. This is most strikingly evident in his attitude to love, which in Mughal society was something which had nothing to do with marriage. In a Persian letter in his youth he had expressed how deeply he had been distressed when his first love died, and how he had come to realize that one should never allow oneself to be too attached to one beloved. His Urdu letters of a much later period show that he never changed this view. In 1860 he heard of the death of a courtesan who had been the mistress of one of his close friends. He wrote to him:

Mirza Sahib, I received your letter with its grievous news. When I had read it I gave it to Yusuf Ali Khan Aziz to read, and he told me of your relationship with her—how devoted to you she was and how much you loved her. I felt extremely sorry, and deeply grieved. Friend, we 'Mughal lads' are terrors; we are the death of those for whom we ourselves would die. Once in my life I was the death of a fair, cruel dancing girl. God grant both of them His forgiveness, and both of us, who bear the wounds of our beloveds' death, His mercy. It is forty years or more since it happened, and although I long ago abandoned such things and left the field once and for all, there are times even now when the memory of her charming ways comes back to me, and I shall not forget her death as long as I live. I know what you must be feeling.

> *We have no means of knowing how long an interval elapsed between this letter and the next, but it seems that his friend could not overcome his grief, and Ghalib adopts quite another tone in an effort to rally him:*

Mirza Sahib, I don't like the way you're going on. I have lived sixty-five years, and for fifty of them have seen all that this transient world of colour and fragrance has to show. In the days of my lusty youth a man of perfect wisdom counselled me, 'Abstinence I do not approve: dissoluteness I do not forbid. Eat, drink and be merry. But remember that the wise fly settles on the sugar, and not on the honey.' Well, I have always acted on his counsel. You cannot mourn another's death unless you live yourself. And why all these tears and lamentations? Give thanks to God for your freedom, and do not grieve. And if you love your chains so much, then a Munna Jan is as good as a Chunna Jan. When I think of paradise and consider how if my sins are forgiven me and I am installed in a palace with a houri, to live for ever in the worthy woman's company, I am filled with dismay and fear brings my heart into my mouth. How wearisome to find her always there!—a greater burden than a man could bear. The same old palace, all of emerald made: the same fruit-laden tree to cast its shade. And—God preserve her from all harm—the same old houri on my arm! Come to your senses, brother, and get yourself another.

> Take a new woman each returning spring,
> For last year's almanac's a useless thing.

His sense of the limitations which life imposes also led him to a more admirable conclusion—that life as such, all of life, is to be enjoyed. Five years earlier, in a letter to the same correspondent, he had written:

First I want to ask you a question. For several letters past I have noticed you lamenting your grief and sorrow. Why? If you have fallen in love with some fair cruel one, what room for complaint have you there? Rather should you wish your friends the same good fortune and seek increase of this pain.

At this point he starts writing of himself as if he were someone else—a common device among poets, perhaps from the habit of doing so in the final couplet of the ghazal, where it is obligatory to introduce their pen name. And ironically he uses of himself words always used of a saint after his death:

In the words of Ghalib (God's mercy be upon him!)

> You gave your heart away; why then lament your loss in
>   plaintive song?
> You have a breast without a heart; why not a mouth
>   without a tongue?

> kisi ko de ke dil koi navaasanj e fughaan kyon ho?
> na ho jab dil hi seene mein to phir munh mein zabaan
> kyon ho?

And what a fine second couplet!—

> Is this affliction not enough to work one's ruin utterly?
> With you as friend, what need is there for fate to be an
>   enemy?

> ye fitna aadmi ki khaana veeraani ko kya kam hai?
> hue tum dost jis ke dushman us ka aasmaan kyon ho?

And if—which God forbid—it is more mundane griefs that beset you, then my friend, you and I have the same sorrows to bear. I bear this burden like a man, and if you are a man, so must you. As the late Ghalib says:

> My heart, this pain and sorrow too is precious; for the time
>   will come
> You will not heave the midnight sigh, nor shed your tears
>   as morning dawns.

> dila, ye dard o alam bhi to mughtanim hai, ki aakhir
> na girya e sahri hai na aah e neemshabi hai

What cannot be helped, he thinks, must be accepted, and accepted serenely. He writes to another friend:

You've spent all you had in the bank, and what will you live on now? My friend, nothing that I suggest and nothing that you think of will make any difference. The heavens keep turning and what is to be, will be. We have no power, so what can we do?... Look at me—neither bound nor free, neither well nor ill, neither glad nor sad, neither dead nor alive. I go on living. I go on talking. I eat my daily bread and drink my occasional cup of wine. When death comes I will die and that will be an end of it. I neither give thanks nor make complaint.

He can even look at himself through others' eyes and empathize with their feelings:

I watch myself from the sidelines and rejoice at my own distress and degradation. In other words I see myself through the eyes of my enemy. At every blow that falls I say, Look! Ghalib's taken another beating! Such airs he used to give himself! I am a great poet, a great Persian scholar. Today for miles around there is none to match me!' Let us see *now* what he has to say to his creditors. Ghalib's finished; and call him Ghalib if you like; I call him atheist and infidel, and that's the truth! I have made up titles to confer upon him. When kings die they write after their names, Whose abode is in Heaven, or Who rests in Paradise. Well, he thought himself King of the Realm of Poetry, and I've devised the forms Who dwells in Hell, and Whose Station is Damnation to follow his name.

Come along, Star of the Realm! [A title bestowed upon him by the Mughal king.] One creditor has him by the scruff while another reviles him. And I say to him, Come, come, My Lord Nawab Sahib! How is it that you—yes, you a Seljuk, and an Afrasiyabi—are put to such indignity? Well, where is your tongue? Say something! Wine from the shop, and rosewater from the druggist's, and cloth from the draper's, and mangoes from the fruiterer's, and loans from the banker's—and all on credit all the time. He might have stopped to ask himself where he'd get the money to pay it back.

His poetry never won the appreciation which he knew it deserved. He wrote to a friend:

...by my faith I swear to you, my verse and prose has not won the praise it merited. I wrote it, and I alone appreciated it.

And, a year or two before his death:

Sir, your humble servant has given up writing verse and given up correcting it. The sound of it he can no longer hear, and the sight of it he cannot bear. I am seventy-five years old.* I began writing verse at fifteen, and babbled on for sixty years. My odes have gone unrewarded and my ghazals unpraised. As Anwari [a Persian poet] says:

> Alas! there is no patron who deserves my praise.
> Alas! there is no mistress who inspires my verse.

I look to all poets and to all my friends not to write my name in the roll of poets and never to ask my guidance in this art.

Asadullah Khan, poetically named Ghalib, entitled Najm-ud-Daula [Star of the Realm]—God grant him His forgiveness.

---

* He was in fact seventy years old.

In his last years he loses some of his buoyancy. In a letter to Salik:

'God sends His blessings by stealth.' I hear that you are fit and well. We must be thankful that we are alive. 'If you have your life, you have everything.' They say that to despair of God's help is to be an infidel. Well, I have despaired of Him and am an infidel through and through. Muslims believe that when a man turns infidel, he cannot expect God's forgiveness. So there you are, my friend: I'm lost to this world and the next. But you must do your best to stay a Muslim and not to despair of God. Make the text [of the Quran] your watch-word: 'Where there is difficulty, there is ease also.'

> All that befalls the traveller in the path of God
> Befalls him for his good.

The word for 'traveller' in the original is salik, which, in a letter to Salik is particularly appropriate.

His last years were indeed miserable ones. For at least fifteen to twenty years before his death he had been quite hard of hearing, and towards the end he was completely deaf. And this was not all. Extracts from his last letters give a distressing picture.

I don't employ a clerk. If a friend or acquaintance calls, I get him to write the replies to letters. My friend, I have only a few more days to sojourn in this world... I have had a detailed account of my condition printed in the newspapers, and asked to be excused answering letters and correcting verses. But no one has acted accordingly. Letters still come in from all sides demanding answers to previous letters and enclosing verses for correction; and I am put to shame. Old, crippled, completely deaf and half-blind, I lie here day and night, a chamber-pot under the bed and a commode near it. I don't have occasion to use the commode more than once in every three or four days; and I need the chamber-pot...five or six times in every hour.

I am near to death. I have boils on both my hands and my leg is swollen. The boils don't heal and the swelling doesn't subside. I can't sit up. I write lying down.

A year and a half later he was dead.

THE 'NEW LIGHT': RESPONDING TO SOCIAL CHANGE

The 'New Light':
Responding to Social Change

British reaction to the great revolt of 1857 brought about fundamental changes in India, and not least in Indian literature. Urdu culture and its aristocratic exponents were affected particularly deeply. To understand the extent of these changes, you need to know something about the historical background.

In the eighteenth century, the period of the first flowering of Urdu classical poetry, India was the battleground of many contending powers, some Indian, and some foreign; some seeking to establish virtual independence in a particular region, some aiming at an all-India supremacy. This was nothing new in Indian history. Indians had been accustomed for centuries to seeing this as a normal state of affairs, and not one of the contending powers was seen as significantly different from any of the others. From 1757 when the East India Company became de facto masters of Bengal, the British too become a major power in northern India, and were initially seen as nothing more than that. In the Urdu-speaking regions their impact upon cultural life was minimal. Though the British took political control over Oudh (the area around Lucknow) in 1765 and occupied Delhi in 1803, they allowed the old Mughal elite to continue in its traditional lifestyle.

Early in the nineteenth century, however, the situation changed, as it became evident that the British would defeat all their rivals and emerge supreme over the whole of India. Even so, this might have brought about no substantial change in Indian attitudes had it not been for the fact that British policy was now increasingly influenced by people who were so convinced of the immeasurable superiority of British institutions over those of all other nations, that they set about attacking the very foundations of the Indian social order and attempting to remould it in their own image. Mass resentment rapidly grew until it exploded in 1857.

Most British writers still call this revolt 'the Indian Mutiny', but although it began in the army it was much more than a mutiny. It convulsed the whole area of the northern plains between Bengal in the east and Punjab in the west—the area which was the base of the old Mughal elite and of its Urdu culture. Up to 1857 nearly all the independent Indian powers had formally acknowledged the sovereignty of the Mughal king, and so too had the British. After the crushing the revolt, the British not only ceased to give formal allegiance to the Mughal king but declared that the Mughal Empire had ceased to exist, proclaimed themselves retrospectively the only legitimate sovereign power, tried the king for rebellion against them and exiled him to Rangoon. They also took drastic punitive measures against those they thought, rightly or wrongly, had inspired and led the revolt. Their distrust of all those who had been members of the old, predominantly Muslim, Mughal elite was intense.

This class felt the loss of its former influence keenly. Its leading elements began to think strenuously about what the Muslims needed to do to regain it. They quickly divided into two opposing camps, and conflict between them dominated the last decades of the nineteenth century. Those in the first camp maintained their strong (if now mainly silent) hostility to the British, withdrawing from the political arena and clinging firmly to their traditional religion and culture in the hope that conditions might one day emerge in which they could regain their former dominance. The other camp took a very different stand, calculating that the old Muslim elite could never fully regain its old ascendancy, but *could* hope to persuade the English to take them on as junior part- ners provided that they made a complete break with the past, and identified their interests completely with those of the British. To do this they needed to acquire modern education and adopt, wholesale, British cultural norms. It should be stressed that it was not merely to win British approval, fundamentally important to them though it was, that they took this view. They were convinced that it was the mastery of modern science and the adoption of the modern ways of life that had been the basis of British preeminence, and that their own Muslim community would never prosper or win a place of honour in the modern world unless it did likewise.

Upholders of these opposing views were dubbed respectively as champions of the 'Old Light' and propagandists for the 'New Light'.

Outstanding among the champions of the New Light was Sir Sayyid Ahmad Khan (1817–1898) a man who stood head and shoulders above all his contemporaries and was their unchallenged leader. He expounded his ideas in an unceasing stream of essays and books, and gathered around him a band of supporters who did likewise. As part of their modernizing impulse they championed the use of Urdu over classical Persian, and the writing of these men enormously enriched the stock of Urdu prose literature. Within something like thirty years, from about 1870 to the end of the century, prose literature of every kind—essays and polemics on religious, social and political themes, literary criticism, biography and the novel among others—had found a permanent place in the literature.

There was no aspect of religious, social and political life and thought that did not engage Sir Sayyid's attention, though his main efforts were devoted to the creation of a college at Aligarh where modern education would be imparted to the sons of the old ruling elite and so create a force capable of changing the whole outlook of the community and winning a place of honour for it in social and political life. The movement which he inspired and led is thus generally referred to as the Aligarh movement. In 1875 it had gathered the necessary resources to establish the Mohammedan Anglo-Oriental College, which in the course of time (after Sir

Sayyid's death) became the Aligarh Muslim University and continues to this day as one of the major Indian universities.

This section represents the energy of this new movement through extracts from the writing of Sir Sayyid Ahmad Khan and two of his most articulate followers, Altaf Husain Hali (1837–1914) and Nazir Ahmad (1836–1912), both of whom were young men at the time of the traumatic events of 1857. Hali started as a ghazal poet (the last section had extracts from his memoir on Ghalib); but quickly became a fervent supporter of Sir Sayyid and put his poetic and critical skills at the service of the new movement. Nazir Ahmad was a versatile writer—novelist, essayist, and writer of many works on religion. (I shall say more about him in the section on *The Novel*.) I have also included an extract from an early novel by Ratan Nath Sarshar (1846–1902) which describes a young man determined to be 'modern' in the style of the New Light.

The chapter that follows is on Akbar Ilahabadi (1846–1921), an accomplished poet who turned his satirical eye on both Old and New, and the changing norms of society.

Sayyid Ahmad Khan and the Aligarh Movement

The proponents of the New Light faced a formidable task, and Sir Sayyid made the running for them. He was an impressive figure, a man of an old aristocratic family whose grandfather had held high positions both in the old Mughal administration and the new British one. He was determined in the radically changed circumstances of the post-1857 world to win a similar position of honour for himself and his fellows, and he bent all his formidable energies to this task, completely undeterred by the enormity of it. He was ready to assail every traditional belief and every social convention that presented an obstacle to the acceptance of modern science and to Muslim-British understanding.

~

'The Sick Man of Islam'
Neither Sir Sayyid nor his followers felt any easy optimism about what they were attempting. He wrote:

> The Hindus and Muslims of our part of the country are still sunk in ignorance and will remain so for a long time to come. In fact, the Muslims may remain in this state so long that it will be too late for them to progress and civilize themselves. They are sick with a disease which may prove to be incurable... They recall the tales of their ancestors and conclude that no one is superior to them, and this blinds them to the garden which is now before their eyes and to the flowers that bloom in it.

Hali makes the same point bitterly at the start of a long poem which Sir Sayyid encouraged him to write:

> A man went to Hippocrates and asked him
> 'What ailments in your view are always fatal?'
> He said, 'The world has yet produced no ailment
> For which God has not granted us the cure—
>> Except when the sick man will take no notice
>> Thinking that what the doctors say is nonsense.
>
> Explain its causes and its symptoms to him—
> He will pick holes in the best diagnosis
> Refuse to take his medicine, or to diet
> And let his illness gradually grow stronger
>> Make sure he keeps his distance from the doctor
>> Until he has no hope of life left to him.
>
> This is the state in this world of that people
> Whose ship has slowly moved into the whirlpool
> The shore is far away; the storm is raging;
> It seems the ship may sink at any moment
>> And yet the crew sleep on, sunk in oblivion
>> Sleep soundly, unaware of any danger.
>
> The black storm clouds are gathering above them
> And all the signs of imminent disaster
> Hover above them like a flock of vultures
> And from all sides a voice is calling to them,
>> 'What were you once? And what have you become now?
>> Once you were waking, you who now are sleeping.'
>
> But this voice cannot rouse this heedless people
> Content as ever in its degradation
> Reduced to dust, but arrogant as ever.
> Morning has dawned, but it sleeps on serenely
>> Neither bemoaning its abject condition
>> Nor envying the lot of other peoples.

~

Reinterpreting Islam

Central to the ideas of the New Light was the question of how to reconcile traditional Islamic learning with an acceptance of modern scientific education. Sir Sayyid argued for a thorough going re-interpretation of Islam. Like all Muslims, he believed that the Quran was the word of God; but he laid equal stress on their belief that the universe was the work of God, and argued that those who, like the British, were making ever fresh advances in discovering its laws—as the Muslims, alas, had long ceased to do—were discovering the will of God. Because the work of God and the word of God could not possibly be in confict, he argued that if there were passages in the Quran which seemed to contradict the findings of modern science, then that contradiction could only be apparent. The task was to re-interpret such passages so as to bring the interpretation into line with the findings of science. The attempt to do so was expressed not only in Sir Sayyid's own writings, but in essays and articles by many of the best prose writers of the time.

One was Nazir Ahmad, a powerful propagandist of the new movement. He was by no means an uncritical supporter of everything Sir Sayyid said. He once compared Sir Sayyid's more laboured efforts at a modern interpretation of Islam to the efforts of a man trying 'to touch his buttocks with his ears'. But this makes his support for the main thrust of Sir Sayyid's argument all the more striking:

~

Nazir Ahmad on The creation of Adam

The story in the Quran of the Creation of Adam tells us of God's object in creating humankind and of the nature of humankind.* God, with some design which only He knows, created this splendid workshop of the universe and established the laws that govern it. Then, with some design which only He knows, He desired that

* For the full story, with much colourful detail, see p.124.

man should be his deputy and vicegerent and by His command should exercise certain limited powers in ordering the affairs of this workshop in accordance with the laws of nature, and should, to a limited extent, make use of its resources. God gave him intelligence, so that he might know and understand the law. Now let us see how man's perception of his role as God's vicegerent, and his education in learning the names of things and his awareness of his stature as the 'best of created things' has progressed. Man is not God, but there is in him without a doubt a reflection of God, because he rules over all that is in the world. To level the mountains, dry up the seas, break the force of turbulent rivers, make the barren plains bloom, beat off the attacks of fierce animals like the elephant and the tiger, subdue the strong, rebellious forces of steam and electricity—all this is child's play to him. Yes, he is God's servant, but when you see the authority he wields and the power he holds it seems that other created things are *his* servants. But in order to bring into full play the authority and the power which God has prescribed for him he needs to know the laws of nature, because no matter what the authority he wields and no matter what the power he exercises, he remains subject to these laws. He cannot by so much as a hair's breadth transgress their bounds or exercise any power over them. He stands in the same relation to these laws as the rider does to his horse. It is not the rider that completes the journey; it is the horse. But the rider has put a bridle in the horse's mouth and a saddle on its back; he has a whip in his hand and spurs on his heels; and the horse carries him where he wants to go. In the same way if we look at the workings of the world we see that man both commands and is himself commanded by it, is at once a cause and an effect, an origin and an outcome. At all events, man has been granted sufficient power to understand the properties and the uses of things or, in other words, the intelligence which enables him to understand the causes of things, and by furnishing these causes, to obtain the results he desires. And this is the essence of what human vicegerency, human deputyship means. And then this vicegerency which God in His majesty and glory has bestowed upon man has been bestowed on every human being, without distinction of country or community, on every human being *as* a human being. And in this respect every one of the children of Adam is God's vicegerent. Granted that there are degrees of vicegerency... The deeper and more perceptive a man's knowledge of the laws of nature is, the more extensive is his power, the more sweeping his authority and the higher and more exalted his rank and status as vicegerent will be. In our time there are about two hundred and sixty million people on the face of the earth. And Hindus, Muslims, Christians, Jews, idolaters—each one of them—no matter who he is or where he is from or what his colour or his appearance and his faith—each one is the vicegerent of God. Even so, it is of course true that people differ from one another: 'one is a diamond, another a pebble'. There are the British and American vicegerents who beat the drum of 'to me is the power in these days' and there are the Muslim vicegerents who are being shattered more and more in the explosions of 'Just see the difference between this and that!'* And now the question arises of where this difference comes from. It comes from a failure to understand what God's vicegerency means. It comes from man's ignorance of his destiny. It comes from his failure to recognize his own worth. It comes from the fact that, living in the world of cause and effect he has not sought out the causes of things.

> While all of us were spending time in useless disputation
> The men of Europe leapt into the void of God's creation.

> Time was when their condition was more miserable than
>   ours
> But now the wealth of all the world rains down on them in
>   showers.

> Now God Himself has moved to share his secrets with
>   these nations
> Because they have perceived the mode of Nature's operations.

---

* A Persian verse. He means, 'Just see how completely conditions have changed.'

To sum up: God has made man His vicegerent, which means that in this law-governed universe he is to bring into play, while subjecting himself to the laws of nature, a limited authority and limited powers. In order to fulfil the conditions of his role properly as vicegerent, it is necessary to know the laws of nature. And his ability to do this depends on education—not the old-style education in which there is nothing but verbiage and intellectual hypotheses, but the new education which the British, in their great kindness and generosity, are propagating. It was this education that enabled the British themselves to rise in the world. By ill fortune, Muslims have, for ages, out of ignorance and religious prejudice, thought of this education as that of infidels and renegades. When 'the sparrows had gleaned the field',* then a few of them—not all—began to feel disturbed at the state of affairs and began to think about it. Their rivals had almost reached their goal when they sensed that they were suffering 'loss both in this world and the next', as the saying goes, and began reluctantly to move slowly from the stand they had taken. What we have 'lost in this world' is everywhere plainly visible. Be it government service, trade, agriculture or any other means of livelihood, the Muslims lag behind. As for what we have 'lost in the next world', whether Muslims accept it or not, I am fulfilling my responsibilities when I tell them that every created thing worships God by realizing the aims and objects for which it was created. For example, the sun worships God by giving light and warmth to the earth, and the earth by growing grain for those who live on it... In the same way man's effort to fulfil his duties as God's vicegerent, which is what he was created for, is an act of worship. In the light of this, look at [the verse of the Quran which says] 'Without doubt the most Godfearing among His servants are the learned' and the Tradition,† 'Without doubt the acquiring of knowledge is the duty of every Muslim man and

---

* The second part of an Urdu proverb, 'It is no good repenting now that the sparrows have gleaned the field'—i.e. it's no use crying over spilt milk.
† Traditions: see note p. 85.

every Muslim woman'—and then decide whether Islam regards the acquisition of modern education as justified or unjustified, as a duty or as a sin!

~

Sir Sayyid on the Need to Become 'Modern'

Sir Sayyid's social and political writings evidence the same qualities as his religious writings, including quite often an extremism which most of those reading him nowadays would find unacceptable and occasionally quite absurd. He often regarded most of the current conventions and fashions of the British society of his day as essential features of modernity, and argued that his own community should adopt them wholesale. He also tried to shock his readers into a realization of their backwardness by contrasting them with the British in the most unfavourable terms—and by so doing gave deep and wholly understandable offence not only to his opponents but also to his supporters.

It helps us to see this in context if we bear in mind that such extremism was not confined to India. Kemal Ataturk, the creator of modern Turkey, evinced an equally astonishing extremism well into the twentieth century, insisting to his fellow countrymen that only if they changed their dress, wore boots or shoes on their feet, trousers on their legs, shirt, tie, jacket and waistcoast on the upper part of their bodies, and a 'cover with a brim' on their heads—('this head-covering is called a hat,' he explained to them) could they regard themselves as civilized. Even Sir Sayyid did not go as far as that!

In 1869 Sir Sayyid travelled to England to see the marvels of English civilization at close range, and wrote an account of his journey to the secretary of the Scientific Society, which he himself had founded, for serial publication in its journal:

~

I have received your kind letter dated 9th September 1869. You are not pleased with me because I have not sent you any [further] account of our journey; I ask your forgiveness for this and acknowledge that I am at fault. But I had heard that some members of your Society disapprove of the freedom with which I wrote, and are displeased with me. It is not in me to conceal, out of fear of the members of your society, the impressions which I form in the course of this journey or the honest conclusions I draw from them. If I did that I would myself be committing the very sin of which I accuse my fellow Indians. So I decided it would be better to stop writing. If you think that publishing my independent opinions and statements will not harm your Society, and if you are not afraid of the displeasure of the members of the Society (and indeed of anyone but God), then I have no objection to continuing to send you full accounts of events, and of the wonders of this country, and of the lessons and warnings we should take from them.

If you will print this letter just as it stands in your journal and give your frank opinion on the matter I have just mentioned, then I will continue to send you letters as before.

For the present, to make amends, I am writing you an account of the outcome so far of the past six months... It is about six months since I arrived here. During that time, despite the fact that there were many things that shortage of money has made it impossible for me to see, I have at any rate seen some things. I have been in the society of lords and dukes, have taken part in their great banquets and assemblies, have met nobles of lower rank, had friendly relations with gentlemen of middle rank—people who, so to speak, have the same sort of rank and status as we have—and taken part in their dinners and assemblies. On each occasion I have met their ladies, educated and talented ladies of their class. I have met gentlemen who are rich, others who have modest means, and yet others who are poor. More than that, I have seen the homes of people of extremely humble status, and seen the way they live. I have also seen great merchants and their factories, merchants of middle rank and their shops, their warehouses and the way they conduct their buying and selling, and the way they behave with, and talk to, their customers. I have also seen craftsmen and labourers, imposing houses and museums, engineering factories and shipyards, armaments factories, factories that manufacture the cables that lie under the sea and connect one world with another, and warships (on board one of which I have travelled several miles). I have attended meetings of some societies, and have participated in dinners and meetings at some clubs.

He then announced the conclusion he had drawn from this experience—
in words so harsh that even the most bigoted white racist would hesitate
to use them today:

This is the conclusion I have drawn from all this: In India we used to say that the British behaved extremely rudely to Indians (and I do not acquit them of this charge even now), and that they look upon Indians as no more than animals. [But] this is what we really are. I tell you without exaggeration and with complete sincerity that Indians, from the highest to the lowest, rich and poor alike, traders and craftsmen alike, from the most learned and accomplished to the most ignorant, when one compares them with the education and training and cultured ways of the British, bear the same resemblance to them as a filthy wild animal does to an extremely talented and handsome man. And do you think any animal deserves to be treated with honour and respect? So we have no right (even if we have reason) to object if the British in India look upon us as wild animals.

He returned later to the point about British attitudes in India:

I say that the British in India behave extremely badly in their dealings with Indians, and they ought not to. This is not because I think that the Indians are so cultured that they deserve better treatment, but because when the British, with all their culture, behave like this they discredit their own culture and education, and put obstacles in the way of the general spread of culture.

He knew that he would get a hostile reception:

My fellow countrymen will think that these are exceedingly harsh words, and will ask in surprise, 'In what are we wanting?' And 'in what ways do the British surpass us?' that I should write like this. Their surprise is nothing to be surprised at. They know nothing about anything here; and it is a fact that everything here is beyond the grasp of their imagination... Any of my fellow countrymen who cannot think that what I have written can be true and factual, is, I assure you, like the frog in the story of the frog and the fish.

A living fish that an angler had caught fell into a well in which there were frogs living. One of these, seeing this fair new arrival, shining like silver, welcomed him and asked him where he came from. He said, 'I come from the River Ganges.' The frogs asked him, 'Is your country like ours?' He said, 'Yes, but there it is much, much lighter; it is a fine country over which the gentle breeze blows, and there are waves in the water in which we move like people in a swing... It is a vast, broad country in which we swim about.' At this one of the frogs moved about a hand's breadth from the wall of the well and asked, 'As broad as this space between me and the wall?' The fish said, 'Even broader.' The frog moved out another hand's breadth and asked the same question. 'Even broader,' said the fish. The frog continued to move, repeating the same question and receiving the same answer until he reached the other wall of the well. There he again asked 'As broad as this?', and when the fish replied, 'Much broader than even this,' he said, 'That's not true. How can it be broader than this?' At this point someone lowered a bucket into the well, and the water moved. The frog said, 'Are your waves like this?' The fish laughed and said, 'Why ask about something you have never seen, that you cannot imagine and that cannot be described to anyone who has never seen it?'

~

Maintaining Self-respect—Hali on Sir Sayyid

This sort of writing may well give a false impression to modern readers. Hali, in his biography of Sir Sayyid, *Hayat i Javed*, makes clear that he wrote in this way not to flatter the British but to goad his fellow countrymen; and his admiration for the British and their works was not a servile one. Throughout his life it was the interests of his own community which dominated his thinking, and his policy of identifying with British interests was pursued not for the sake of the British but because he saw this as a means of enhancing the achievements and status of his fellow countrymen.

In his personal dealings with the British he had a very proper regard for his self-respect and did not hesitate to protest publicly against behaviour that accorded him and his fellow countrymen less respect than he felt they were entitled to. The following extract from Hali's biography gives some instances of this:

In February 1867 a grand exhibition took place at Agra. Sir Sayyid and a number of other distinguished Indians were members of its organizing committee, along with a number of British members. All of them had equal powers, and there was no distinction made between the British and the Indians. On the last day of the exhibition, a *durbar* was to be held, and arrangements for this were in the hands of Mr Pollock, district magistrate for the Agra district. He had had chairs arranged for the participants in the durbar in an open space near the exhibition ground. One part of this open space was somewhat higher than the rest, and one line of chairs had been set out there, with a canopy erected over them to keep off the sun. A parallel line of chairs was on lower ground, and there was no canopy over them. Sir Sayyid had assured the Indian participants that it was the government's wish on this occasion that no distinction should be made between the Indians and the British, and that all would be treated alike.

One distinguished Indian participant happened to be passing that way perhaps a day before the durbar was due to be held, and he chanced to sit down on a chair in the upper line. A clerk came and moved him off, telling him that the lower line was for him. He went straight to Sir Sayyid, told him what had happened, and said, 'You were mistaken in thinking that the Indians and the British were to be treated equally.' Sir Sayyid was taken aback, and felt extremely embarrassed at having given an assurance which was now proved to be wrong. He at once went to the durbar ground and deliberately took a seat in the upper line. The clerk came to him too and rebuked him. He got up, went straight to the government secretary Mr James Simpson who was issuing tickets, and told him the whole story. He too disapproved of what had been done and told Sir Sayyid he should see Mr Pollock about it. At this point Mr Thornbull [an important British official] arrived. When he was told what had happened he was extremely angry with Sir Sayyid and said to him, 'During the Mutiny you people behaved as if there was no ill treatment that was too bad for us. And now you want to sit side by side with us and our womenfolk?' Sir Sayyid replied, 'Everything that has gone wrong is because you people have always despised and humiliated us Indians. But for that, things would never have come to this pass.' Mr Thornbull got even more angry. In the end Mr Simpson persuaded Sir Sayyid that it was no good continuing this conversation. Sir Sayyid went away and took no part in the durbar.

Information reached the Lieutenant-Governor, and he too disapproved of the arrangements that had been made. He issued orders to the effect that no significant change could be made at this stage but that the British officials in charge of every district and divison should sit in the lower line with the Indian gentlemen and officials of their respective districts and divisions. After the durbar all the European officials who met Sir Sayyid asked him what had happened, and were very put out when he told them. Sir Sayyid concluded that it was not advisable for him to stay on, and left for Aligarh the same night. A few days later he received a letter from the local government secretary demanding to know why he had not attended the durbar, and why he had left for Aligarh without permission. Sir Sayyid wrote and explained why he had left Agra, and apologized for not having attended the durbar. After that no further enquiry was made. Before this exhibition Lord Lawrence, Viceroy and Governor-General, had ordered the award of a gold medal to Sir Sayyid. Since Sir Sayyid had not attended the durbar the Lieutenant-Governor gave the medal to the Commissioner of the Meerut division so that on his way to Meerut he could stop off at Aligarh and present the medal with his own hands. When the Commissioner arrived at Aligarh railway station, Sir Sayyid, in accordance with instructions that had been sent to him, was there. The Commissioner took him to one side, and because he was offended by the blunt words Sir Sayyid had used to Mr Thornbull, said, 'I would not have been willing to hang this medal round your neck with my own hands, but I am under government orders.' Sir Sayyid replied, 'I too am under government orders,' and then bent his neck, put the medal on, and left.

I have heard from reliable sources that this happened at a time when the government had decided to award a substantial increase in salary to sub-judges, but that because of Sir Sayyid's behaviour it was a long time before this increase materialized, and Sir Sayyid and his fellow sub-judges had to do without it.

~

Sir Sayyid on his stay in London

The historian W. Cantwell Smith, said aptly of Sir Sayyid's visit to England that 'he suddenly saw European civilization in full swing and was overwhelmed by it, dazed like a young child.' But reading his account of it we feel the strength of his conviction that his fellow countrymen needed to acquire the good things that the English had and his ardent desire that he and they should bend all their efforts in acquiring them:

I want to write a little about my private life here; this will probably be of interest to my countrymen and will either astonish them, or excite their ridicule, or provide them with another arrow of censure to loose at me.

When I reached London I stayed three or four days in Charing Cross Hotel. I had not enough money to be able to rent a house, buy furniture for it and engage a servant; and so I rented lodgings. Lodgings means that the owner of a house lets some rooms in it. He provides the necessary furniture, including even beds and bedding. The owner is called the landlord and his wife the landlady. Food too is provided by her, and she arranges for servants to look after us. Every week she gives a bill for us to pay, and we live in complete comfort.

The house we live in belongs to Mr J. Ludlum. He has a wife, Mrs Ludlum, and she has two sisters, Miss Ellen West and Miss Fanny West, who sometimes come to stay as their sister's guests for two or three weeks. Mr Ludlum has all the capabilities and accomplishments which you would expect to find in the most able gentlemen. He is well versed in numerous branches of knowledge and is so interested in them that when he has time he goes at night to meetings of various societies to hear lectures on chemistry or biology or zoology or other subjects. (Societies like these are formed by ordinary people; people attending lectures pay a fee of a few coppers, and this covers the expenses of the hall, the equipment and the lecturer's fees. In this way ordinary people have acquired an education such as the greatest philosophers in India never had.)

Six months have passed, but in my room I have never so much as heard his voice and have never encountered him except for occasional chance meetings when we exchanged a few words or greeted each other as I was leaving or going into my room. What courtesy!—to bear in mind all the time that there are others in the house who should not be put to any trouble. Anyway, I do not want to describe Mr Ludlum's virtues, because it is possible that others here may not possess them, and what I want to write is a sketch which will give my fellow countrymen some picture of the state of education here.

Mrs Ludlum is such a highly capable, highly educated, highly cultured, and good lady that no words of mine can describe her. She is the incarnation of culture, courtesy and human goodness. She personally attends with the greatest efficiency to all the work of the house and all the household management, and Mr Ludlum does not have to concern himself with anything other than going to his office and attending his lectures.

Her two sisters are just as cultured and just as accomplished. One of them, Miss Ellen West, is very fond of reading. These days I am writing a book on the Muslim religion, and have got together a number of English books on the subject—some in favour of it, and some against it, and some by completely irreligious people who do not believe in any religion and reject them all. Some days ago Miss Ellen West fell ill—really very ill. On the next day, when she felt a little better, but still very weak, so that she could not easily get out of bed and move about, she sent a message to me asking if I could send her one of the books I had recently bought so that she could pass the time in reading it. I said I hadn't any book of that kind, only religious books, and these too full of argument and controversy. She said, 'No matter, send me one of them.' So I did. Within two days she had finished it, and when she had completely recovered and emerged from her sick room she made some very good points about this book.

From this you should understand how well-educated women of something lower than middle-class status are. Is it not amazing that a sick woman should pass the time in reading a book of this kind? Have you seen anything like this in the home of any nobleman, nawab, rajah, or gentleman in India? If in India a woman were to go out into the street and walk around completely naked, how amazed and flabbergasted our countrymen would be. I tell you without exaggeration that people here are no less amazed when they learn that the women in India cannot read and write and are given absolutely no education.

These days I am living in a very interesting house... We have six rooms in it—four bedrooms (one for each of the four of us). Hamid, Mahmud and Mirza Khudadad Beg's bedrooms are rather better than mine and are more fully furnished than mine, because they read in these rooms in the evenings. In my room there are only the things I need to sleep there... I have a room to write and read in, and to do my literary work in. And we have our meals and our tea in this same room. Then there is a big furnished room called a sitting room—that is, a reception room. We sometimes sit there together and amuse ourselves, and it is there that we receive any friend who comes to visit any of us.

Our kind landlady has engaged two maidservants to attend to our needs. One is called Anne Smith and the other Elizabeth Matthews. The latter is a young girl from a poor family, and does all the odd jobs. The other is an extremely intelligent, capable, well-educated girl—who can read books, write to the extent that is necessary and with a neat handwriting, and read the newspapers. And she enjoys doing all these things. She does her work with all the regularity and efficiency of a machine.

We get fully dressed in our bedrooms, and at about eight o'clock go to the reading and writing room. Meanwhile Anne Smith has cleaned both rooms, and dusted everything—chairs, tables, shelves, pictures, writing materials, books—and put everything in its proper place. She lights a fire in the fireplace when it is cold enough to make this necessary. If any letter has come for anyone she looks to see who it is addressed to and puts it in front of that person's seat. If a newspaper comes she puts it in the middle, and whoever wants to read it first can do so. In short, we come into the room and find everything arranged ready for us. At about nine o'clock she comes and knocks at the door to ask permission to come in, and when this is given she comes in, lays a cloth on the table and sets out the breakfast things. She speaks in a very proper way, respectful and yet at the same time pleasant... She is extremely polite; she calls us all 'Sir', addresses Hamid as 'Mr Hamid', Mahmud as 'Mr Mahmud', and Mirza Khudadad Beg as 'Mr Beg'. She has found out that this is not Mirza Khudadad Beg's full name, and has once or twice said, 'Sir, please pardon me; your full name is very difficult.' This amuses us and now we all call him 'Mr Beg'. Anyway, in this way everything is ready on time, and it is the same with dinner and supper... And all of this is the result of education.

Just look at this youngster Elizabeth Matthews. Despite the fact that she earns only a very small wage, she regularly buys a half-penny paper called *The Echo* and reads it in her spare time. Sometimes she picks up a copy of *Punch*, looks at the pictures of women's manners and customs and enjoys the editor's oblique comments on them.

Above all the shops there are signboards bearing the name of the owners in large gold letters, or letters in other colours. The maidservants can read them all, and do all the shopping there.

The cabmen and coachmen all keep a newspaper under their seat. The moment they set down their passenger they get it out and read it. Think of it. Their status is comparable to that of the ekka*—drivers that ply for hire in Benares. Until general education is developed to this degree, civilization and culture will never come, and our nation will never be respected.

The whole secret of all this progress in England is only this: here everything, every branch of knowledge, every art, is conveyed in the language which everyone, or nearly everyone, speaks.

It follows that all those who genuinely seek the well-being of India and want it to progress must be convinced that the well-being of India depends entirely on this: all branches of knowledge, from the lowest to the highest, must be imparted in the language of the people. I think that as an admonition for the future, these words should be engraved in huge letters on the peaks of the Himalayas: 'Unless all branches of knowledge are imparted to Indians in their own language, India will never attain the rank of an educated and cultured nation. This is true! This is true! This is true!'

The government faces a very great difficulty here. The language of the government is not the language of the country, and, that being so, people feel very little incentive to pay any attention to the vernacular; because it is still the case that no one in India feels any other motive for study but the desire for government service. No one wants to acquire knowledge because he values it.

But, all you who wish India well, do not expect anyone else to do the job for you. Rely upon yourselves; support one another, raise money, and extend the teaching of all branches of knowledge, high and low, throughout the country. Then when you have acquired knowledge, education and culture, the greed for employment in government service will count for nothing in your eyes. I hope

* Ekka: see note p. 87.

that sooner or later that day will come, will certainly come, will be sure to come!

~

The New Men and the Old

The views of Sir Sayyid and his supporters met with virulent opposition from the powerful conservative forces in Indian Muslim society. Sir Sayyid's occasional extremism provoked an equally extreme response, but it would be a grave mistake to regard this as the major cause of this response. To the pillars of the Old Light the mere fact that an idea was new was sufficient to condemn it.

By the time of Sir Sayyid's death in 1898 the New Light had become the predominant ideology of the leaders of the Muslim community. Whatever the Old Light could offer in hopes of a restoration of Muslim glory in some indefinite future, it clearly had no solution for the problems of the here and now. The New Light clearly did offer a solution, and in the absence of any clear alternative, it gained increasing acceptance.

Sarshar: The Tale of Azad

There is an amusing illustration of the clash of attitudes in a work of fiction by Ratan Nath Sarshar (1846–1902) entitled *The Tale of Azad* (*Fasana i Azad*). Azad, the hero, is a determined and enthusiastic champion of the New Light. His henchman, Khoji, though personally loyal to Azad, is an equally firm upholder of the Old. The form of the book in itself reflects the influence of the changing attitudes. It has elements of the traditional Persian dastan (disconnected episodes in the life of a highly romanticized, long-ago, hero), but Sarshar's intention is to write a contemporary story reflecting the realities of daily life:

> Azad and Khoji are on a railway journey from Lucknow. When they reach the station Azad finds the refreshment room. There is nothing at all exaggerated in the account that follows:

Azad was delighted with what he saw; everything was spotlessly clean and in its proper place. From one end of the room to the other were tables with chairs arranged round them, and glasses set out upon them. Lamps were burning brightly on all sides. Azad sat down. 'Bring me something to eat,' he said. 'But, mind you, no wine, and nothing with pork in it.'...The waiter, spick and span in his clean uniform, and with a turban on his head, brought him all manner of English dishes [sic] which he served from costly plates of the most expensive kind. Azad plied his knife and fork with a will, and finished off with lemonade and soda-water. When he came out, there was Khoji, his bedding unrolled on the platform, eating parathas and kababs.

'You look as though you're doing all right,' said Azad, 'the way you're scoffing those kababs.'

'That's right,' said Khoji, 'some of us like kababs and some of us like wine.'

'What do you mean, "Some of us like wine"? Do you think I've been drinking wine? I never touch the stuff. I'll swear on the Quran I haven't touched a drop. You might as well accuse me of eating pork.'

Khoji smiled, 'Right!' he said. 'You wouldn't let *that* chance slip. "You might as well say I've been eating pork!" he said. Well said! You have to think these things forbidden or repulsive to keep off them. But both are allowed to you. You think it's a great thing to have them. Well done, my friend! Today you've really shown what you're capable of.'

'Have you finished? Or do you want to go on abusing me? I tell you, you can put me on oath. I've not so much as put my hand to wine; I've not even looked at pork.'

'You put that well. All right, you haven't put your hand to wine. But it went down your throat, I'll be bound. And anyway, who takes any notice of *your* oaths? An oath means nothing to you. I can't make out to this day what your religion is... Oh well, we shall all get the reward of our deeds. Why should I worry about it?'

'You're not going to admit you're wrong, are you?'

'Why should I? Didn't I see you with my own eyes using a knife and fork?'

'Well? Do you think you drink wine with a knife and fork?'

'How do I know how you drink wine? Better ask one of your drunken friends about that. But I'm sorry you're so far gone. What a pity! What a shame!'

'Do just one thing for me: just go into the refreshment room and see for yourself.'

'What, me? Me, a true Muslim, go into a refreshment room? God forbid! God save us! You go if you want to. But me? Go into a refreshment room? May God protect me!'

Azad left Khoji to his kababs and strolled along the platform. A gentleman with a beard a yard long accosted him, 'Well, sir, may I know your name?'

'Azad.'

'Azad.'* He smiled. 'Yes, indeed. The name suits you. Freedom and free-thinking are written all over you. And your religion?'

[Azad quoted a Persian verse and then replied] 'Respected sir, your humble servant is a Muslim. Islam is my faith, and I observe the shariat. And *your* name, Maulvi Sahib?'

'Never mind *my* name. Allow me to express my sorrow.'

'Please do. Burst into tears if you like. But remember that Muharram isn't far off. You'll be able to weep then to your heart's content. Why so impatient?'

'You say you are a Muslim and observe the shariat, and yet you go into a restaurant and drink wine. God have mercy on us! My good man, do you never think of Judgement Day?'

'Respected sir, what can I say? I have no more to say to you. God save us!'

'Pardon me if I am rude; but think of yourself when you say "God save us!" Well, you have done Satan's work, but praise God that your better self reproaches you.'

---

* Azad means free, but its senses range from liberty to license to 'free-thinking'.

'Maulana, I swear by God I took only food in the restaurant, and that too only what Islam permits. Be fair! What is wrong with that? After all, in Istambul everybody—including the most eminent doctors of Islam—dine with Christians. Why on earth is it that in India Muslims think it a sin?'

'Listen, I'll explain it all to you. To eat in a restaurant is not creditable to a Muslim. If you'd spread your mat and had the same food brought out to you, that would have been all right. That too would have been open to objection, but not to the same extent. Then again, you may swear as many oaths as you like, with the Quran raised in your hand, but no one will *believe* that you didn't have pork and wine. If you trade in coals your hands will get black. And don't talk to me about Istambul. The Shah of Persia drinks wine and orders the most expensive brandy. But does that make wine-drinking permissible? Let the Turks eat with Christians as much as they like. That doesn't mean that *we* should. It's against our traditions to do so. Have you got to live in Istambul? Or have you got to live here in India? When you're *in* Istambul, do as they do. But are we talking about Istambul or are we talking about India? After all, there's no lack of food outside the restaurant—kababs, parathas, biscuits, everything. So what was to be gained by going there? Why make yourself conspicuous and get yourself laughed at for nothing?'

'My dear sir. First, the food in there is fine and tasty. Secondly, the place is spotlessly clean. Then you can sit and *enjoy* the food. There's a man to pull the fan. The fan is clean. The plates are clean. The tables are clean. There are four waiters standing ready to serve you. Can I get all that outside? God save us!'

'The food may be fine according to *your* taste. And for the fan, out here you can pay a pice and get yourself fanned for an hour at a time. And what do you want with cleanliness when you are travelling? Besides, it's not as though things out here are filthy dirty. If *you're* over-particular, that's quite another matter. Anyway, it's your business and you can get on with it. But youngsters should listen to what their elders tell them. I've told you. But you must do as you like.'

Azad thought to himself, 'I shan't do such a stupid thing again. It's up to me whether I eat in a restaurant or not, but I don't have to advertise the fact. From now on I'll be more discreet.'

'Well', said Khoji, '*now* what about it? You thought you could make a fool *of me*; but now the Maulvi Sahib has told you off. I bet you won't go again in a hurry!'

~

The Impact of Hali's Musaddas

A great role in winning acceptance for Sir Sayyid's ideas was played by a long poem of general referred to as Hali's *Musaddas*, because it is in the musaddas form, that is, in stanzas of six lines. First published in 1879, its actual title is *The Flow and Ebb of the Tide of Islam* (*Madd o Jazr i Islam*). The first stanzas were quoted earlier; after that Hali goes on to contrast the present benighted state of the Muslims with the past glorious achievements of Islam, recounting the social and religious revolution that the coming of Muhammad brought to Arabia and the cultural achievements in subsequent centuries which put the Muslim world far in advance of contemporary Europe. Then he returns to themes of the present decline, and urges his contemporaries to take inspiration from their glorious past and again make their mark in the world.

The poem quickly won widespread popularity. It owed much of its success to two things. First, just because it was a poem, and while the new prose was still trying to establish itself, poetry had an immediate appeal as the medium of serious literature. Secondly, it celebrated the past glories of Islam. This would strike a chord in the hearts of the conservatives and would predispose them to listen, however reluctantly, when he went on to draw the contrast between past glory and present decline and to prescribe the cure.

A movement which set out to re-examine everything in the Muslim heritage could hardly ignore poetry, and both Nazir Ahmad and Hali turned their attention to it. Their assessment of it is startling. Nazir Ahmad writes:

What is there in our poetry except indecency and playing at love?

Hali is even more vitriolic. Here is the relevant section of the musaddas (given here in a prose translation):

> That foul collection of verses and odes, which stinks worse than a cesspool, which has an impact in the world no less than an earthquake, and which makes the angels in heaven feel shame at it, has been the ruin of learning and religion. Such is the role among our arts and sciences of the art of literature. If there is any punishment for the composing of depraved verse, if the telling of vain lies is impermissible, then that court in which God is judge, and in which retribution of good and bad deeds is decreed, will release all other sinners and fill hell with our poets.

There is a certain unconscious irony in these passages. The theme of Nazir Ahmad's article on God's vicegerency echoes one of the major themes of Urdu poetry. As for Hali, he was himself a ghazal poet, and a good one. Among Hali's later works is *Poetry and Poetics* (*Muqaddama i Sher o Shairi*), published in 1893, in which he undertook a critical assessment of the whole body of Urdu poetry, with proposals for reform in the light of the demands of the new age which had now dawned. In it his tone was much more restrained than it had been in his musaddas; and it is significant too that, although he wrote *Poetry and Poetics* as an (inordinately long) preface to a collection of his verse, that verse still includes much that does not conform to his prescriptions. It is not surprising that these strictures on poetry were generally ignored. Classical poetry continued to make a universal appeal—as it still does.

But in other respects, the impact of the musaddas was unquestioned. Sir Sayyid himself rated its value to the New Light extremely highly, so much so that he wrote to Hali:

> Yes, it was I who urged you to write it, and I rate this so high among my stock of good deeds that when (on Judgement Day)

God will ask me, 'What have you brought here?' I will say, 'I have brought the musaddas which I got Hali to write: nothing more.'

Satire in a Changing Society

AKBAR ILAHABADI

The Aligarh movement did not win all its battles. The passionate hopes that Sir Sayyid expressed in his letters from London were to a great extent unrealized. He himself virtually abandoned his aim of spreading modern knowledge through the medium of Urdu, and the language of instruction in the Aligarh College, except in the traditional 'Oriental' subjects, was English (and still is in the Aligarh Muslim University). His ideal student who 'wants to acquire knowledge because he values it' was a rarity, and for the most part the student who came to Aligarh continued the tradition that he had deplored, and was still one who did not feel 'any other motive for study but the desire for government service'. By the time the first generations of students had passed through the Aligarh College, reflection on their experience had produced a reaction against the wholesale acceptance of Sir Sayyid's views.

This found its most effective expression in the satirical verse of Akbar Ilahabadi, a poet who looks at the conflict between the New Light and the Old but refuses to give indiscriminate support to either. For Sir Sayyid's efforts to improve the lot of the Muslims and to make them see the advantages of learning from the British, he has a genuine respect. But he does not think Sir Sayyid's efforts are in any way adequate to produce the results he wants. He is opposed to the extremism that maintains the old just because it is old or embraces the new just because it is new. But in the conditions of

his time, he understandably concentrates his fire on the excesses of
the New Light.

~

*Akbar shares with both the Old Light and the New a sense of traumatic
change:*

> The minstrel and the music—both have changed
> Our sleep has changed, the tale we told has changed
> The nightingale now sings a different song*
> The colour in the cheeks of spring has changed
> Another kind of rain falls from the sky
> The grain that grows upon our land has changed
> A revolution has brought this about
> In all the realm of nature all has changed.

*He also shares with the New Light the conviction that changed times
demand changes in outlook; but at the same time Muslims must be loyal
to all that is best in the legacy of the past and must make their own active
contribution to the process of change:*

> Akbar does not deny the need for moving with the times
> But understand that loyalty has its importance too.
> Why feel so proud because the times have changed you?
> True men are those whose efforts change the times.

He portrays himself humorously as caught in the crossfire between the two:

> I wear a loincloth—and am looked at with suspicion and
>   contempt.
> I put on trousers—and arouse men's anger and hostility.
> Perhaps I'd better drop them both and go around with
>   nothing on—
> Then maybe men will feel my charm and I shall feel their
>   sympathy.

---

* Nightingale: see p. 83.

He disapproves of Sir Sayyid's complete identification with British aims, for he is alarmed at the prospect of the evils which this identification is likely to produce:

> Sir Sayyid sought—no doubt of it—well-being for us Muslims.
> But lectures and subscriptions? How can these set us on course?
> Mere nails and tacks will not avail to mend the throne of honour;
> Do not expect great horsemanship from him who shoes the horse.
> Sir Sayyid had an intellect that radiated learning
> And strength enough to vanquish any foe you care to mention
> And I for one would readily have counted him a prophet
> But that there never was a prophet yet who drew a pension.*

The British, says Akbar, did not (as Sir Sayyid liked to argue) come to India as the Muslims' friends. They hold all the power, and they use it in their own interests:

> The Englishman can slander whom he will
> And fill your head with anything he pleases.
> He wields sharp weapons, Akbar. Best stand clear!
> He cuts up God himself into three pieces.†

The British have the impudence to accuse the Muslims of having spread Islam by the sword. Akbar retorts:

> You never ceased proclaiming that Islam spread by the sword:
> You have not deigned to tell us what it is the gun has spread.

---

* A reference to Sir Sayyid's income from British official sources—not pension in the sense of retirement pension.

† In other words, he believes in the doctrine of the Trinity which, to the Muslim, is at best ridiculous, and at worst blasphemous.

If they promote those Indians who support them, this does not alter the overall picture, no matter how much their supporters praise the New Light:

> The light that only lights the path to plunder
> I will not call 'refinement's radiance'.
> You ruin thousands to promote a hundred:
> I'll not call that 'humanity's advance'.

and

> If fifty to a hundred of them get good posts, what of it?
> No nation yet was ever based on fifty to a hundred.

For the old Muslim elite, he wryly says, British rule has brought only deprivation:

> You have no gold: how can you live in style?
> You have no mistress: how can you have fun?
> And if you want to end it all—all right—
> But then how can you when you have no gun?

He comments on the founding of the Mohamedan Anglo-Oriental College with a somewhat sardonic humour and a warning against neglecting the importance of spiritual values:

> God confer on Aligarh a cure for every malady
> And on its students, scions of the gentry and nobility
> Refined, and elegant, and smart, and clean, and neat, and
>   radiant,
> Hearts full of good intentions, minds blessed with originality,
> They ride the highways of the East, and plod along the
>   western ways,
> Each one of them, without a doubt, everything you would
>   have him be.
> No Indian fair, no English miss, diverts them from their
>   chosen path;
> Their hearts are innocent and pure; their books absorb
>   their energy.

All of them dwell in College, still without experience of life;
They do not know what lies ahead, nor what should be
    their destiny.
The flame of faith burns in their hearts, but those who
    guard it are not firm
And logic's winds may blow it out, or youthful immaturity,
Ensnaring them, and teaching them to hold religion in
    contempt
And, seeking fame, to bring to nought the ways of their
    community.
I pray then: May the boons of knowledge and of
    understanding be
Bestowed on them by their professors and their God—
    respectively.

With the passing of time he felt that events were proving that his fears had been warranted:

What our respected Sayyid says is good.
Akbar agrees that it is sound and fair.
But most of those who head this modern school
Neither believe in God, nor yet in prayer
They *say* they do, but it is plain to see
What *they* believe in is the powers that be.

And indeed faith in the rightness of all things British did indeed become, for many, their strongest article of faith. For others, their traditional faith was overlaid by Western values:

His rosary is sandalwood. Alas!
Its fragrance is imprisoned in French polish.

For Akbar, it is obvious that science cannot explain everything, because as he puts it, God is beyond the range of telescopes. He simply cannot understand why people should want to question this:

Why all this concentration on the problem?
You ask what God is? God is God. What else?

*He mocks the modern student whose knowledge is preserved not in his
head, but in his notebooks, and imagines his embarrassment after death
when according to Muslim belief two angels visit the grave to interrogate
him:*

When the angels both appeared inside the grave to
     question me
I myself intended to explain things comprehensively.
Delving in my pocket for my notebook, I was shocked to
     find
I had lost it on the way there—or, perhaps, left it behind.
Much confused I said, 'I really *must* apologize to you,
I have left my notebook in the world—there's *nothing* I can
     do.'

*Such students think that their modern syllabus encompasses all knowledge
and that the application of this knowledge is sufficient to solve all difficulties:*

Poor fellows, how can they believe that there's a throne of
     God?
It wasn't on the maps they studied in geography.
No more they fear the day of retribution;
They concentrate on doing what they like.
What if the bridge to Paradise is narrow?
They say they'll ride across it on a bike.

*On occasion he sarcastically enlists their most profoundly held beliefs of the
British and their admirers to support his conclusion:*

Today when my petition was rejected
I asked the Sahib, feeling much dejected,
'Where shall I go to now, Sir? Kindly tell.'
He growled at me and answered, 'Go to Hell!'

I left him, and my heart was really sinking;
But soon I started feeling better, thinking,
'A European said so! In that case
At any rate there must *be* such a place!'

*Or he plays with concepts familiar to them in order to score off them. Thus,
he represents an Indian as telling his British superior,*

Fate favoured you, kind sir: *you* grew from monkeyhood to
    manhood.
See *our* ill-luck: once men, we grow more monkey-like
    each day.
You say 'There's nothing after death'? What nonsense!
Just look at us. *We're* dead, and *we're* still here.

*Sometimes his mockery is extremely bitter. He sees a generation of men
arising whose whole aim is to forget all that their forefathers valued and to
learn only what they need to learn to get a post, however menial, in the
British administration:*

We do not learn the things we ought to learn—
And lose what was already in our keeping;
Bereft of knowledge, plunged in heedlessness,
Alas! We are not only blind but sleeping.

He jeers at them:

Give up your literature, say I; forget your history
Break all your ties with shaikh* and mosque—it could not
    matter less.
Go off to school. Life's short. Best not to worry overmuch.
Eat English bread, and push your pen, and swell with
    happiness.

---

* Here the word simply means an elder of the Muslim community,
without the pejorative sense it bears in the Urdu ghazal.

He sums up their great achievements:

> What words of mine can tell the deeds of men like these,
>   our nation's pride?
> They got their B.A., took employment, drew their pensions
>   and then died.
> So great is their refinement now, they've bid their parents'
>   home goodbye.
> They spend their lives in hotel rooms and go to hospital to
>   die.
> What do they want with parents, or with maulvis, or with
>   God?
> They owe their birth to doctors and their schooling to the
>   state.

He believes that modern education undermines morality:

> Praise be! Both wife and husband are refined.
> She feels no shame: he feels no indignation.

More humorously, he depicts a male graduate addressing a female one:

> Both you and I have passed our graduation—
> Lie down, let's have a learned conversation.

By the time Akbar had got into his stride, self-important Indians who held minor posts in the service of the British Raj were fairly numerous. He ridicules their pretensions, their motives, and their methods of gaining advancement:

> Look at the owl! What airs and graces! What a way to talk!
> Because the British told him he's an honorary hawk!

> *(The owl, in Urdu idiom, is a symbol of foolishness, not of wisdom.)*

> Perched in their park the crow makes loyal speeches
> One day they'll make him honorary nightingale.
> I'm actually a nightingale, but since I want to eat
> I pretend to be a parrot and accept a council seat.

He is disgusted with what such people will do for the sake of a little cheap fame:

> They changed their fashions, left their homes, and got into
>   the papers.
> But after all it doesn't last. Death ended all their capers.

When at a somewhat later stage political leaders emerged who expressed respectful criticism of British policies, he felt just as great a contempt for them and for their pathetic belief in the power of the press against so formidable an adversary. Their policy, he says, is,

> Faced with a gun, bring out a newspaper.
> The country swarms with editors and leaders
> Who can't find any other games to play.
> They used to say the pickpocket is brother to thief
> They tell us now the editor is brother to the leader.

Such leaders make great play with their deep sympathies for their suffering people. Akbar is not impressed:

> He made his speech with copious tears—and that is known
>   as 'policy'
> I thought he was my well-wisher—and that is called
>   'stupidity'.
> In mourning for their nation's plight they dine with the
>   authorities.
> Our leaders suffer deeply for us, but they suffer at their ease.
> I must not be ungrateful: see the trouble that he takes—
> After each meal he eats he sends a photo of the cakes.

Akbar sees this lack of genuine feeling for the poor as a characteristic of the well-to-do in general—as indeed it was. Sir Sayyid's movement, for example, was concerned almost exclusively with the old Muslim elite. Their religion ought to impel them to do better:

> Reward in heaven calls to you, 'If you want me, then help
> them.
> I lie concealed within the thirst and hunger of the poor.'

*It is religion that he looks to to give him and his countrymen the comfort
and the strength they need to meet the challenges of the age in which they
live, and though he is a Muslim he urges his fellow Hindu countrymen to
look similarly to their religion:*

> Akbar, in all the verse you write make this your theme
> repeatedly:
> Muslim, take up your rosary, and Brahmin, wear your
> sacred thread.

But these externals must be the symbols of something deeper:

> They think that circumcision is the essence of religion:
> Men claim that they are Muslims who have never said their
> prayers.

The Hindu pandits and Muslim maulvis are no better. And so, he concludes:

> Away with pandits and with maulvis too.
> I do not want religion, I want faith.

THE NOVEL

The Novel

The most substantial contribution to the prose literature of the New Light is to be found in the fiction of the early novelists like Nazir Ahmad, Sarshar and Sharar.

The work of the Sarshar and Sharar is for the most part of greater social and historical than of literary importance. Ratan Nath Sarshar (1846–1902) is best known for *The Tale of Azad* (*Fasana i Asad*), of which you saw an extract in the last section.* It appeared between 1878 and 1885 as a serialized novel. At his best he writes with vivid realism but he is a very uneven writer and does not often reach this level. Abdul Halim Sharar (1860–1926)† is famous mainly as the author of numerous historical romances which exalt the past glories of Islam and contrast these with the evil deeds of the Christians of that period. It is generally considered that the best is *Flora Florinda* (the title is the names of the two central characters), published serially between 1893 and 1899. He is a clear and fluent writer but not a great one. His appeal for his contemporaries was similar to that of Hali's *Musaddas*—he reminded his fellow Muslims of their glorious past; but his simplistic characterization and melodramatic story lines are not likely to appeal to a modern Western reader.

Nazir Ahmad (1836–1912) is in another class altogether. He was a man of many parts—a powerful and immensely popular public speaker, a writer of educational books, a good letter-writer,

* See p. 310.
† See p. 250.

a scholar of Arabic, a talented translator (both from Arabic and English), and a voluminous writer on religious themes.* Of all his writings his 'novels' are best known. The first, *The Bride's Mirror* (*Mirat ul Arus*) appeared in 1869. They are not novels in the now generally accepted sense of the word, and he never claimed that they were—he himself made clear that they were stories written to point a moral. But the realism of his characterization and his ability to keep the reader engaged ensured their popularity. The best known is *The Repentance of Nasuh* (*Taubat un Nasuh*), which begins with a vivid description of a cholera epidemic, and the effect on Nasuh of thinking that his last days have come.

Nazir Ahmad's mastery of Urdu prose is astounding, and far surpasses that of any of his contemporaries. For the most part the language is that of vigorous, near-colloquial speech (because this is what his themes generally demand). But he has an equal command over the formal, elaborate style which the older literary canons prescribed, and where he thinks it appropriate to employ this style he does so with much of the same power as Ghalib did in his Persian prose. Unfortunately the very passages which make the greatest impact on Urdu readers defy effective translation into English and for that reason his novels are not represented in this selection. Their power derives from a skilful use of a range of literary devices which, for the most part, are unfamiliar and unappealing to contemporary English-speaking readers. To people of my generation the nearest parallel is the solemn and sonorous prose of, for example, the general confession in the Book of Common Prayer or such passages as that on faith, hope and love in the Bible. Strongly marked rhythms, alliteration, and the multiplication of near synonyms ('erred and strayed', 'devices and desires') are features of such passages, and Nazir Ahmad's prose shows these features too. But it also shows many more—self-consciously poetic diction, hyperbole, play upon words, rhyming phrases, and successive, parallel statements on a single theme expressed first in splendid language abounding in

* See p. 295.

Arabic and Persian loan words and then in the homely language of indigenous colloquial speech. The contemporary English-speaking reader would be disconcerted to come upon passages in this sort of style in a modern novel. But Nazir Ahmad's readers, people whose first acquaintance with the written word was made through the poetical prose of the Quran, people in whom the love of poetry and an appreciation of just such literary devices was universal, would have enjoyed reading such prose as much as he must have enjoyed writing it.

There is however one outstanding nineteenth-century novel, *Umrao Jan Ada* by Mirza Muhammad Hadi Rusva (1858–1931), first published in 1899. Rusva was a man of extraordinarily wide interests and talents. His works include long theological treatises, translations from English, cheap thrillers written to earn money, and three serious novels. *Umrao Jan Ada* is the story of a Lucknow courtesan, whose name forms the title of the book. It takes the form of her autobiography, as related to the author, and there are some grounds for thinking that in essentials it is a true story. It was an immediate success and has remained popular ever since.

The story spans the years 1840–1870—that is, the decades spanning the great watershed of the revolt of 1857. In that period courtesans of Umrao Jan's class, besides being expert singers and dancers, were highly educated in the traditional culture of their day and were quite often poets, as Umrao Jan herself was—'Ada' is her takhallus, her poetic name.* They played a role in Lucknow society closely comparable to that of the hetaerae in ancient Athens. In India, as in ancient Athens, respectable women were not permitted to reach the educational and cultural level which would have enabled them to give anything more than sexual satisfaction and domestic comfort and affection to their husbands, and cultured men who could afford it commonly kept a courtesan mistress as well as a wife. The courtesan would move freely in cultured society, and through her experiences one could see something of the social

* Takhallus: see p. 149.

and cultural history of the times. It was Rusva's intention that this should be so. In the preface to another novel he brackets *Umrao Jan Ada* with two others and writes of them, 'My novels should be regarded as a history of our times, and I hope it will be found a useful one.' Rusva shows Umrao herself as being aware of the relevance of her experience to an understanding of the historical period through which she lived. Each chapter begins with a verse— the one where she starts to tell her story begins:

> Which is the story you would rather hear?
> The story of my life or of my times?

In this selection, it seems sensible to let the Urdu novel be represented by substantial extracts from this one novel, rather than by a number of shorter extracts from the whole range.

Umrao Jan Ada

RUSVA

1

The novel begins with Rusva's account of how it came to be written:

Ten to twelve years ago a friend of mine named Munshi Ahmad
Husain who lived near Delhi came on holiday to Lucknow. He
took a room in the Chauk* near Sayyid Husain Gate, and in
the evenings friends of his would often visit him there. These
were very enjoyable occasions. Munshi Sahib had an excellent
understanding of poetry; he occasionally wrote poetry himself,
and it was good poetry; but generally he preferred to listen to
others reciting theirs. So poetry would be the usual theme of our
gatherings.† There was another room adjoining his which was
occupied by a courtesan. But her style of living was completely
different from that of most courtesans. No one had ever seen her
sitting on the balcony overlooking the street‡ and there were no
comings and goings to her room. Both doors were curtained,
day and night, and the door which opened onto the Chauk was
always closed. There was another door which opened onto a little
side street, and her servants would come and go by this door.
Were it not for the fact that one could sometimes hear the sound

---

* Chauk: One of the main thoroughfares of Lucknow, in which many
courtesans lived.
† See the description of a mushaira on p. 148.
‡ and thus soliciting customers.

of singing coming from the room one would not even have
known that the room was occupied. In the room in which we sat
there was a little hatch connecting our room with hers, but it was
secured by an iron ring.

One day we were assembled as usual, reciting our ghazals to
one another and acknowledging one another's praise. When my
turn came I recited a couplet, and it was immediately greeted
by a 'Wah!' from the other side of the hatch. I stopped reciting
and everyone turned that way. Munshi Ahmad Husain called out,
'Absent praise is not appropriate! If you like poetry please come
and join us.' There was no response to this, and I began to recite
again. We had dismissed what had happened until shortly afterwards a maidservant presented herself, paid her respects to us, and
asked, 'Which of you gentlemen is Mirza Rusva?' They pointed me
out and the girl then said, 'My lady has asked if you would please
come to see her for a moment.' I said, 'What lady? Who is she?' The
girl said, 'She told me not to tell you her name. Otherwise I am at
your service.' I felt rather reluctant to go with her, and my friends
began to chaff me about it. 'Oh yes! You must be old acquaintances!
That's why she's sent for you.' I was wondering who it could be
behaving so familiarly when the girl spoke again. 'My lady knows
you well, sir. That is why she has sent for you.' In the end I had to
go, and when I got there I saw that it was Umrao Jan.

The moment she saw me she said, 'Well, Mirza Sahib, it seems
that you've forgotten me completely.'

'How did I know where you'd been carried off to?' I replied.

'I've often heard your voice, but I could never pluck up the
courage to send for you. But today your ghazal made such an
appeal to me that I couldn't help myself, and without thinking I
called out. Someone said, "Come and join us," and I was overcome
with embarrassment. I thought I'd best keep quiet and leave it at
that. But I couldn't persuade myself. So in the end, bearing in mind
our closeness to each other in days gone by I put you to the trouble
of coming here. Please forgive me... and do please just recite that
couplet again.'

'I shall certainly not forgive you. And I shan't recite the couplet either. If you feel so pleased, come and join us.'

I'd have no objection, but I feel that your host or some of his guests might not like it.'

'Are you mad? Would I invite you anywhere where you weren't welcome? We're all familiar friends, and if you come we'll enjoy ourselves even more.'

'Maybe so. But I hope no one will get *too* familiar.'

'No one will. No one there except me can behave familiarly with you.'

'All right then, I'll come tomorrow.'

'Why not today?'

'You can see for yourself. I'm not dressed for the occasion.'

'You aren't going there to perform.'

'Mirza Sahib, your arguments are unanswerable. Very well then. You go. I'm coming.'

I left her, and soon afterwards, after she'd changed her clothes and made herself presentable, she came. I introduced her in a few words, praising her taste in poetry and her mastery of music. Everyone was very pleased, and now that she had come it was decided that all of us would recite verse turn by turn and that she would do so too. In short it was a very enjoyable occasion, and after that she often came. We would meet for an hour or two, and sometimes it would be poetry, while at other times she would sing for us...

On one occasion she was the first to recite, and she recited this couplet:

'Ada, who is there who will hear the tale I have to tell?
I went astray; and thus I saw all that this age could show.'

'What a couplet, Umrao Jan Sahiba!' I exclaimed. 'It really reflects your own experience. Recite us some more.'

'Thank you, Mirza Sahib, but I swear to you that this is the only couplet of that ghazal I can remember. And God knows how long ago I wrote it. I can't remember it by heart, and I've lost the book in which I wrote my ghazals down.'

'What was the couplet?' Munshi Sahib asked. 'I didn't hear it.'

'How could you?' I said. 'You were busy getting ready to entertain us.'

And Munshi Sahib really had done all that needed doing to make our gathering a success. It was summer. An hour or so before sunset water had been sprinkled on the open roof, so that by evening it would be cool. A carpet had been laid down, and on it a gleaming white covering; pitchers of brand new earthenware had been filled with fragrant water and set out along the parapets, each with an earthenware drinking vessel on top of it. Ice too was provided. There were little paper cups, each containing seven cones of paan wrapped in a red cloth soaked in fragrant water. There was scented chewing tobacco, hookahs with their tubes soaked with water and wrapped in garlands of flowers. It was a moonlit night with little need for much artificial lighting. So a single candle to be passed round had been lit in a glass shade. By eight o'clock everyone had assembled—Mir Sahib, Agha Sahib, Khan Sahib, Shaikh Sahib, Pandit Sahib* and the rest. First everyone was given a cup of milk jelly, and then the poetry session had begun.

Now Munshi Sahib again asked, 'What was that verse?'

'I'll recite it again,' said Umrao, and did so.

When the mushaira was over, the other guests dispersed, and Munshi Sahib, Umrao and I sat down to a meal. Munshi Sahib asked Umrao to recite again the couplet she had recited at the beginning of the mushaira. She recited it:

'Ada, who is there who will hear the tale I have to tell?
I went astray; and thus I saw all that this age could show.'

---

* 'Sahib' is a polite, but still quite familiar form of address, and is used following the name or title of the person addressed. 'Mirza' is for a person of Turkish descent. 'Mir' for a Sayyid, and so on. 'Pandit' is for a Brahmin.

At this Munshi Sahib, said, 'The story of your experiences would certainly be most interesting. I have been thinking so ever since you recited that couplet. Your life story would be a very interesting one.'

I seconded this. Umrao was evasive, but in the end his eagerness and my encouragement overcame her reluctance, and she agreed to tell us her story.

Umrao Jan spoke excellent Urdu, as one would expect. She was well-read, and had been brought up among high-class courtesans, moving in the society of princes and noblemen. She had had access to the royal court, and had seen with her own eyes things that others had probably not so much as heard of.

After every instalment of her story, I would, without letting her know, write it down, and when the story was complete I showed her the manuscript. At first she was very angry with me, but what was done, was done, and after a while she thought it over and changed her attitude. She read through the manuscript and made good occasional omissions.

I have known Umrao Jan ever since the time she met the Nawab Sahib. In those days I too often used to visit her. I feel not the slightest doubt that her story is true in every detail. But this is my personal opinion. It is for my readers to form their own.

2

Umrao's Story Began

There would be no point in my telling you what sort of family I came from, and the fact is that I don't remember. I do remember that our house was in a muhalla on the outskirts of Faizabad. Ours was a brick-built house. All the others were just huts, or mud houses. The people too were lower-class people—water-carriers, barbers, washermen, potters and so on. The only other brick-built house was Dilawar Khan's.

My father was employed at the tomb of Bahu Begum. I don't

know what he did or how much pay he got. All I remember is that people called him jamadar...*

When I was nine years old I had been engaged to be married to my cousin, and his parents were now pressing for the marriage to take place. My aunt† had married a man who owned land and lived in Nawab Ganj [in Lucknow]. Their house was much bigger than ours—mud-built, but very large. I'd been there several times before my engagement had been arranged. They had cows, oxen, buffaloes, and plenty of everything you could want to eat and drink... I'd seen my fiancé too—had played with him, in fact. My father had already got my dowry together and the wedding date had been fixed. When my father and mother used to talk about it at nights I used to listen secretly and feel extremely happy. My bridegroom-to-be was better looking than Kariman's. (Kariman was the cotton-carder's daughter and the same age as me.) Hers was really dark, and mine was really fair. Hers had a great long beard, and my bridegroom's moustache was only just starting to grow. Kariman's dressed in a grubby loincloth. Mine dressed in fine clothes...

Their neighbour Dilawar Khan had a grudge against Umrao's father. He was mixed up with a gang of armed robbers and had just come out of jail after serving a twelve-year sentence; and it had been the evidence of Umrao's father that had convicted him. One day he tricked Umrao into coming into his house:

As soon as I was in he locked the door from the inside. I wanted to scream, but he stuffed some wadding into my mouth and tied my hands tightly together. There was a door at the back of the house. He sat me down on the floor and then went to that door, opened it, and called out, 'Pir Bakhsh!' Pir Bakhsh came in. Then the two of them pushed me onto an ox-cart and got moving. I was terrified. I didn't know what to do. There was nothing I *could* do. I was at the

---

* Jamadar: Literally, one who commands a small body of men, but the word is used vaguely as a title of respect.
† The cousin's mother.

mercy of these two brutes. Dilawar Khan, with bloodshot eyes, and a knife in his hand, seated himself inside the cart, holding me fast under his knees. Pir Bakhsh was driving, and driving the oxen fast. Soon it was nightfall, and there was darkness everywhere. It was winter, and a bitter wind was blowing, I was shivering from head to foot, and weeping continuously, and thinking, 'Daddy will be home by now and looking for me. Mummy will be frantic. My little brother will be playing. He won't know what trouble his sister's in.' I could see my father and mother and my brother, the house and its courtyard and kitchen as clearly as if they had been before my eyes. And at the same time I was terrified that they were going to kill me. Dilawar Khan kept on brandishing his knife and I thought that at any moment he'd plunge it into me. He'd taken the wadding out of my mouth, but I was too frightened to speak. And there were they, Dilawar Khan and Pir Bakhsh, talking and laughing together, and cursing my father and me at every breath. 'Do you see, friend Pir Bakhsh?' said Dilawar Khan. 'We soldiers take our revenge even after twelve years. What a state the bastard will be in now!'

'Yes, you've proved it. It must be all of twelve years since you were sent to jail.'

'Yes, a full twelve years. My friend, you don't know what I had to put up with in Lucknow. Anyway, this'll give the bastar something to remember. And this is only the start of it. I'll kill him before I've finished.'

'What? You're going to kill him too?' said Pir Bakhsh.

'Of course I am. If I don't I'm no Pathan.'

'You're a man of your word. If you say you'll kill him, you will.'

'Yes. You'll see.'

'And what are you going to do with *her*?'

'What do you *think* I'm going to do with her? Kill her somewhere near here, bury her, and be back home while it's still night.'

Now I was *sure* they'd kill me. My tears stopped. My heart gave a jump. I went all limp. Dilawar Khan saw the state I was in, but even then he showed no pity. He punched me hard in the back, and I cried out.

'All right,' said Pir Bakhsh, 'so you'll kill her. And what about my money? Where are you going to get it from? I had a different idea.'

'Let's get back home. If I can't raise it any other way I'll sell my pigeons and pay you.'

'You're a fool. Why sell your pigeons? Shall I tell you what I think?'

'All right, tell me.'

'All right, I'll tell you. We'll go to Lucknow and raise money on the girl.'

Once I'd felt sure I was going to be killed, I'd not listened much to what these two brutes were saying, I'd felt as though I was listening to people talking in a dream. But now what Pir Bakhsh had just said made me hope that I wasn't going to die after all. In my heart of hearts I blessed him. But now I waited to see what Dilawar Khan would say.

'All right, we'll see,' he said. 'For the present keep going.'

'Why don't we stop here for a while? There's a fire burning over there under the tree. Let's get some coals and light the hookah.'

Pir Bakhsh went off to the fire, and I felt afraid again in case Dilavar finished me off before he got back. I was so frightened I screamed.

Dilavar Khan at once slapped my face hard two or three times. 'Keep quiet you little bastard, can't you? I'll soon knife you if you don't. Kicking up that row!'

Pir Bakhsh wasn't yet far off. He shouted out, 'No, my friend! Don't do anything of the sort! Just let me bring the coals.'

'All right then.'

Pir Bakhsh was soon back. He lit the hookah and gave it to Dilavar Khan. Dilavar Khan took a puff at it and said, 'How much will we get for her? And who'll arrange to sell her? If we're caught at it we'll be in worse trouble than we are now.'

'*I'll* take care of that. Good God! What's the problem? Who's going to catch us? In Lucknow things like this go on all the time. You know my brother-in-law?'

'Kariman.'

'Yes. He earns his living by it. He's kidnapped dozens of boys and girls and got good money for them in Lucknow.'

'Where is he these days?'

'Where is he? He's in Lucknow. His in-laws live across the Gomati. He'll be there.'

'Well, what does a child fetch?'

'It depends on what they look like.'

'Well, what will this one fetch?'

'A hundred to a hundred and fifty. Depends on your luck.'

'What are you talking about, my friend? A hundred to a hundred and fifty? She's nothing to look at. We'll be lucky to get a hundred.'

'Well, what of it? Let's go. Killing her's no use.' Dilavar Khan then leaned over and whispered something which I couldn't hear. Pir Bakhsh said, 'Of course! I knew *that*. Would you be such a fool?'

The cart went steadily on throughout the night. I was in agonies of uncertainty. The prospect of death was before me. All my strength was gone. My whole body was numb. You know what they say, that even on the gallows you can't fight off sleep. I soon dozed off. Pir Bakhsh had the decency to put the oxen's blanket over me. Several times in the night I woke with a start. I would open my eyes, but I was too frightened to speak. In the end I pushed the blanket off my face, and saw that I was alone in the cart. I peeped through the curtain and saw that there were some mud houses in front of me. And a corn chandler's shop at which Dilavar Khan and Pir Bakhsh were buying something. The oxen were eating bran under a banyan tree. Two or three rustics were sitting round a bonfire warming themselves. One was smoking from a clay hookah bowl. Pir Bakhsh came and brought me some parched gram to eat. I'd had nothing to eat all night. A little later he brought me a lota of water. I drank a little and then lay down again quietly.

We stayed there a long time. Then Pir Bakhsh yoked the oxen, Dilavar Khan, smoking his hookah, came and sat by me and we set off. Today I wasn't treated so badly. Dilavar Khan didn't pull out his knife, or punch me, or scold me. He and Pir Bakhsh stopped quite often to see to the hookah. They would talk until they got tired of talking, and then sing—that is, one would sing and the other would listen. Probably he wasn't listening but thinking of something to say next. Then they would start talking again. Quite often they would start swearing at each other. They'd roll up their sleeves ready to fight. And then they'd calm down, forget about what had happened, and be friends again. One would say to the other, 'What on earth were we fighting about?' And the other would say, 'Yes, it was nothing.' And they would tell each other to forget it.

Well, that was how I spent my first night of captivity. I shall never forget as long as I live how completely helpless I felt. It still amazes me that I survived it. Well, Dilavar Khan in this world was eventually brought to book. But do you think that satisfied me? I'd have cut the brute up into little pieces and fed him to the kites and crows without turning a hair. I know that now he's dead he'll be suffering the tortures of the grave, and on Judgement Day, God willing, he'll get worse than that.

What must my father and mother have felt? I can't imagine their distress...

Mirza Sahib, that's enough for today. I'll go on with my story tomorrow. My heart's too full for words, and I feel as though I could scream and never stop crying.

I'm telling you my shameful story. But what will you do with it? Why not leave it at this? I wish now that Dilavar Khan *had* killed me. The grave would have preserved my honour, my parents would not have been put to shame, and I would not have been disgraced in this world and the next.

I saw my mother once again—ages ago now. I don't know now whether she's still alive. I've heard that my young brother has a son. God bless him, the boy'll be fourteen or fifteen now. And he has two girls. I can't help wishing I could see them all. Faizabad isn't all that far away. One rupee will get you there. But there's nothing I can do about it. I can't go.

In those days there was no railway, and from Faizabad to Lucknow was a four days' journey. But Dilavar Khan was afraid my father might come after him, and God knows what out of the way roads he travelled by. It took us something like eight days to get there. I, poor little wretch, had no idea where Lucknow was, but I could gather from what Pir Bakhsh and Dilavar Khan said that that was where they were taking me. People had talked about it at home, because my grandfather worked there as one of the armed guards at one of the big houses, and people used to talk about it. He visited us once in Faizabad, and brought me a lot of sweets and toys...

In Lucknow, on the far side of the Gomati, Karim's in-laws lived. They set me down there. It was a small mud house. Karim's mother-in-law, who looked as if she was at death's door, took me in and shut me in a little room. We'd reached Lucknow early in the morning. I stayed shut up there until midday, when the door opened and a youngish woman (Karim's wife) came in, put down three chapatis, a spoonful of lentils in an earthenware cup, and a small pot of water, and went out again. Even that was a godsend to me at that time. I'd not eaten home-cooked food for eight days. During the journey here nothing but gram and *sattu*.* I drank about half of the water and then lay down and went to sleep. God knows how long I slept, because in the dark room you couldn't tell whether it was night or day. I woke up a few times, but there was darkness everywhere and no sign of anyone anywhere near. So I would cover my face and go to sleep again. When I woke up for the third or fourth time I stayed awake, and lay there until Karim's mother-in-law, looking like a witch, came mumbling and grumbling into the room. I sat up.

'How the little brat sleeps!' she said. 'During the night she screamed until she was hoarse. I had to keep shaking her to wake her up. She was hardly breathing. I thought she'd been frightened by a snake. Well, well! She's sitting up again.'

I said nothing, and when she'd finished grumbling she said, 'Where's the cup?' I picked it up and handed it to her, and she went out and shut the door behind her. After a little while Karim's wife

---

* Sattu: Ground wheat mixed with sugar and milk.

came in. There was a window in the room and she now opened the shutters. She led me out of the room into some broken-down ruin, and here I could see the sky. After a little while she took me back into the same black hole and shut me in. Today I got different kind of lentils and some millet porridge.

Two days passed like this. On the third day they brought in another girl, a year or two older than me, and shut her in the room with me. God knows where Karim had enticed her away from. The poor girl was sobbing all the time. Her coming was a comfort to me. When she'd stopped crying we talked quietly together. She was a corn chandler's daughter. Her name was Ram Dai. She came from a village near Sitapur. It was too dark to see what she looked like, but on the following day they opened the window as usual and we could see each other. She had a very fair complexion and very beautiful features, and was rather on the slim side.

On the fourth day she was taken away. I was left where I was, and again had to pass the time alone for two full days. On the night of the third day Dilavar Khan and Pir Bakhsh came to fetch me. It was a moonlit night. We walked across an open space and then through a street of shops. We came to a bridge under which the water was flowing fast. There was a cold wind blowing and I was shivering. After a while we came to some more shops, and after that turned into a long narrow lane. My legs were tired. Then we came out into another street of shops. It was crowded, and it was only with difficulty that we could make our way. And now we came to the door of a house.

3

Mirza Rusva Sahib, you'll have guessed where that was. It was the street where my honour was to be sold, the Chauk, and this was the house where I was to get all that was coming to me in this world— disgrace, honour, notoriety, fame, humiliations, triumphs. In other words it was Khanam's house. The door was open. In front of us was a stairway. We went up it to the upper storey. I passed through the courtyard and went to Khanam who was sitting in a spacious room next to the main room.

You must have seen Khanam. At that time she must have been about fifty years old. What a dignified old lady she was! Her complexion was rather dark, but I've neither seen nor heard of any other woman of such imposing presence, and so well-dressed. Her hair had gone completely white at the temples but it framed her face very attractively. She was wearing a muslin dupatta of the finest, most delicate cloth, and a purple paijama with wide legs. Heavy gold bangles fitting tightly on her wrists, and two plain gold earrings on her ears enhanced her charm all the more. Bismillah's* complexion and features were exactly like hers, but she was not nearly as attractive. I can remember to this day what she looked like then. She was sitting on the carpet, with her back against a small bed.

A light was burning in a globe shade. A large, engraved box for paan was open before her, and she was smoking a long-tubed hookah. A rather dark-complexioned girl (Bismillah) was dancing before her, but when we arrived the dancing stopped, and everyone else left the room. Of course, everything had been settled beforehand. She asked Dilavar Khan, 'Is this the girl?'

'Yes,' he said.

She called me to come to her, made kissing noises and sat me down. Then she raised my face and looked at me.

'Very well. The sum we agreed on is ready for you. And what about the other girl?'

'We've already disposed of her,' Pir Bakhsh said.

'How much did you get for her?'

'Two hundred.'

'Oh, well. Who did you sell her to?'

'A lady bought her for her son.'

'She was a good-looking girl. I'd have been willing to pay that for her, but it seems you were in a hurry.'

---

* Khanam's daughter.

'What could I do? I did all I could to persuade my brother-in-law but he wouldn't agree.'

'This one's good looking too,' said Dilavar Khan. 'But it's up to you.'

'Well, she's a girl.'

'And, such as she is, she's here.'

'Very well then. As you please.'

And she called Bua Husaini. A plumpish, dark, middle-aged woman came in. Khanam told her to 'bring the box' and she went out and brought it. Khanam opened it and counted out a lot of rupee coins in Dilavar Khan's presence. I learnt later that it was a hundred and twenty-five rupees. Pir Bakhsh counted out some of them (I was told later it was fifty rupees) and tied them up in a cloth and Dilavar Khan pocketed the rest. After which both bade a respectful farewell and departed. And now Khanam, Husaini, and I were alone in the room.

'Husaini,' Khanam said. 'You don't think I paid too much for the girl?'

'Too much? I'd say you got her cheap.'

'Well, not all that cheap either. Anyway she looks a simple sort of girl. God knows whose daughter she is. What a state her parents must be in! God knows where these wretches get hold of these girls. The fear of God means nothing to them. Bua Husaini, *we're* not to blame in this at all. It's those wretches that'll have to answer to God for it, not us. And after all, if we'd not bought her somebody else would have done.'

'Khanam Sahiba, she's better off here. You must have heard the things ladies do to their slave girls.'

'Yes, of course I have. It's only a day or two ago that I heard how Sultan Jahan Begum saw her slave girl talking to her husband. She branded her with hot irons and then killed her.'

'Ladies like that can do as they like in *this* world. They'll stand condemned on Judgement Day.'

'Stand condemned! They'll burn in hell fire.'

After that Husaini said very earnestly, 'Lady, let *me* look after this girl. She's yours, but I'll look after her.'

'Very well,' said Khanam. 'You look after her.'

All this time Bua Husaini had remained standing. Now she came and sat down beside me and began to talk to me.

'Where do you come from, child?'

'Bangla,' I said.

Husaini turned to Khanam, 'Where's Bangla?' she said.

'Are you a child?' said Khanam. 'Don't you know that they call Faizabad Bangla too?'

Husaini turned to me again. 'What's your daddy's name?'

'Jemadar.'

'You expect too much of her,' said Khanam. 'How on earth would she know his name? She's only a child.'

'All right, what's *your* name?' Husaini asked me.

'Amiran.'

'Oh, I don't like that name,' said Khanam. 'We'll call you Umrao.'

'Do you hear, child?' said Husaini. 'You answer to the name of Umrao. When the lady calls "Umrao!" you answer.'

And from that day I was Umrao. Later, when I became a courtesan, people began to call me Umrao Jan. Khanam continued to call me Umrao to her dying day. Bua Husaini called me Umrao Sahiba.*

After that Bua Husaini took me to her room, gave me nice food, and then sweets to eat, washed my hands and face and put me to bed beside her. That night I dreamt of my mother and father. Daddy had just come home from work, bringing a leaf-cup of sweets. My brother was there playing, and daddy gave him some of the sweets. He asked where I was, thinking I must be in the other room. Mummy was in the kitchen. I saw he was there and came running to give him a hug. Then I told him everything that had happened to me, weeping all the time.

---

* Jan means 'life', 'soul', and as a term of affection, 'darling'. It was commonly attached to a courtesan's name.

In my dream I cried so much that I couldn't stop sobbing. Bua Husaini woke me up, and when I opened my eyes I saw that I was not in my home. No room. No daddy. No mummy. I was in Bua Husaini's arms crying. She was wiping my eyes. The lamp was burning, and I could see that she was crying too.

Bua Husaini really was a good, kind woman. She gave me such affection that within a few days I had forgotten my father and mother. And after all, that was only natural. In the first place, I couldn't help being where I was. And then everything was new— new ways, new colours, the very best food to eat, such as I'd never tasted before. Clothes finer than I had ever dreamt of, let alone seen. Three girls—Bismillah Jan, Khurshid Jan and Amir Jan—to play with. Dancing to watch and singing to listen to day and night. Parties, shows, festivals, visits to the parks—everything I could want to give me pleasure.

Mirza Sahib, you'll think that I must have been very hardhearted to forget my mother and father so quickly. But though I was still very young, as soon as I arrived at Khanam's house I somehow realized that this was where I was to spend the rest of my life. I felt exactly as a new bride does when she goes to her in-laws and knows that come what may she is there for life.

~

Khanam's establishment was a huge house, with an expensively furnished room for each of the ten to eleven courtesans, each with a full complement of servants to attend on her. Khanam catered for a clientele drawn from the richest and most influential classes in Lucknow society, and her courtesans were equipped accordingly, bedecked with jewellery and dressed in the most expensive clothes. The courtesans, of course, earned not for themselves but for Khanam, although clients might sometimes give them money or jewellery without Khanam's knowledge. Their beauty, their skill as dancers and singers, and their education to a cultural level where they could appreciate, and in some cases compose poetry, were all assets to be valued. They possessed these in varying measure. Thus Khurshid Jan was exceptionally beautiful, but danced poorly and was useless as a singer. Umrao was quite good looking, quickly developed a real talent for music and singing, and took such an interest in her education that she quickly mastered some of the classics of Persian literature, learnt elementary Arabic, acquired a good taste in poetry and herself began to write it, with Ada as her takhallus.

The playmates of her early days there were launched in their profession before she was, and she greatly envied them and eagerly awaited the time when she too would be a full-fledged courtesan.

She goes on to describe her own initiation and early experiences with various clients and then devotes two successive chapters to Bismillah Jan and Khurshid Jan, letting their character appear through their own words and actions. Bismillah is the complete courtesan, skilled in all the accomplishments of her profession, completely mercenary and completely callous.

Khurshid on the other hand is not fitted to be a courtesan at all. She wants to love and be loved. She falls in love with a client, Pyare Sahib, and when his marriage is arranged she is both furious and heartbroken.

Umrao never makes the point explicitly, but it is clear that her accounts of Bismillah and Khurshid are intended to clarify her own position. She accepts that a courtesan cannot afford to fall in love (although in fact she does fall in love on two occasions), but does not accept that she must be callous and unfeeling.

4

It was a late afternoon in the month of Savan. The rain had stopped and here and there sunlight fell on the tall houses and walls of the Chauk. Fragments of clouds were moving across the sky and you could see the colourful glow of the sunset spreading in the west. Crowds of people, all dressed in white, were building up in the Chauk, unusually crowded today because it was Friday and people were going off eagerly to the Aish Bagh* Fair. Khurshid, Amir Jan, Bismillah and I were dressing up for the fair. Dupattas dyed bright green were just back from the dyers, and we were having

* Aish Bagh: 'Pleasure Garden', a famous Lucknow park.

them crinkled, and combing and plaiting our hair, and getting out our heavy jewellery. Khanam Sahiba was there, reclining against a bolster. Bua Husaini had just brought her her hookah and was standing behind her. Mir Sahib[*] was sitting facing her and urging her to go to the fair; and she was saying, 'I feel lazy today. I shan't go.' We were all praying that she wouldn't, so that we could really enjoy ourselves.

Khurshid was looking her most attractive. Her fair complexion contrasted with her bright green muslin dupatta. In her heavy purple paijama with its wide legs, and her tightly fitting kurti she looked completely stunning. She was wearing delicate jewellery on her neck and on her wrists, a diamond nose stud and gold earrings, heavy bangles, and a pearl choker, and looking at herself in the full-length mirror in the room opposite. I can't tell you how beautiful she looked. If I had had her beauty and seen it reflected in the mirror I'd have been afraid of the evil eye.[†] But not her. She was bemoaning the fact that no one so much as looked at her these days. Pyare Sahib had fallen out with her, and her sadness showed in her face. But that too only enhanced her appeal. A beautiful woman is always beautiful, no matter what her mood. I can't describe how I felt as I looked at her—as if I were savouring some passionate verse of a good poet I'd just heard.

Bismillah was quite good-looking, with her nut-brown complexion, symmetrical features, straight nose, big dark eyes and slim figure. She was wearing a suit of heavily embroidered cloth, a moss-green crepe dupatta, with a braided border, and a heavy yellow paijama, and was loaded from head to foot in valuable jewellery. And to complete the effect, a garland of flowers. She looked just like a bride on the fourth day of her marriage.[‡] Moving about in the fair with bold and mischievous words on her lips, making faces at one, making eyes at another, and once she had attracted his attention, turning away.

---

[*] One of Khanam's old admirers.
[†] i.e. I'd have been inordinately proud of myself and so invited misfortune.
[‡] A special ceremony is performed on that day.

Oh, I forgot to tell you that when we'd finished making up we'd been taken in palanquins to the fair.

The crowds were such that you could have thrown a metal tray over their heads and it couldn't have fallen to the ground. Everywhere there were toy-sellers, and sweet-sellers, stalls, people moving about selling things from trays, fruit-sellers, people selling garlands and paan and preparing hookahs—all the things one always sees at a fair. I wasn't interested in all this, but I've always been interested in studying people's faces, especially at fairs and shows. Some are happy, some sad; some poor, some rich; some stupid, some intelligent; some learned, some ignorant; some of good family, some not; some generous, some mean. And their faces tell it all. Here was a man marching proudly along in his long coat of fine cloth and purple waistcoat and pointed hat, and paijama fitting close at the knee, and velvet shoes with raised heels. Another has tied a dupatta dyed the colour of sandalwood on his head, set at a rakish angle, and is moving around staring at the courtesans. Another has got himself to the fair, but he looks very cross; he's frowning and muttering something under his breath as he passes us. He looks as though he's just quarrelled with his wife, and is thinking of all the things he would have said to her if he'd thought of them in time. Here's a man holding his little boy's hand and talking to him as they move around. They're talking all the time about 'Mummy'. Mummy must be doing the cooking. Mummy isn't feeling well. Mummy must be asleep. Mummy must just have woken up. You musn't be naughty or mummy will have to go to the hakim.* Another has dressed up his little seven- or eight-year-old daughter in red clothes. She's riding on his shoulders, a little nose-ring in her nose, her hair plaited tight on the top of her head and tied with a red hair ribbon. She has silver bangles on her wrists and he's grasping them so tightly with both hands that her wrists are hurting. He's afraid someone might slip them off her wrists and go off with them. In that case, why did he have to bring her here?

---

* i.e. Your naughtiness will make her ill.

And here are two friends vying with each other to see who can swear most colourfully: 'Come on, have a paan!' says one of them, and throws the money onto the paan-seller's stall, showing his friend how rich he is, and how the odd coin means nothing to him. Then he at once calls to the hookah man, 'This way! Is the hookah ready?' Another of his friends turns up. They swear affectionately at each other as good friends do, 'Well, get me a paan, then!' It's interesting to see that he is a Muslim and his friend a Hindu. When the paan-seller held out the paan he at once took hold of it, and then remembered that he shouldn't have.* 'Oh, I'm sorry; I forgot.' The other looked put out. He took out a coin and told the paan-seller, 'Here you are. Give me two paans. Put some cardamom in, but not too much lime.† Then, to his friend, 'Here you are. Now let me have a smoke.' As soon as he took the clay bowl from the hookah the hookah man glared at him. He at once gave it back, took some money from his pocket and paid him.‡

Gauhar Mirza§ had laid down a carpet beside the Moti Jhil.¶ We went there, moved about a bit among the trees and then decided to go back home. We'd been at the fair from early evening until well after dark. We each got into our palanquin—and then noticed that Khurshid Jan's was empty. At first we thought that maybe she was walking among the trees somewhere. We looked for her everywhere, and sent our servants running off to look for her. Gauhar Mirza searched all through the fair for her, but in the end we had to give up and go home.

As soon as she heard it Khanam beat her head. The whole house

---

* Because of the Brahminical belief that one cannot eat anything that has been touched by someone of a lower caste or by a Muslim.

† The betel leaf would be rolled up into a cone containing other ingredients.

‡ He could not use the mouthpiece in case it had been used by a Muslim. But the hookah man objected to him removing the clay bowl, so he gave it back and paid the man, but did not smoke.

§ A man who had spent his boyhood with the courtesans and was on familiar terms with them.

¶ 'Pearl Lake': the name of a lake in the park.

was shocked by it. I too cried all night. A servant was sent to Pyare Sahib's house, and the poor man came running and swore a thousand oaths that he knew absolutely nothing about it, saying that he hadn't even been to the fair; his wife was ill, and he couldn't. And in fact there was no reason to suspect him, and after he'd sworn to all this no one suspected him any longer, because once he had got married he was so devoted to his wife that he'd stopped coming to the Chauk altogether. In fact he never went out at night at all. It was partly because of his former love for Khurshid and partly because of his regard for Khanam that he'd somehow found it in him to come.

Six weeks after Khurshid had disappeared a man walked straight into my rooms, and sat down at the edge of the carpet. He was dressed in the style of the young bloods of Lucknow. Nut-brown complexion, slim, a large shawl tied around his waist and another around his head. I guessed he wasn't quite a gentleman, or at any rate was new to cultured society, and hadn't often visited courtesans. I was alone at the time, and I called Bua Husaini. As soon as she came into the room he stood up, somewhat familiary took her hand, took her aside and said something to her. I only heard snatches of their conversation. Then Bua Husaini went to Khanam. When she came back they talked again, and finally she said, 'You'll have to pay for a month in advance.' He took a bag of rupees from his waistband. Bua Husaini opened her knees and he threw the coins into her lap.

'How much is that?' said Bua Husaini.

'I don't know. Count it.'

'I can't count.'

'I know how much there is. Seventy-five rupees. Maybe one or two more or less.'

'And how many is seventy-five?'

'Three twenties and fifteen. Twenty-five short of a hundred.'

'Twenty-five short of a hundred. So how many days' pay is that?'

'Fifteen days. I'll bring the other seventy-five tomorrow. That'll be a full hundred and fifty on the nail.'

When he said 'on the nail' I didn't like it at all. I was convinced now that he was a very ordinary sort of man. But courtesans can't please themselves. They get their orders from someone else. What was I to do?

Bua Husaini went off and took the money to Khanam. Khanam must have been in a good mood that day, because she at once agreed to what he had said. I was surprised. Normally she'd make no concession even for a moment, not even to the richest noblemen; and here she was agreeing to a day's delay.

When all this had been settled he stayed the night with me in my room. About three hours before dawn it seemed as though someone knocked at the door below my room. He got up at once. 'I'm going now,' he said. 'I'll be back tonight.' As he left he gave me five gold coins and three rings, one of gold set with a ruby, one diamond ring and one of turquoise. 'Keep these for yourself,' he said. 'Don't give them to Khanam.' I was very pleased. I put the rings on and admired how they looked on my fingers. They looked really beautiful. Then I opened my box and put them and the five gold coins in the secret drawer.

The next evening the same man came again. I was practising singing with my teacher at the time. He sat down at the edge of the carpet and listened. Then he gave the musician five rupees. My teacher and the sarangi player began to flatter him. My teacher was after the shawl tied around his waist, and when hints had no effect, he asked for it outright. But it was no good. He wouldn't give it to him.

'Ustad ji he said, 'You can have money and anything else you want, but not this shawl. It's a keepsake from a friend.'

The ustad ji couldn't say anything.

When the lesson was over he handed over the other seventy-five rupees to Bua Husaini, and gave her five rupees for herself. She went off, and when he and I were left alone in the room I asked him where he had seen me, that he favoured me in this way.

'Two months ago,' he said, 'that Friday at the Aish Bagh fair.'

'And it's only now you've come—two months later?'

'I was away. And I'm going away again now.'

At that I began to practice the courtesan's wiles. 'So you're going to leave me?'

'No, I'll be back soon.'

'Where do you live?'

'My house is in Farrukhabad. But my work brings me here a lot. In fact I really live here. I go away for a few days and then come back.'

'And this shawl. Whose keepsake is it?'

'No one's.'

'Oh yes! I understand. It's your lover's.'

'No it's not. I swear to you I haven't got a lover. Only you.'

'Give it to me then.'

'No, I can't do that.'

I was very put out, but he at once produced a necklace of large pearls, with emeralds hanging from it, and a pair of diamond-studded bracelets and two gold rings and laid them down in front of me. I was very pleased. I picked them up and opened my box to put them away. But I wondered why he casually gave me all these things, which were worth thousands, but wouldn't give me the shawl. The fact was I didn't particularly like the shawl, that I should press him to give it to me. I knew what I was about.

5

His name was Faiz Ali. He used to come quite late at night, sometimes not till midnight. Sometimes he'd leave an hour or two before dawn. During the month to six weeks he came to me I would sometimes hear a knock at the door or a whistle, and he'd at once get up and go. By that time my box was full of jewellery, plain and jewel-studded, and of gold coins and rupees more than I could count—some ten to twelve thousand worth of things that Bua Husaini and Khanam knew nothing about.

I didn't love Faiz Ali, but I didn't hate him either. Why should I? He was not bad-looking. And when you're constantly being given presents it has a remarkable effect on you. I tell you truly that I would watch the door for his coming... People who used to come to me had gathered that I now had one particular client. So they'd leave early, and if any of them looked like staying on, I'd find some excuse to get rid of him.

I forgot to say that search was made everywhere for Khurshid, but no trace of her could be found.

In those days Faiz Ali really came to love me, and if my heart had not been given elsewhere I'm sure I would have come to love him too and given my heart to him. As it was I did all I could to please him, and to all appearances nothing was lacking. I'd convinced him that I was in love with him, and the poor man was well and truly trapped. No one else had the slightest knowledge of all the things he'd given me. Sometimes, on Bua Husaini's and Khanam's intructions, I had to ask him for gifts, and these demands too he regarded as his duty to fulfil. He wasn't bothered about money. I've never encountered so generous a man, not even among nobles and princes.

At this point Rusva interrupted her. 'Naturally,' he said, 'what you get free you can give away freely. How could anyone compete with him?'

'What do you mean?' she asked. 'What you get free?'

'Do you think then that it was his mummy's jewellery he was giving you?' he asked.

'How was I to know?' she said.

Among those who used to come to me in the evening was one Panna Mal Chaudhry. He would stay for an hour or two and then leave. He liked company, and if he received due attention, wasn't bothered by others coming and going too. He paid two hundred rupees a month in cash, and presents as well. During the days Faiz Ali was coming to me he came less often. Before that he'd come every day, but now he was coming only every second or third day. Then he didn't come for two whole weeks. When he did come he looked thoroughly depressed. He'd give short answers to your questions and then fall silent again.

'Haven't you heard the news?' he asked me.

'What news?'

'I'm ruined. The house has been robbed. All our ancestral wealth has gone.'

I was startled. 'Good God! How much was stolen?' 'Everything. There's nothing left. Jewellery worth two hundred thousand.'

In my heart of hearts I was laughing at him. Everyone knew that his father Chutta Mal was a millionaire. Two hundred thousand is a lot of money of course, but to them it was nothing. But I put on an expression of regret.

'Yes,' he said. 'There's a lot of thefts in the city, these days. Nawab Malika-e-Alam has been robbed. And Lala Prashad. Things are really bad. They say the thieves come from outside the city. Mirza Ali Beg,* poor man, is at a loss what to do. He summoned all the known thieves in the city. None of them could tell him anything. They all swore it wasn't them.'

The following day I was sitting in my room when I heard a great uproar down in the Chauk. I went and stood by the screen. I could see a good crowd had gathered there.

Someone said, 'They've caught them, haven't they?'

'Yes,' said another. 'What a man! He's the kind of *kotwal* you want!'

'Have they traced any of the loot?' said someone else.

'Yes, a lot of it. But there's still a lot more.'

'Have they caught Miyan Faizu too?'

'Here he is, coming now:'

And I could see for myself that there was Miyan Faizu, with his arms pinioned, being brought along under guard, with crowds pressing in on all sides. He'd covered his face with a dupatta, so you couldn't see what he looked like. All this happened during the morning.

Faiz Ali, as usual, came late at night. He and I were alone in the

* The name of the *kotwal*, a sort of chief of police, the official responsible for law and order in the city.

room. He at once said, 'Today I'm going away. I'll be back the day after tomorrow. Listen, Umrao Jan. Don't let anyone know what I've given you. Don't give it to Bua Husaini and don't show it to Khanam. It'll be useful to you. I'll be here the day after tomorrow without fail. And now tell me: can you come away with me for some days?'

'You know very well that that's not up to me. It's up to Khanam. You'll have to ask her. If she agrees then of course I don't object.'

'It's true what people say,' he said. 'You lot aren't true to anyone. I'd give my life for you, and that's how you answer me. All right then, call Bua Husaini.'

I did, and she came in.

Faiz Ali pointed to me and said, 'Can she leave Lucknow for some days?'

'To go where?'

'Farrukhabad. I'm no ordinary man. I have my estate there. At present I'm going there for two months. If Khanam agrees, I'll pay her in advance for the two months—and if she wants more than that I'm ready to give it to her.'

'I'm not at all sure that she'll agree.'

'Anyway, go and ask her.'

And Bua Husaini went.

I knew it was pointless to send her to Khanam. I was quite sure she'd never allow it.

Faiz Ali had been so good to me that if it had been in my power I wouldn't have hesitated to go with him. I thought, 'When he's treated me like this here in my own home he'll do even more for me in his own place.' I was thinking this when Bua Husaini came back. She told him that my going away was absolutely out of the question.

Faiz Ali said, 'What if I pay double?'

'Not if you pay four times over,' Bua Husaini said. 'We won't let her go.'

'Very well then...'

Bua Husaini went off and I saw that he was weeping. I felt

very sorry for him. When I used to read stories of the fickleness of women towards their lovers I used to feel sorry and think badly of them. And now I thought, 'If I don't stand by him, that'll prove beyond doubt that I'm a faithless and ungrateful woman.'

'I'll go with you,' I said.

'You will?'

'Yes I will, whether they let me or not.'

'How?'

'Without their knowing.'

'All right then. I'll come the day after tomorrow at night. And we'll go an hour or two before dawn. Mind you, don't go back on it, or you'll regret it.'

'I'm telling you I'm going of my own accord. I've promised you and I'll keep my promise. You'll see!'

'All right, we'll see.'

That night Faiz Ali left me before dawn, even earlier than usual. After he went I began to think hard. 'I've promised him, but shall I go, or shan't I?' When I thought of his love for me and the promise I had made him I thought I should go. But it was as though I could hear another voice telling me, 'Don't go! God knows what may happen to you.'

I was still in this state of uncertainty when morning came. I couldn't make up my mind one way or the other, and kept thinking about it all day. As it happened, no one visited me that evening. I was alone in the room with my thoughts. It was late before I went to sleep and I woke up late. All day I felt as if I had a hangover. I quarrelled with Bua Husaini about something or other.

Oh, now I remember what it was. Someone had asked me to go and perform somewhere. Bua Husaini asked me if I'd go. I had a headache at the time and I flatly refused. Bua Husaini said, 'What a one you are! You're always refusing! Do you think you can do that in this profession?' I said, 'I've told you. I'm not going.' Bua Husaini said, 'You'll *have* to. They've especially asked for you and Khanam has promised you and taken their money.' I said, 'I'm not going. Give them their money back.'

'You know Khanam,' Bua Husaini said. 'Have you ever known her give money back?'

'No,' I said. 'She doesn't care whether you're well or not. If she won't return their money, *I* will.'

'Oh ho! You're a rich woman now, are you? Come on then, let's have the money.'

'How much is it?' I asked.

'A hundred rupees.'

'All right, but stop pestering me.'

God knows what had got into Bua Husaini that day. She said, 'If you're such a fine lady, give it to me now.'

'I'll give it to you this evening,' I said.

'They're waiting outside. They won't agree to wait until evening.' Bua Husaini was thinking I wouldn't have that much money, and that if she went on pestering me I'd have to agree to go and perform whether I liked it or not. In my box I must have had not less than a thousand to a thousand five hundred in gold coins, besides all the jewellery. But I couldn't open it while she was there.

'Go away, I'll give it to you in an hour's time.'

'Oh yes! You'll earn that much from clients in an hour.'

'Yes, I will. Go away, my dear. Don't bother me now. I'm not feeling well.'

'Why, what's the matter, girl?'

'I feel as though I've got a temperature, and I've got a bad headache.' Bua Husaini felt my forehead. 'Yes,' she said, 'your body is burning. But you'll have to go and perform, say, the day after tomorrow. You won't, God forbid, still be ill then. So why should we return their money?'

Before I could reply, Bua Husaini got up and went off. This argument with her had made me very angry, and it was then that I decided. I thought to myself, 'These people think only of themselves. They don't care whether I'm ill or not; so it's no good staying here.' But I couldn't decide whether to go or not, and until Faiz Ali came that night I still hadn't taken a really firm decision.

I took it when he appeared and I saw how well prepared he was. And yet I tell you truly that as I was leaving I felt as if someone was whispering in my ear, 'Umrao, don't go! Do as I tell you!' And as I went downstairs I'd hardly reached the third step when I felt as though someone had taken hold of my arm and was pulling me back and telling me not to go. But I did go.

6

They made their escape from Khanam's house to where an ox-cart was standing ready for them. A little further on Faiz Ali's groom met them with his horse and he rode with them.

By dawn we reached Mohan Lal Ganj, and we stayed in an inn there till midday. We had the innkeeper cook us a meal.

> Lentils without a grain of salt in them
> And not a whiff in them of fragrant ghee.

On the third day we reached Rae Bareilly, and here we bought clothes for the journey. I got two suits made and parcelled up the clothes I'd come from Lucknow in.

We now dismissed the ox-cart that had brought us from Lucknow, and hired another one. Then we set off for Lal Ganj, a small town some twenty miles from Rae Bareilly. We got there the same evening and put up at an inn. Faiz Ali went off to the bazaar to buy things we needed. In the room next to ours a village prostitute was staying. Her name was Nasiban. She was properly bedecked with jewellery and her clothes were of good quality. Though she was a villager her Urdu was good, spoken with the accent you hear in country towns. We conversed together at length.

'Where have you come from?' she asked.

'Faizabad.'

'My sister Piyaran lives in Faizabad. You must know her.'

I saw that she had realized that I too was of her profession.

'No,' I said. 'How should I?'

'There's none of us in Faizabad that doesn't know her.'

'I've been living with him for a long time. He lives in Lucknow, so for most of the time I live there too.'

'But you were born in Faizabad?'

'Yes, I was born there but I left when I was a child.'

'So you don't know anyone in Faizabad?'

'No. I don't know anyone.'

'What brings you here?'

'I'm with him.'

'And where are you going?'

'To Unnao.'

'And you've come via Lucknow?'

'Yes.'

'Then why didn't you come direct instead of by this out-of-the-way route?'

'He had some business in Rae Bareilly.'

'I asked you that because this route is a dangerous one. So much armed robbery that people have stopped coming this way. You'll have to go by Pulia to get to Unnao, and dozens of people have been robbed there. There are only three of you—two men and one woman. And you're wearing jewellery. I ask you, what can you do against them? They even attack wedding parties.'

'We'll have to trust to our luck.'

'You're very bold.'

'What else can I do?'

Well, we chatted about this and that. I don't need to tell you it all, and anyway I don't remember. Oh, yes, I asked her where she was going.

'We're out on *gadai.*'

'I don't understand.'

'What? You don't understand? What sort of a prostitute are you?'

'Sister, how should I know what it means? Gadai usually means begging.'

'Never! *That's* not what we do. Although to tell you the truth a prostitute *is* a beggar, no matter how rich and independent she is.'

'You're right. But I don't know what gadai means.'

'Once a year we leave our base and go round the villages. We go to the rich people's houses, and they pay us what they like. Sometimes we have to perform, sometimes not.'

'So that's what it means.'

'Yes, you understand it now.'

'Are you going to some rich man near here?'

'Yes. Not far from here is Raja Shambhu Dhiyan Singh's fort. I've been there. He's been ordered by the King to do something about the robbers, so he's not there. I waited some days for him to come back and then got fed up and came here. About four miles from here there's a village called Samriha. It's a prostitutes' village. My aunt lives there. Tomorrow I'm going to her.'

'And then?'

'I'll stay there until the Raja comes back, and then go to the fort. There's lots of others waiting for him too.'

'Does he like song and dance performances?'

'Yes, very much. But he's brought a prostitute from Lucknow and doesn't care about us any more.'

'What's her name?'

'I don't know her name. I've seen her. She's got quite a fair complexion and is quite good looking.'

'And she sings well?'

'Not at all. She's no good at singing. She dances quite well. The Raja's crazy about her.'

'How long has she been there?'

'Must be about six months.'

That night I told Faiz Ali about the danger of the route we were taking. He said, 'Don't worry. I've taken care of that.'

The next day we left before it was properly light. Nasiban's cart was following ours. Faiz Ali was on horseback and Nasiban and I talked to each other. It was not far to Samriha. Nasiban pointed it out before we got near it. There were fields at the roadside. Some country women were watering them while others were weeding them. There was a well with a big leather bucket hauled up by

oxen. A strapping woman in a loincloth was driving the oxen
and another managing the bucket. Nasiban told me that all of
them were prostitutes. I thought to myself, 'What an occupation!
Prostitution, and on top of that the kind of heavy labour that even
men would find it difficult to do. So why be prostitutes as well?'
But they looked like women who are suited to such work, exactly
like the women in Lucknow who come and milk your animals and
bring your yogurt and knead your dough.

Nasiban left us here and we went on another four miles until
we came to a big hollow. Rough ground, and, here and there, caves.
We could see a river bank in front of us and lines of trees growing
close together on both sides. The sun was well up when we got
there. It must have been about three hours after sunrise. No other
travellers in sight. Everywhere quiet and deserted. As we neared
the river Faiz Ali urged his horse forward, and although I did my
best to stop him, in no time at all he was a long way off. For a little
while his horse disappeared, and then reappeared on the other side
of the river.

Our cart continued to move forward, with the driver urging
the oxen on and the groom running behind the horse. Now the
driver and I were on our own. Suddenly I saw in the distance ten
to fifteen villagers running towards us. 'May God keep us safe!'
I thought. Soon they reached the cart and surrounded it. All of
them were wearing swords and had muskets on their shoulders and
linstocks* burning.

'Stop the cart,' said one of them. 'Who have you got in the cart?'

'A passenger from Rae Bareilly,' said the driver. 'We've hired it
as far as Unnao.'

'Stop the cart!'

'What for? The passenger is the Khan Sahib's lady.'

'No man riding with her?'

'The men have gone on ahead. They'll be back soon.'

'Lady, you must get down.'

---

* Staffs with fire at the top to ignite the charge in the musket.

'Pull back the curtain and pull her out,' said one of them. 'She's only a bloody prostitute. Why would *she* be in purdah?'

Another of them came forward, pulled the curtain aside and told me to get down. Three men stood guarding me. Suddenly we could see dust rising from the direction of the river and hear the sound of horses' hooves. As they drew nearer I could see Faiz Ali's horse out in front and ten to fifteen other riders behind him. As soon as they saw them the villagers fired off a volley, and two of the riders fell. They drew their swords, and then the riders were upon them. They too had drawn their swords, and blows were exchanged. Three of the villagers fell to the ground wounded and one of our men fell too. Then they ran off, calling out, 'You won't get far! You'll see what happens on the other side of the river!'

After they'd gone I got into the cart again. The wounded man had his wounds bandaged and he was put into the cart with me. We set off again, with a rider on either side of the cart, and others riding in front and behind.

Faiz Ali said to his companion, 'There was no way we could have got away from Lucknow before we did. I can't tell you the trouble we had.'

'Why don't you admit you stayed on to enjoy yourself?'

'Yes, that's what you *would* say.'

'What else? And you've brought your prize with you; let *me* take a look at her too.'

'Do. Do you think I'd keep her in purdah from you?'

'I'll wait till we get to the camp. Then I'll look at her to my heart's content.'

By this time we'd reached the river bank. The bank was steep, and I had to get out of the cart and walk. We had a lot of difficulty in getting the cart across to the other side. The jolting had opened the wounds of the wounded man, and there was blood all over. When we had got across his wounds were bound up again and the cart washed clean. It was now about midday and I was extremely hungry. The cart moved on as before, and their camp was nowhere in sight. About eight miles on next to a village we came to a park where little tents were pitched, horses were tethered and people were moving about. Some of them were getting food ready. Here the cart stopped. As soon as he saw the riders with us a man came forward and whispered something to his companion, who was called Fazal Ali. Fazal Ali looked anxious. He rode up to Faiz Ali and talked quietly to him.

'All right,' said Faiz Ali, 'We'll see.'

'We haven't time to eat,' said Fazal Ali. 'Let's go while the going's good.'

'We'll eat while they're striking the tents and saddling the horses.'

I got out of the cart. A cloth was spread on the ground behind a mango tree, and the pans of food were brought, and with them great piles of chapatis in big baskets. The three of us—Faiz Ali, Fazal Ali and I—ate together. They seemed anxious, but were laughing and joking too.

By the time we'd finished the tents had been loaded onto ponies and the horses saddled. Then we moved off.

We'd not gone more than five or six miles when we found ourselves surrounded by a body of men, some on horseback and some on foot. We on our side were prepared for this, and bullets began to fly from both sides. While the fighting went on Faiz Ali never went far from my cart. I sat there offering up prayer after prayer with my heart beating fast and violently, and hoping for the best. Every now and then I moved the curtain away to see what was happening. People falling, people dying... There were many wounded on both sides. We had fifty to sixty men with us, but the other side had many more—something like ten to one. (I learnt later that these were Raja Dhiyan Singh's men.) Fazal Ali and Faiz Ali took the chance to escape. About a dozen on our side were taken prisoner, and I among them.

7

The driver of the ox-cart pleaded with his captors to let him go, and they did. He took the wounded man from the cart, put him down on the ground by the dead men, and made off for Bareilly, glad to escape with his life. The other captives' arms were pinioned, and we set off for the raja's fort, which was about ten miles away. After a little while the raja and some of his companions came to see me. He was on horseback, and we moved ahead of the others. He gestured towards me and asked, 'Is this the lady from Lucknow?'

I replied with hands respectfully folded, 'Your honour, I am at fault, and yet if you consider the matter, not so greatly at fault. We women know little of fraud and deception. I knew nothing of what was happening.'

'Don't try to prove your innocence. Your guilt is proven. Just answer the questions I shall ask you.'

'As you command.'

'Where did you live in Lucknow?'

'In Taksal.'

The raja beckoned to one of his men and told him to get an ox-cart brought from the fort. 'This lady is a Lucknow courtesan, not one of our country prostitutes who can dance before an audience all night and still go on dancing for twenty miles as they accompany the wedding party.'

The ox-cart came, and I was handed into it. The rest of the prisoners, arms still pinioned, walked beside it.

When we reached the fort the others were sent off somewhere and I was invited in, and allotted a clean place to stay. Two men were given the task of looking after me. They brought me food—puris, sweets, and all kinds of pickles, and today, for the first time since leaving Lucknow, I ate my fill. Next morning I learned that the other prisoners had been sent off to Lucknow, but that I was to be set free. But the raja sahib was not yet willing to let me go. Later in the morning he sent for me.

'I'm releasing you,' he said. 'Faizu and Fazal Ali turned out to be rogues. All those other good-for-nothings will go to Lucknow and get their punishment there. You are certainly not to blame, but in future don't mix with people like that. If you wish you can stay here a few days. I've heard that you sing very well.'

I remembered what Nasiban had told me—that the raja had a Lucknow courtesan with him. It must have been she who'd praised my singing. I asked him who had told him.

'You will find that out,' he said.

After a while the 'Lucknow courtesan' was sent for. Khurshid Jan. She ran to me and hugged me and we both started crying, but from fear of offending the raja sahib, we quickly separated and sat down respectfully before him. Musicians were called. When I had been told that I was to be released I had composed a ghazal suited to the occasion. I'll recite all the couplets I can remember, though there were many more. At every couplet the raja sahib and all the others present expressed their great appreciation. Everyone was entranced. Here is the ghazal:

She then recites a ghazal—a continuous one—on the theme of a captive bird whom the fowler is about to release. The bird is in love with its captor, and is sad because it is being released. The closing couplet includes the takhallus Ada.

The raja sahib then asked whose takhallus Ada was. 'It's hers,' said Khurshid. 'It's her own ghazal.' The raja sahib was even more pleased. He said, 'If that is how you feel I shall certainly not let you go.'

'Your honour,' I said, 'the ghazal will have told you that I do indeed regret it. But you have issued orders and your handmaid is free.'

The gathering then dispersed and the raja went off to take his meal.

Khurshid and I had a lot to say to each other.

'Look,' she said, 'I'm not to blame for anything. Khanam Sahiba and the raja sahib had been at loggerheads for ages. The raja sahib had asked for me several times, but Khanam had always flatly refused. So in the end he had his men waiting at the Aish Bagh fair and they brought me here by force. I've been here ever since. They can't do too much for me. I have every comfort I need.'

'You mean to say you like it here among all these rustics?'

'Well, that's true. But you know what I'm like. I hate the idea of having to go to a different man every day, and that's what I had to do there. You know what Khanam's like. And here I have only the raja to deal with, and everyone is at my command. Besides this is where I was born; I like *everything* here.'

'So you don't intend to go back to Lucknow?'

'I certainly don't. I'm well-off here. In fact why don't *you* stay here too?'

'No. I shan't stay here unless I'm forced to.'

'You'll go back to Lucknow, then?'

'No.'

'Where *will* you go then?'

'Wherever God takes me.'

'Well, stay here for a few days.'

'Yes, for the present I will.'

I stayed there two weeks, and saw Khurshid every day. She'd become attached to the place, but I got very bored and restless. In the end I went to the raja and told him, 'Your honour has given orders for my release.'

'So? What of it? Do you want to go?'

'Yes. Please give me leave to go. I will come again.'

'That's true Lucknow talk. Where will you go then?'

'Kanpur.'

'Not Lucknow?'

'Your honour, how could I show my face there? I'd be ashamed to face Khanam. And all the others would laugh at me.'

In the first place, I really didn't intend to return to Lucknow. And secondly I thought that if I told the raja I was going there he would probably not let me leave, because if I did, Khanam would learn what had happened to Khurshid and make trouble about it.

The raja sahib was very pleased with my decision.

'You'll never go back to Lucknow, then?'

'There's no one there who is close to me. Singing is my profession. No matter where I settle I shall find people to appreciate me. I don't want to live in Khanam's custody any more. If I'd wanted that I wouldn't have left.'

I convinced him that I would never go back there, and three days later he gave me leave to depart. He gave me ten gold coins, a shawl, a kerchief and a stylish conveyance with three oxen. In short he set me up as an independent courtesan. He gave orders for a driver and two men to accompany me, and I set off for Unnao. There I put up at an inn, and sent the raja's two men back to him, keeping only the driver with me.

8

In the evening I was sitting outside my room watching people pass by and listening to the inn-keepers calling to them. 'Travellers, this way! This way! A clean, well-swept room is waiting for you. The hookah, good food, everything for your comfort! Shade beneath the neem tree for your horses and ponies!' Suddenly I saw Faiz Ali's groom coming towards me. When he got to the door of the inn he caught sight of me. Our eyes met, and he came and started talking to me. He asked me how I was, and I asked how Faiz Ali was.

'He's heard of your coming to Unnao,' he said. 'You can be sure he'll come to you late tonight.'

This made my heart beat fast. I didn't want to be with Faiz Ali any more. After what had happened at the raja's fort I'd thought I was free. I'd no idea I'd again run into Faiz Ali in Unnao. I thought to myself, 'Trouble again. Let's see what happens. He won't let me go if he can help it.' It was quite late at night when he descended upon me. We talked for a while about this and that and then discussed for a long time how we should get away from Unnao. In the end we thought it best to dismiss the driver of the cart. The groom could drive it and Faiz Ali himself would see to the horse. Then we decided to leave the cart with the inn-keeper and cross the Ganges by night. What was I to do now? I was in Faiz Ali's power, and had to agree with what he proposed whether I liked it or not. He summoned the innkeeper, took him aside and talked to him for quite a long time. Then, at about midnight, he put me up onto the horse with him and we left the inn. We had ten to twelve miles to travel through the night, and I began to ache in every limb, and feel constant pain. Finally we got somehow to the Ganges, with great difficulty found a boat, and got to the other side. Faiz Ali said, 'We're safe now.' By dawn we reached Kanpur. Faiz Ali installed me in an inn and went off to look for a house. He was soon back, 'It's not a good idea to stay here,' he said. 'I've arranged for a house. Let's go.'

He hired a sedan chair, and we soon stopped at the door of an impressive brick-built house. I got out, and we went in. In front of us was a sitting room with two ordinary bed-frames in it, strung with rough cords. On the floor a piece of matting and a weird and wonderful hookah the very sight of which would have put you off smoking for ever. I felt revolted by it all. After a while Faiz Ali said, 'I'll go and get us something to eat from the bazaar.'

'All right,' I said, 'but don't be long.'

He went off and I was alone in the house.

And now let me tell you what happened next. Faiz Ali didn't come back, and it seemed to me as though he never would. Half an hour, an hour, three hours. Midday came; evening came. I'd had nothing to eat since early evening the day before in Unnao. I was aching from the night's journey on horseback, and half-drunk from lack of sleep. Since morning I hadn't had so much as a cupped handful of water to freshen my face, and not a morsel to eat. I was half dead with hunger. Soon the sun went down, and darkness came on. Now it was night and I didn't know what to do... All alone in this huge, desolate house, I began to hear things—as though someone was coming out of a room; someone was walking in the sitting room opposite me; I could hear footsteps up on the flat roof; slippers clacking as someone came down the stairs. Most of the night had passed. Up till now there had been moonlight on the walls and in the courtyard. Now the moon went in, and it was pitch dark. In the end I pulled my shawl up over my face and lay down. But I again felt afraid. It seemed as though the night would never pass. But eventually morning came.

My feelings were indescribable, and now I realized what Lucknow had meant to me. I thought, 'What have I got myself into?' I remembered all the comforts I'd enjoyed there. I'd had my own room. I'd only to call out and a servant would at once present himself. The hookah, paan, food and drink—the moment I wanted any of them they were there.

Anyway, it got to be midday and Faiz Ali had still not come back. In that condition if I'd been a virtuous lady, living my life in purdah within the four walls of my home, I'd have died. As it was, although I still behaved with a certain reserve, I'd been in the company of hundreds of different men, and if I didn't know Kanpur, I at any rate knew most of the lanes and byways of Lucknow. Here too I had seen the inn and the bazaar. I wasn't going to stay any longer in this empty house. I quietly drew the bolt back and stepped into the street. I had not gone more than ten to twenty paces from the house when what should I see coming towards me but a man in uniform, on horseback, accompanied by ten to fifteen musketeers—and in the midst of them our friend Faiz Ali, with his hands tied behind his back. I was thunderstruck and stood rooted to the spot—as though my feet were too heavy for me to lift them. Luckily none of them noticed me and they passed by and out of sight. I moved on into another lane, and then turned into another narrower one. Here there was a mosque. I thought, 'What better place for me than the house of God? I'll stay there awhile.' The doors were open, and I went straight in.

9

Inside I was confronted by a maulvi. He was dark-complexioned and was wearing a blue loincloth and walking back and forth in the sunlight. At first he probably thought I'd come to make an offering, and was very pleased. But when I went quietly and sat down on the raised platform at one side of the courtyard with my legs hanging down he came up to me and said, 'Well, lady, what do you want here?'

'I'm on a journey,' I said, 'I thought "Here is a house of God" and decided I'd come in and sit down awhile. If this offends you, I'll leave at once.'

He was a very uncouth fellow, but my affectionate gaze and courteous speech had enchanted him. He was too embarrassed to say anything, and looked helplessly about him. 'Good,' I thought, 'I've got him in my snare.'

He soon pulled himself together and said, 'I see. Where have you come from?'

'From somewhere. But for the present I propose to stay here.' He was most embarrassed. 'What, here in the mosque?' he said.

'Not in the mosque. In your room,' I said.

'God save me!'* he said.

'Who from, maulvi sahib? I don't see anyone here but you.'

'Well, yes. But I live here on my own. That's why I asked you what you wanted here.'

'What does that matter? Is there anything to stop anyone else living where *you* live? I don't want anything. What a question! And what do *you* do here?'

'I teach boys.'

'And I'll teach you.'

'God save me!'

'God save you? Why do you keep on saying that? Is Satan after you?

'Satan is man's enemy. We should fear him at all times.'

'We should fear God; what do we want with fearing Satan? And what was it you said? "Satan is man's enemy"? Are *you* a man then?'

'What else?' he said crossly.

'You look like a jinn to me. You live here all alone in the mosque. Don't you get weary of it?'

'What else am I to do? Besides, I'm used to living alone.'

---

* This gives the general sense. The original is an Arabic phrase 'la haula va la quwata,' which are the first words of a sentence which, in full, means, 'There is no strength and power but in God.' The words are always spoken when one is confronted with words or actions that shock or disgust one.

'That's why you have such a wild look. Haven't you heard the verse: "Don't sit alone, for that's halfway to madness"?'*

I'd have gone on teasing him—there are some people you can't help laughing at the moment you set eyes on them—but I was too hungry to keep it up. He was a young man, and not bad looking, but with an expression on his face too stupid for words. He had a beard, which, however, looked extremely uncouth. His upper lip was clean shaven. He'd tied his loincloth very high, and had a great big chinz hat which completely covered the top of his head. He had a very odd way of talking. His mouth opened very quickly and then shut again. He would bring his lower lip up over his upper lip, and his pointed beard would move in a very odd way. Then a sort of 'hoon' sound would emerge from his nose. It seemed as if he was eating and talking at the same time, so he had to take care to shut his mouth quickly in case anything should fall out. He *wasn't* eating, though; just chewing the cud.

Anyway I took out a rupee. He thought I was offering it to him for the mosque, and at once held out his hand, saying at the same time, 'There was no need for this.'

I smiled and said, 'Yes there was—the most urgent need. I am hungry. Please send someone to bring me something to eat.'

He felt awkward now and tried to fool me by saying that he understood—'a lot *you* understand,' I thought—and had meant that *he'd* provide food for me here in the mosque.

'Just be patient for a little while,' he said. 'Food will be here any moment now.'

'To be patient any longer would be distress beyond endurance. Besides I have heard that research has shown that the noble month of Ramzan visits the rest of the world for one month in the year and spends the other eleven here worshipping in this mosque.'

'For the present there's nothing here, but my pupil will be on his way here with food.'

---

* The verse is in Persian. From now on she interlards her words with Persian and Arabic phrases, designed both to impress him and to make fun of him.

'And if we assume that the impossible is made possible and the food does come, it won't be enough for you to keep up your strength, let alone for me to have a share. It's a case of "waiting is worse than death."* You know the saying, "By the time they bring the antidote from Iraq…"'†

'My word, you seem a very talented lady.'

'While you, in my humble estimation, are not in the least talented.'

'You are quite right, but…'

I interrupted him. 'Because my belly is reciting *qul ho vallah*‡ and you are making long speeches.'

'Very well, I'll bring something at once.'

'Well, for God's sake be quick about it.'

I managed to send him off, and in another hour to an hour and a half he came back bringing four cakes of leavened bread and some sort of bluish soup in an earthenware cup. These he set down before me. I looked at it and glared at him. He mistook my meaning and at once took out fourteen pice and a heap of cowries§ which he'd tied in the corner of his shawl and put them down in front of me.

'Listen, lady,' he said. 'Four pice for the bread, and one for the soup. A *dhela* to the man for giving me change. The rest is here. Count it before you eat.'

I again stared at him, but hunger drove me on, and I began to eat quickly. I swallowed two mouthfuls and then addressed him.

'Maulvi Sahib, is this the best this benighted city can produce?'

'This isn't Lucknow where you can get pulao and sweet rice twenty-four hours a day.'

'There must be a confectioner's.'

'Yes, right beneath this mosque.'

---

* An Arabic saying.
† A Persian saying.
‡ See p. 139.
§ Cowries are small shells formerly used as the smallest units of currency. *Dhela* (below) is another small coin.

'Then why did you have to go eight miles? It was afternoon before you got back. And you brought food fit only for a dog.'

'Don't say that. People eat it.'

'People like you eat it, I suppose. Stale bread cakes and dark blue soup.'

'It's not blue. Shall I bring you some yogurt then?'

'No, forget it. I'd rather do without.'

'Don't worry about the money. I'll pay.'

And before I could answer he rushed out, came back with a bowl of bitter yogurt that must have been made God knows how long ago, and set it down in front of me as though, compared to him, Hatim* was nothing.

Anyway I managed somehow to get the four bread cakes down and to drink about a jugful of water. I didn't touch the soup or the yogurt—left them lying where they were and got up. I left the money there too.

I'd got up to go and wash my hands, but the maulvi sahib thought I was leaving.

'Take the money with you,' he said.

'Keep it to buy oil for the lamps,' I said.

After I'd washed my hands and face I came back and began to talk to him.

Thanks to him I was able to settle comfortably in Kanpur. Through him I rented a room, and bought a comfortable bed, a carpet, a white carpet-cover, curtains, copper cooking pots and everything else I needed. I took on a maidservant to cook for me and another to do odd jobs, and two servants besides, and began to live in style. And now I began to look for good musicians. There were plenty who applied, but I didn't like the style of any of them. In the end I found a tabla-player from Lucknow, a man who'd been a pupil of Khalifa ji's school. He suited me very well, and through him I got two quite good sarangi players from Kanpur. Now everything was ready. It soon became known that there was

* A legendary Arab, famous for his great generosity.

singing and music to be heard in my room till late at night. The news spread that 'a courtesan from Lucknow' had come. Men began to visit me, and there was poetry too. Hardly a day passed without my being called to perform somewhere and requests for a full performance came in abundance. In a short time I had got together a large sum of money. I didn't like the Kanpur ways or the Kanpur accent, and often missed Lucknow, but here I lived an independent life and this was so much to my taste that I had no desire to go back. I knew that if I returned I'd again have to enter Khanam's establishment, because so long as I continued in my profession there was absolutely no way I could move out. In the first place, all Lucknow courtesans acknowledged her power. If I moved out, no one would come near me. Secondly, it would have been difficult to get good musicians, and I couldn't have mounted song and dance performances. I had access to influential families, but this too had been gained through Khanam. I was regarded as one of the best singers in Lucknow, but there are plenty others, and besides, only a select few can tell the difference between the good ones and the bad ones. It's your name that makes them willing to pay. The rich and influential go for the best establishments. No one would have bothered about me. Here in Kanpur my reputation was higher than I had dared to hope. There was no big wedding at which I was not invited to perform and where it was not considered a matter of pride to have me.

Umrao stayed on in Kanpur for six months. By then word of her had reached Lucknow, and Bua Husaini, accompanied by a male escort, came to take her back. Thereafter she spent the rest of her life in Lucknow, except for a brief period during and after the revolt of 1857.

10

Throughout the narrative Umrao breaks off from time to time to talk to Rusva about thoughts arising from her experience, or he interrupts her to comment on, and quite often dispute with her about things she has said. These conversations are set out as in the text of a play:

Umrao: Mirza Rusva Sahib, have you ever been in love with anyone?

Rusva: No, God forbid! *You* must have loved hundreds, and it's your story we want to hear. We want you to tell us about these things, but you don't.

Umrao: But that's my trade. We courtesans know all the ways to trap a man... But I tell you truly, I've never been in love with anyone, and no one has ever been in love with me.

Much later in her narrative she speaks of Akbar Ali Khan, a crooked lawyer who, unscrupulously but successfully, defends her when a false charge has been brought against her.

Umrao: He had a sort of love for me. It's my experience that even bad people aren't wholly bad, and that there is usually someone or other who they are good to. During the months of Ramzan and Muharram* he did so many good deads that they cancelled out his wrongdoing for the rest of the year. At least, rightly or wrongly, that was what he believed.

Rusva: This is a question of religious belief, so just allow me to say that he was wrong.

Umrao: Yes, I think so too.

Rusva: Wise men have divided sins into two kinds. The first are those which affect only the sinner, and the second those whose effect extends to others. In my humble opinion the first are minor sins and the second are major sins (although others may think otherwise); and sins that affect others can be forgiven only by those whom they have harmed. You know what Hafiz† says:

> Drink wine, and burn the Holy Book, and set fire to the Kaba:
> Dwell in the idol temple—but don't harm your fellow men.

---

* Muharram: see note on p. 73.
† The verse is proverbial, but is not in fact by Hafiz. See p. 190.

Remember this, Umrao Jan: to harm one's fellow men is the worst of sins. This is a sin for which there is no forgiveness, and if there is, then God preserve me, His godhead is in vain.

Umrao: I have lived a life of sin, but I too shrink from that.

Rusva: Yet you've brought pain to many hearts.

Umrao: But that is our profession. That's the way I've earned thousands—and spent thousands too.

Rusva: So what will your punishment be?

Umrao: There ought not to be any punishment, because in the kind of pain we bring to men's hearts there is a sort of pleasure too, and that makes up for it.

Rusva: A fine argument!

Umrao: Suppose someone catches sight of me at a fair. He falls for me. He hasn't a penny to his name. Unless he pays he can't have me. His heart is wounded. Is that *my* fault? Another wants to come to me, and is willing to pay. I'm committed to someone else, or I don't want him. I have my own tastes. He goes into a decline. Well? What's that to me? Some men come and want me to love no one but them. I don't. They've no monopoly over me. They're hurt. So? To hell with them.

Rusva: Yes all of them should be shot, but for God's sake don't put *me* in any of these categories.

Umrao: God forbid! You take life easy. You don't love anyone and no one loves you. And yet you love everyone and everyone loves you.

Rusva: What on earth does that mean? It's so, and it's *not* so. How can that be?

Umrao: I've not studied logic very deeply, but it can. It can when there are two forms of a simple phenomenon. Wise men love in one way and fools in another.

Rusva: For example?

Umrao: An example of the first kind is the way you love me and I love you.

Rusva: Only I know how I love. And the way *you* love is clear because you've just confessed it. Go on, give me an example of the other kind—the way fools love.

Umrao: The way Majnun loved Laila.*

Rusva: What an ancient example!

Umrao: Well, then like Nazir ...

Rusva (interrupting): No, spare us *that* example... Go on with your story.

At another point in the story she is speaking of a younger courtesan and Rusva praises her beauty.

Umrao: Were you too a candidate for her affection, then?

Rusva: Listen, Umrao Jan, and remember this. Whenever you see a beautiful woman think of me, and if possible put me down as a candidate for her...

Umrao: And if I see a beautiful man?

Rusva: Put your own name down for him and mine for his sister— provided that the shariat does not forbid it.

Umrao: Wonderful! Bringing the shariat into it!

Rusva: There's nowhere where religion does *not* come into it, especially so all-embracing a religion as ours. Umrao Jan, it's a principle

* See p. 82.

of my life that I look upon a virtuous woman as my mother or my sister, no matter what their religion or community, and any action that offends against their chastity, shocks me deeply. I think that men who try to entice them and lead them into evil ways ought to be shot. But I think it no sin to enjoy the bounty of bounteous women.

Umrao: Good God!

When Umrao has completed her story, Rusva gives her the manuscript. She describes her reaction.

Mirza Rusva Sahib, when you first handed me the manuscript of my life-story and asked me to revise it, I was so angry that I felt like tearing it into little pieces. I kept thinking to myself, 'Have I not suffered enough shame in my own lifetime that now my story should be written down, so that people will read it and curse me even after I am dead?' But my own dilatory nature, and a regard for the labour you had spent on it, restrained me.

Last night at about twelve o'clock I was dropping off to sleep when suddenly I felt wide awake. As usual, I was alone in the room. The servants were all asleep downstairs. The lamp was burning at the head of the bed. For a long time I kept tossing and turning, trying to get to sleep; but sleep would not come, and in the end I got up and made myself a paan and called the maidservant to come and get the hookah ready. I lay down again on the bed and began to smoke. I thought I might read a story. There were plenty of books on the shelves at the head of the bed, and one by one I picked them up and turned the pages. But I had read them all before several times, and could not arouse any interest in any of them. Then my hand fell upon your manuscript. I again felt deeply agitated, and, I tell you truly, I had quite made up my mind to tear it up when it seemed as though some unseen voice said to me, 'Very well, Umrao. Suppose you tear it up, throw it away, burn it. What difference will it make? The recording angels of God—a just and mighty God—have by His command written down in every detail a clear account of all the deeds of your life. And who can destroy *that* record?' I felt myself trembling in every limb, so that the manuscript nearly fell from my hand, but I managed to rally myself. Now all idea of destroying it had left me, and I wanted to put it down again and leave it as it was. But as though without my own volition, I began to read. I read the first page and turned over, and before I had finished the next half-dozen lines I was seized with so consuming an interest in my story that the more I read the more I wanted to. No other tale had ever engrossed me so completely. When you read other stories the thought is always with you that all this is invented, and did not really happen; and this thought lessens the pleasure you feel. But your whole narrative was made up of things which I myself had experienced, and it was as though they were all returning to pass before my eyes. Every experience seemed as real to me as it had been at the time, and I felt more vividly than words can describe all the emotions which it had aroused in me. If anyone could have seen me then, he would have thought me mad. Sometimes I would burst out laughing; at other times the tears would overflow and drop on to the page. You had asked me to make corrections as I read, but I was too absorbed even to think of it. I read on and on until daybreak. Then I performed my ablutions, said the morning prayer, and slept for a while. I woke again at about eight o'clock, washed my hands and face, and again began to read. By sunset I had finished the whole manuscript.

The book concludes with the account of a final session together in which Umrao tells Rusva her own reflections on the experience of her life.

EDITOR'S NOTES

Urdu Pronunciation

Many sounds in Urdu cannot be represented accurately using the English alphabet, and academic texts use special symbols to indicate these sounds. We have refrained from doing so, for readers familiar with the sounds of Urdu will be able to follow the transliterations. For those who do not know Urdu, here are a few pointers.

VOWELS

3 pairs of short/long vowels:
> **a** = short, unstressed, as in English 'about'
> **aa** = long, as in English 'park'
> **i** = short, as in English 'ship'
> **ii** = long, as in English 'sheep'
> **oo** = long, as in English 'shoot'

Other vowels:
> **e** = as in English 'end'
> **ai** = as in English 'hat'
> **o** = as in English 'close'
> **au** = as in English 'awesome'

CONSONANTS

Most consonants are pronounced as in English. But note the following:

'**n**' at the end of a word, following a vowel:

Often this is not pronounced as an English 'n' but just shows that the vowel is nasalized

(i.e. the sound comes through the nose.)

E.g. **main** [I] **nahin** [not/no]

There are some sounds in Urdu which are not found in English:

'q' is a guttural 'k' made at the back of the throat

E.g. **qalam** [pen]

'kh' in some words is like the last sound in Scots 'loch'

E.g. **khaandaan** [family]

'gh' in some words is a rougher **'kh'**, similar to the rolled 'r' in French

E.g. **ghazal** [kind of poem]

When '**h**' follows a consonant it can represent a number of different sounds.

Apart from the two special sounds above, it usually just indicates that the consonant should be pronounced with a small puff of breath. For example:

bh	**bhai** [brother]
dh	**dhobi** [washerman]
kh	**khaana** [food]
gh	**ghar** [house]

Sometimes the oddity of English spelling makes this confusing. So note:

th	**thoda** [a little]

The 'th' is just 't' with breath; it is <u>not</u> pronounced as in the English 'that'.

ph	**phool** [flower]

The 'ph' just 'p' with breath; it is <u>not</u> pronounced like 'photo' in English.

To avoid confusion, we have followed English spelling/ pronunciation in the following:

sh	**shaam** [evening]—**'sh'** as in English 'short'

Further Reading

If you would like to read more by Ralph Russell, here is a list of his major works on Urdu literature:

The Pursuit of Urdu Literature: A Select History (OUP India, 1992 & 2003): A companion volume to this anthology, with more on the historical context. It includes chapters on the novels of Nazir Ahmad, and on two great twentieth-century poets not included in this anthology, Iqbal and Faiz.

The Famous Ghalib: The Sound of My Moving Pen: Ghazals Selected and Explained by Ralph Russell (Roli Books, 2015): Includes a detailed introduction to the themes of Ghalib's ghazals, with over 200 ghazal couplets. Translations are given with the original in three scripts—Urdu, Roman and Devanagri.

Three Mughal Poets: Mir, Sauda, Mir Hasan (with Khurshidul Islam, OUP India, 1991): Introduces three eighteenth-century poets writing in different genres: Mir Hasan's *masnavis,* long romantic narrative poems; Mir's ghazals; and Sauda's satire on contemporary society.

Ghalib: Life and Letters (with Khurshidul Islam, OUP India, 1994): Ghalib's life told mostly through extracts from his own letters.

How Not to Write the History of Urdu Literature, and Other Essays on Urdu and Islam (OUP India, 1999): Includes an essay on the Progressive Writers' Movement & on concepts of Islam in Urdu literature.

The Oxford India Ghalib: Life, Letters and Ghazals (OUP India, 2003): A compendium volume including the full collection of Ralph's translations of Ghalib's ghazals (without the Urdu originals); chapters on aspects of Ghalib's life and times; and a slightly shortened version of *Ghalib: Life and Letters* (with Khurshidul Islam).

Autobiography:

Two parts of Ralph Russell's autobiography were completed by the time of his death and published by Three Essays Collective, India, (2010):

Part 1: Findings Keepings: Life, Communism & Everything (1918–1946) describes his introduction to Urdu during World War II, when he was posted to India.

Part 2: Losses, Gains (1946–1958) describes studying Urdu at the School of Oriental and African Studies, his early contacts with Urdu writers in India and Pakistan, and the start of his collaboration with Khurshidul Islam.

The Annual of Urdu Studies (www.urdustudies.com) includes many articles by Ralph Russell, including these which are autobiographical:

1996: *Urdu and I*

1998: *Urdu, Khurshidul Islam and I*

Articles in The *Annual* by others, about his contribution to Urdu studies:

2009: *Remembering Ralph Russell: A Tribute*, a special section of the *Annual* in the year after his death, has articles by Urdu scholars, teachers and those who studied with him.

1987: *Ralph Russell: Teacher, Scholar, Lover of Urdu*, by Marion Molteno

~

In recent years there has been a dramatic increase in published translations, particularly of twentieth-century short stories and poetry. The internet has made it possible for any interested reader to find them.

Two particularly useful websites are:

www.urdustudies.com
The Annual of Urdu Studies, edited from the USA and online from 1993 to 2014, published translations of poetry, short stories and literary criticism.

www.rekhta.org
Rekhta has an extensive collection of Urdu poetry, presented in the Urdu script with transcriptions in Devanagari and Roman scripts, and in translation. It also has some translations of short stories.

UNCERTAIN LIGHT

Marion Molteno

'Epic breadth and intimate detail.' —*Sunday Times*, London

'A moving and necessary book.' —Alastair Niven, Judge of the 2014 Man Booker Prize

High in the mountains of war-torn Tajikistan, rebels abduct inspirational UN peace negotiator, Rahul Khan. The lives of his closest friends begin to unravel.

Tessa, now married with two children, has never stopped loving Rahul. Lance, a dedicated aid worker, has used Rahul's friendship to avoid facing up to the gaps in his own life. Hugo, his UN supervisor, feels responsible for the abduction and is driven to uncover the truth. Tajik translator Nargis owes Rahul a personal debt but has secrets she cannot share. As hopes for Rahul's survival fade, each must find a way to begin again.

Set in Central Asia following the collapse of the Soviet Union, *Uncertain Light* vividly evokes a sense of place and an almost tangible atmosphere. With an authenticity and attention to detail that perfectly capture the nuanced compromises of relationships, Marion Molteno deftly weaves the strands of these interlocking worlds into a story of intimacy, hard choices, heartache and courage.

NINE: POEMS

Anupama Raju

A debut collection of poems by an acclaimed young poet.

'Anupama Raju has mastered the right simile, the apt image, the terse line. Love, poetry, journeys, places, moods, relations: her poetry is inclusive and intimate; her verbal iconography, rich with resonances. She can be passionate without being sentimental, ironic without being cynical and economic without being soulless and dry.' —K. Satchidanandan

'Urgent and passionate, these poems circle age-old preoccupations of love and longing. This is perilous terrain where the danger of cliché lurks at every turn. However, without resorting to the easy distancing strategies of irony, the poet plunges into psychologically fraught zones of "poetry, perfidy and Pandora", ready to give voice to the vulnerability and confusion attendant on such an exploration. A quiet blend of authenticity and artistry sees her through, transforming familiar tropes of blood and longing, pain and death, into the "burnt letters" of warm, pulsating verse. Anupama Raju cuts close to the bone in this debut collection of poems.' —Arundhathi Subramaniam